Social Media and Society

An Introduction to the Mass Media Landscape

Regina Luttrell

Syracuse University

Adrienne A. Wallace

Grand Valley State University

Rowman & Littlefield

Lanham • Boulder • New York • London

Acquisitions Editor: Natalie Mandziuk
Assistant Acquisitions Editor: Sylvia Landis
Marketing Manager: Kim Lyons
Sales and Marketing Inquiries: textbooks@rowman.com

Credits and acknowledgments for material borrowed from other sources, and reproduced with permission, appear on the appropriate pages within the text.

Published by Rowman & Littlefield
An imprint of The Rowman & Littlefield Publishing Group, Inc.
4501 Forbes Boulevard, Suite 200, Lanham, Maryland 20706
www.rowman.com

6 Tinworth Street, London SE11 5AL, United Kingdom

British Library Cataloguing in Publication Information Available

Library of Congress Cataloging-in-Publication Data
Names: Luttrell, Regina, 1975– author. | Wallace, Adrienne A., 1976– author.
Title: Social media and society : an introduction to the mass media
   landscape / Regina Luttrell, Syracuse University, Adrienne A. Wallace,
   Grand Valley State University.
Description: Lanham : Rowman & Littlefield, 2021. | Includes bibli-
   ographical references and index.
Identifiers: LCCN 2020049955 (print) | LCCN 2020049956 (ebook) | ISBN
   9781538129081 (cloth) | ISBN 9781538129098 (paperback) | ISBN
   9781538129104 (epub)
Subjects: LCSH: Social media—Social aspects. | Social change. | Com-
   munication and technology. | Technology and civilization.
Classification: LCC HM851 .L88 2021 (print) | LCC HM851 (ebook) |
   DDC 302.23/1—dc23
LC record available at https://lccn.loc.gov/2020049955
LC ebook record available at https://lccn.loc.gov/2020049956

∞™ The paper used in this publication meets the minimum requirements of American National Standard for Information Sciences—Permanence of Paper for Printed Library Materials, ANSI/NISO Z39.48-1992.

CONTENTS

SOCIAL MEDIA WITHIN MASS MEDIA

It is undeniable that the media and its influence on our society have grown exponentially over the past decade with advances in technology. This growth has had both positive and negative influences on mass media, which must be understood by all members of society, especially future media practitioners. As new media continue to evolve, their impact on the profession changes as well, but a familiar historical pattern can be observed. Each iteration of the technology that we use to communicate (such as print, radio, television and film, and mobile devices) has altered the ways in which individuals communicate with one another and has raised the expectations of the organizations with which they do business. Competing in a global marketplace requires better, faster, and more effective forms of communications. A number of texts on social media exist. However, very few focus specifically on social media and mass communications. Instead, they focus on defining the term "social media" and providing step-by-step implementation, with little attention to where social fits within the large frame of society. In addition, current texts on the market often introduce various social media platforms and then provide examples as evidence supporting their effectiveness.

The goal of this text is to engage students as consumers and creators of social media by providing a framework for understanding the connection among social media, mass communications, and the impact on society. Although the tools may have changed, the purpose and goals of communications have not. Through analyzing both veteran and new brands, highlighting theory in action, and culling examples from popular culture, our text demonstrates a broader arc of the ways in which new forms of media are strategically implemented. It provides students with the ability to identify the shifts that are happening right before their eyes within social media and society. Rather than understanding how to write a 280-character tweet, students can learn the importance behind the ecosystem of the social sphere, allowing them to adapt to any environment.

This text offers a unique perspective that truly orients social media within our society. It contextualizes the social sphere within the mass media landscape and provides evidence of the transition from traditional to new media. We use specific communications content areas to focus social media usage on the three significant areas of communications: *relational*, *societal*, and *self*. This holistic approach helps lead students to a greater understanding of the interactions among technology, culture, democracy, economy, and audience fragmentation, and how they relate to media literacy. Armed with this knowledge, soon-to-be professional communicators can gain more insight into their audiences and the level of influence that their strategies can have on the public.

Within this framework, we explain how social media benefits students and professionals, demands strategic thinking, and requires relationship building, while also issuing cautions about its dark side.

When learning about various social media topics, students often demonstrate their know-how by pointing to usage of their personal social media accounts. However, simple usage of social media is very different from its strategic implementation. The former is a skill that requires little knowledge. The latter, in addition to that skill, includes expertise in targeting specific audiences across multiple media platforms. This distinction is important for careers in fields that require demonstration of effective results, such as communications, business, politics, health, and others. Focused strategic training and practice can yield effective results in all of these fields.

With the increasing trend from mass media to niche media, media literacy and the ability to understand audiences are more important than ever. By identifying key concepts, theories, and practices within each communications area, we emphasize how people seek communications exchanges in a social media world. To this end, our text is divided into three sections:

- Part 1 Social Media Defined, Distinguished, and Delineated
- Part 2 Communication Contexts for Social Media
- Part 3 Suggestions and Advice for Using Social Media

This organization provides clear connections to the underpinnings of social media and its integration with digital media by focusing on achievement of specific learning objectives and presentation of relevant examples and activities.

DISTINGUISHING CHARACTERISTICS

As professors, we find teaching social media to be a collaborative experience. Students bring a wealth of information to the classroom regarding their personal experiences with social media and mass media. They are producers, consumers, and active participants, often from a young age. Their knowledge can result in dynamic and intuitive course discussions. What most students misunderstand, though, is the broader framework for distinguishing how their interactions on social media and within mass media impact themselves, their relationships, and society as a whole.

To that end, we aim to build on students' personal knowledge and experience by providing a text that focuses on the identification of strategic concepts, theories, and practices that can be applied to a multitude of communications areas. In Part 1 our approach initially centers on examining a student's relationship between various components of media and the broader social world. In Part 2 we then turn to the use of social media in different areas of communications. And finally, in Part 3, students will learn how their personal uses of mass media and social media have power on their private life.

Focused on specific learning objectives and coupled with relevant examples and activities, this text contextualizes the social sphere within the mass media landscape to provide understanding of the underpinnings and integration of social and digital media. Each chapter analyzes digital and social media applications through the societal, relational, and self lenses to thoroughly explore each concept.

Each chapter contains the following:

- Chapter-Opening Pedagogy: To help introduce students to central concepts, each chapter opens with Learning Objectives, a chapter-opening scenario, and a chapter introduction.

- Images: Vibrant visuals are integrated throughout to capture key trends and statistics in an accessible and graphically appealing style common to new media.
- Media Literacy: This important concept is integrated within each chapter and is focused on key issues regarding the impact of media on culture and society. Students are encouraged to think critically and analyze issues related to their own consumption of media with examples from popular culture that they will recognize and relate to easily.
- "In Theory": These boxed features describe theoretical applications in some detail, helping attach theory to practice throughout the text. Each one ends with one or more *Think about It* critical-thinking questions to increase assignability and student accountability.
- "Relational/Societal/Self": These boxed features highlight the "red thread" of this text. They offer a unifying perspective to help provide students with a greater understanding of how technology, culture, democracy, economy, and audience fragmentation in the media interact to show that true integration of these concepts can become a hallmark of future practice. Like the "In Theory" features, each one ends with one or more *Think about It* critical-thinking questions.
- End-of-Chapter Pedagogy: The Chapter Wrap-Up, Critical-Thinking Questions, Activities, Key Concepts, and Media Sources help students cement key ideas, assess understanding of key materials, and bookmark information for future use.

CHAPTER SUMMARIES

PART 1 Social Media Defined, Distinguished, and Delineated

Chapter 1 The Framework of Social Media

What is social media and what isn't? Often confusing, the term "social media" is used to describe apps, platforms, and even aggregators. This chapter focuses on laying the foundation on which students can build their understanding of what social media is and articulate the differences among websites, browsers, URLs, applications, networks, email marketing, blogs, aggregators (such as Reddit), livestreaming uses, and social networking sites (including Facebook, Pinterest, Instagram, Snapchat, TikTok, LinkedIn, and Twitter).

Chapter 2 Concerns about the Dark Side of Social Media

Social media is a tool that works in important ways for people and business. Although there is strong evidence for its utility, there's also a downside. Studies show that consumers of social media platforms experience feelings including a loss of control, confusion, distrust, and even depression and anxiety. This chapter explores the dark aspects of social media, with particular emphasis on the complex concerns related to the health of relationships, society, and self.

Chapter 3 Benefits of Social Media

Though social media has its darker side, its use also brings a multitude of benefits. From reconnecting with old friends and finding new ones to improving social and business outcomes, social media is a cheap, fast, and reliable tool to facilitate relationships of all kinds among the masses. This chapter examines the benefits of social media as a communication tool through the lenses of well-being in relationships, society, and self.

PART 2 Communication Contexts for Social Media

Chapter 4 Mass Media to Niche Media

As already noted, the media landscape has changed dramatically over time. From the expansion from a few television channels to multiple cable networks to the birth of digital and online technologies, what was once a "mass audience" has become very fragmented. Through critical exploration of the evolution of media, including the convergence of mass and niche media, this chapter identifies the effects of these changes on audiences and ways in which communicators can develop a strategic media mix of communication that is informative, engaging, and effective.

Chapter 5 Business and Strategic Communications

Business-to-business and internal communications have experienced some of the most dramatic changes as digital and social media have infiltrated the office. Building a strategic communications plan requires demolition of silos. This chapter explores the various fields under the umbrella of business communications (marketing, advertising, public relations, etc.) and discusses how they work together to achieve their goals. By exploring the ways in which organizations leverage the digital space to connect with external stakeholders more efficiently and break down barriers to new markets and audiences, the chapter homes in on efforts by leadership teams to incorporate digital and social media to connect internal stakeholders, increase business efficiency, and enhance employee satisfaction and engagement.

Chapter 6 Crisis Communications

Critical news has never traveled faster than in the modern era of digital communications. This chapter examines the context of crisis or risk, the multiple "publics" or "audiences" that exist in the social media world, direct and indirect dissemination of information across social media, and the integrated relationship between traditional and social media during a time of crisis.

Chapter 7 Sports Communications

The far-reaching and accessible nature of social media has had a tremendous impact on how sports news is obtained and digested by the audience and how sports enthusiasts interact with athletes, journalists, and one another. Sports journalists use social media to communicate directly with their audiences and monitor competition and trends; they also utilize the platforms as additional tools for play-by-play and real-time updates. Sports blogs, which provide a deep dive into issues of importance to the audience, can strengthen the personal connection. By optimizing social strategy and content, universities leverage social platforms as recruitment tools to market their athletic programs, and—like professional teams—to drive revenues and connect with fans. This chapter examines both the benefits and challenges that have resulted from the increased influence of social media in the sports industry.

Chapter 8 Political and Civic Communications

Social media offers opportunities to citizens the world over to come together and share information and ideas, providing long-term solutions and tools that can strengthen civil society and the public sphere. As the percentage of people around the world connected online increases, agents of change across the globe are being empowered like never before to define government and governance, using social media platforms to develop, execute, and sustain modern social movements. This chapter examines the role social media plays in social movement formation through exploring concepts including citizen journalism, viral content, livestreaming, and organizing.

Chapter 9 Health Communications

As the world's population ages and chronic disease and illness become more widespread, particularly in a post COVID-19 world, the need for effective health communications grows. The integration of communications channels has put the delivery of health information literally at our fingertips. This is both empowering and confusing, because sometimes bad information can be spread faster than it can be remedied. For people with limited reading or technical skills, or those intent on self-diagnosis (paging Dr. WebMD), this can pose a challenge; this chapter stresses the importance for public health professionals and communicators of becoming adept at the creation, delivery, and monitoring of consumer health information.

Chapter 10 Entertainment Media

Social media has become an integral component for television and movies. Conversations happen globally surrounding experiences people share based on what they are watching. This chapter explores how consumer behavior with television and film influences social conversations. These interactions translate into actionable social media strategies.

PART 3 Suggestions and Advice for Using Social Media

Chapter 11 Measuring Social Media

New knowledge requires people to lather, rinse, EVALUATE, and repeat. This chapter is designed to provide background on the theories and methods used to inform evaluation of digital interventions. The importance of analytics in both native and third-party applications is examined, as is assessment of the "what now" portion of a social campaign or digital effort. The chapter emphasizes description of the tools and utilization of their findings to present contextualized meaning that can be applied to future environments.

Chapter 12 A Holistic Approach: Keeping Up with Social Media

Keeping current is among the most challenging aspects of digital media. Both skilled social media marketers and enthusiastic newbies with digital curiosity surging through their veins will be required to keep up with trends in this fast-changing field. The chapter offers tips and tricks for strategically managing these changes with grace, speed, and excellence, as well as our thoughts on the future of social media.

ACKNOWLEDGEMENTS

We would like to express our deepest appreciation to our editorial board. Your time and effort in reading each chapter and providing insightful feedback were extraordinarily valuable:

Ai Addyson-Zhang, Education and Marketing Consultant

Lauren Bronson-Petrous, *Boundless & Co.*

Adam Brown, *Deakin University (Melbourne, VIC, Australia)*

Amanda Holdsworth, *Holdsworth Communications*

Keith Quesenberry, *Messiah College*

We give special thanks to Elizabeth Swayze. She was the driving force behind this book coming to fruition. Thank you for believing in us. #GirlBoss

We'd also like to thank Natalie Mandziuk and Deni Remsberg, Michael Tan, and Sylvia Landis for helping us pull the book across the finish line. A very special note of gratitude to Karen Trost for superior editing. We appreciate your experience and wisdom.

To each of the experts who willingly shared their time, including Mike Tirico, Olivia Stomski, Bill Werde, Ulf Oesterle, Derek DeVries, and Jason Dodge: We express our sincerest gratitude.

We would like to acknowledge the special contributions to this book made by Kelly C. Gaggin, MS, APR, a senior public relations consultant with Strategic Communications LLC in Syracuse, New York, and an assistant teaching professor at S.I. Newhouse School of Public Communications at Syracuse University. Her professional background and personal interest in cross-cultural understanding and relationship building was of great value to this project.

REGINA LUTTRELL, Ph.D., is the associate dean of research and creative activities and director of the W20 Emerging Insights Lab at the S.I. Newhouse School of Public Communications at Syracuse University, where she teaches public relations and social media. A contributor to *PR Tactics* and *PR News* as well as peer-reviewed journals, she is a noted speaker, frequently presenting at national and international conferences and business events on topics related to the current social media revolution, the impact of artificial intelligence on news and society, the ongoing public relations evolution, and Millennials and Generation Z within the classroom and workplace. As a Knight Foundation Tow Journalism Fellow, she examines attitudes and awareness of artificial intelligence and its impact on society. She is the author of several books, including *Public Relations Campaigns: An Integrated Approach; The PR Agency Handbook; Social Media: How to Engage, Share, and Connect; The Millennial Mindset: Unraveling Fact from Fiction;* and *Gen-Z: The Superhero Generation.* Prior to entering the educational field, she spent the first portion of her career in corporate public relations and marketing. Her extensive background includes strategic development and implementation of public relations and social media, advertising, marketing, and corporate communications.

ADRIENNE A. WALLACE, Ph.D., is an assistant professor at Grand Valley State University (Michigan) in the School of Communications, where she teaches courses in advertising and public relations. Adrienne has more than 22 years of professional experience in both the public and private sectors ranging in scope from nonprofit, health, education, government, hospitality, politics, lobbying, and finance. She's a frequent contributor to industry publications and conference speaker on all things related to digital/social media strategy, student-run firms, and experiential learning design. Dr. Wallace received her PhD from Western Michigan University (WMU), where she studied the intersections of public relations, participation, and lobbying on the creation/implementation of public policy in the United States. She received degrees in Health Communications/Advertising & Public Relations (BS), Communications (MS), and Government & Non-Profit Administration (MPA), all from Grand Valley State University. She is also a graduate and class president ('15) of the Michigan Political Leadership Program located in the Institute for Public Policy and Social Research (IPPSR) at Michigan State University's College of Social Science. Outside of academia, Adrienne creates and implements campaign strategies for future local politicians and maintains practice as a consultant in integrated communications.

SOCIAL MEDIA DEFINED, DISTINGUISHED, AND DELINEATED

PART 1

The Framework of Social Media

A PEEK INSIDE SOUTHWEST AIRLINES

LEARNING OBJECTIVES

1.1 Explain what social media is, and what it is not.

1.2 Describe the tiers in the social media pyramid.

1.3 Distinguish among social media, social networking, apps, aggregators, and social networking sites.

At Southwest Airlines, the company culture plays a critical role in their social media strategy. According to Linda Rutherford, senior vice president and chief communications officer at Southwest Airlines, because the customer is the DNA of the company, their needs drive most decisions. Curtis Midkiff, a senior adviser for social business strategy for the company, adds that social media is the "hub, with spokes extending into every other department."[1] The company has adopted the mantra that social media is the center of their marketing and communications strategy, making it the epicenter of relationships among departments. Building the structure for social media starts with understanding Southwest Airlines' goals, mission, and culture.[2]

Most of us cannot imagine a day without social media. In fact, probably one of the first things you did when you woke up today was check your phone. At some point, you've probably taken a foodie-pic and posted it on **Instagram**. More than likely, you've sent a Snap to a friend, maybe even taken a photo or video and made it part of your story. You might even have created a Snapcode selfie GIF. Media consumption and interaction is at an all-time high. In fact, as MarketWatch reports,

> Americans spend more time than ever watching videos, browsing social media and swiping their lives away on their tablets and smartphones. American adults spend more than 11 hours per day watching, reading, listening to or simply interacting with media. That's up from nine hours and 32 minutes just four years ago.[3]

The Pew Research Center reports that 88 percent of eighteen- to twenty-nine-year-olds, also known as **Generation Z (GenZ)** (those born after 1997), indicate that they use one or more forms of social media.[4] Their preference, though, is to spend their time on **Snapchat**, Instagram, **TikTok**, and Twitter. GenZ spends approximately 15.4 hours per week on their phones[5]; they use up to five devices simultaneously; and check their social media accounts approximately 100 times a day.[6] This generation is not alone. Seven in ten Americans use social media to connect with one another, read news content, share information, and simply entertain themselves.[7] One thing's for sure, we are a connected society, making a comprehensive framework for social media key in today's ever-evolving digital atmosphere.

You may traverse the Internet with ease, snapping, Tweeting, and posting, but do you utterly understand the differences between being on a website, in an app, or part of a social networking site or platform? This chapter constructs a frame of reference for social media and explains the differences among websites, browsers, URLs, applications, networks, email marketing, blogs, aggregators, livestreaming platforms, and social networking sites including Facebook, Pinterest, Instagram, Snapchat, LinkedIn, and Twitter.

SOCIAL MEDIA EXPLAINED

So, what exactly is social media? This often-confusing term is used to describe everything from apps to platforms, and even news aggregators. Professionals and academics alike have contributed to articulating the meaning of social media. Here are a few definitions:

- "forms of electronic communication (such as websites for social networking and microblogging) through which users create online communities to share information, ideas, personal messages, and other content (such as videos)" (Merriam-Webster)[8]
- "websites and computer programs that allow people to communicate and share information on the internet using a computer or mobile phone" (Cambridge Dictionary)[9]
- "websites and other online means of communication that are used by large groups of people to share information and to develop social and professional contacts" (Dictionary.com)[10]
- "Social media refers to activities, practices, and behaviors among communities of people who gather online to share information, knowledge,

PHOTO 1A Interactions on social media allow people and brands to create and share content while bringing together communities. Social media can be understood as a networked hub of interactions.

and opinions using conversational media. Conversational media are Web-based applications that make it possible to create and easily transmit content in the form of words, pictures, videos, and audios." (Lon Safko)[11]

Although these definitions vary slightly, **social media** can be thought of as forms of electronic communication through which users create online communities to share information, ideas, personal messages, and other content via the social sphere.[12] Think of social media as a networked hub of participatory media in which people can communicate across dimensions, platforms, and geographical regions (see the In Theory feature).

IN THEORY | Applying Theory to Participatory Media

Social media is not a solitary act. What makes social media so effective is the participatory nature inherent in its platforms. Media scholar Henry Jenkins identified the concept of shifting sentiments in what he termed *participatory culture*. A participatory culture has minimal impediments to public engagement, expression, and development and sharing of content, and fosters social connections.[13]

Another media scholar, Howard Rheingold, identified *participatory media* as blogs, wikis, RSS, tagging and social bookmarking, music-photo-video sharing, mashups, podcasts, digital storytelling, virtual communities, social network services, virtual environments, and vlogs. These distinctly different media share three common characteristics: They communicate "many-to-many," demonstrate the power of the people, and have amplified networks. All of these characteristics bring with them the power to carry strategic messages to the masses.

Think about It: How do podcasts exhibit Rheingold's three characteristics of participatory media?

THE SOCIAL MEDIA PYRAMID

Randy Hlavac, lecturer at Northwestern University and author of *Social IMC Social Strategies with Bottom-Line ROI Marketing,* developed what he calls the Social Media Pyramid (see Figure 1.1). He asserts that there are six types of social media, ranked in tiers from top to bottom based on the nature of the conversations: social networking sites, news aggregators, passion connections, video connections, thought leaders, and virtual communities. The conversations happening at the top of the pyramid are short, while conversations occurring toward the bottom are seen as longer term and more substantial.[14]

Social Networking Sites

Social networking sites (SNSs) allow users to share personal information with friends or family. By creating a profile, users can share videos, text, photos, or audio. The most common and well-known social networks are Facebook, Pinterest, Twitter, WeChat, and Instagram.

News Aggregators

News aggregators are Web applications that pull news stories from different Internet sites into a single location that the user can view at their leisure. These include online newspapers, blogs, podcasts, and vlogs. Sites like these present text, video, and audio content targeting their readers:

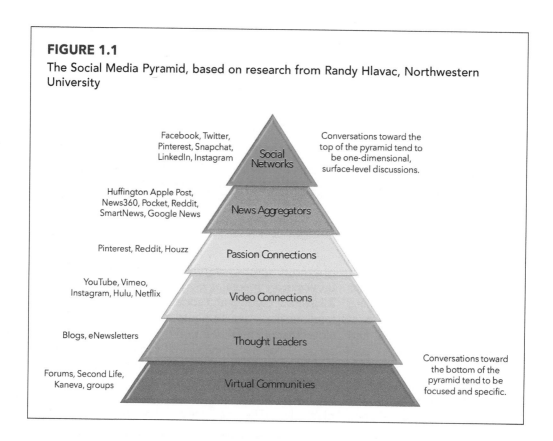

FIGURE 1.1

The Social Media Pyramid, based on research from Randy Hlavac, Northwestern University

Aggregation technology helps to consolidate many websites into one page that can show the new or updated information from many sites. Aggregators reduce the time and effort needed to regularly check websites for updates, creating a unique information space or personal newspaper.[15]

Passion Connection Sites

Passion connection sites are sites centered on our personal interests. For example, Houzz is a passion connection site that shares information about architecture, interior design and decorating, landscape design, and home improvement.[16] Other examples include Listy for booklovers, Bakespace and Foodbuzz for foodies, Lookbook for fashion aficionados, or Nomad for those of us who love to travel. Such sites allow users to make it easy to connect with others who share the same passion.

Video Connection Sites

Video is a powerful medium, and users just can't seem to get enough of **video connection sites**. Branded video content has increased 99 percent on YouTube and 258 percent on Facebook in just one year.[17] According to statistics provided by YouTube, the company claims that more than 1 billion hours of video are watched daily across 88 countries and in 76 languages, while Instagram reports that the site has 800 million monthly active users with 250 million daily stories posted.[18] Not only that, sites like Hulu, Amazon Prime TV, and Netflix have changed the way consumers are viewing movies, television shows, and original content. With analytics and simple easy-to-use tools, social media strategists can pull together a video that reaches a precisely targeted and defined audience with the exact content they want to see.

Thought Leaders

Thought leaders, or bloggers, make up the fifth tier of the pyramid. At the time of publication, there were more than 1.74 billion websites in the world; more than 500 million of these are recognized as blogs.[19] Blogs offer readers perspectives on the social sphere from influential, informative, and engaging experts. There are several types of blogs:

- In *personal blogs,* everyday people express their opinion about what is happening in their lives.
- *Business blogs* deliver content that can boost exposure for the company, drive traffic to owned media channels, and/or help the bottom line through increasing sales or engaging new customers.
- *Niche blogs* focus on a single topic with the goal of providing as much insight as possible.
- *Reverse blogs* host posts written by multiple users rather than a single author. The Huffington Post has built a $14 million monthly empire on reverse blogging.
- *Microblogs,* such as Twitter posts, are meant to be brief and to the point. They often utilize hashtags, photos, or GIFs.

Depending on what they want, readers can find just about any blog to fit their needs.

Virtual Communities

The bottom tier in the pyramid is **virtual communities**, a term coined by Howard Rheingold to designate a set of people sharing common interests, ideas, and feelings over the Internet.[20] Today, this term is synonymous with the broader concept of social media. Often not utilized to their fullest capacity, virtual communities offer focused interactions surrounding a specific topic to an identified audience. Although they can operate within social networking sites, virtual communities are not considered SNSs. Virtual communities thrive on deep conversations and connections between users. For example, Goodreads is one of the largest virtual communities for book lovers. Users can not only create their own library catalog and reading lists, but also join book groups, partake in online discussions, make suggestions, and even blog about books they have read.

THE SOCIAL MEDIA BREAKDOWN

The Social Media Pyramid (see Figure 1.1) helps us understand and frame the tools utilized in the social media sphere. Various tiers within the pyramid may be utilized in a full communications strategy, and social networks, blogs, video, forums, and more may appear in more than one. So then, what is what in the digital world?

Social Media versus Social Networking Sites

In the most general sense, social media can be summarized as a platform for broadcasting information. In contrast, a social networking site (SNS) is a platform for communicating with others. Think of social media as the communications channel and an SNS as a mechanism for two-way communication.[21] Facebook, Twitter, Pinterest, LinkedIn, Instagram, and Snapchat are all social networking sites; their users can register, develop a profile, connect with others, and comment on topics.

Website versus Browser

A **website** is defined by Merriam-Webster as "a group of World Wide Web pages usually containing hyperlinks to each other and made available online by an individual, company, educational institution, government, or organization"; it defines a **browser** as "a computer program used for accessing sites or information on a network."[22] Websites and browsers are not considered social media. Brands' company pages are set up to communicate with a target customer audience in much the same way that ordinary people connect with one another. However, social media platforms such as Facebook and LinkedIn can be accessed using the Internet via a browser, and blogs are often hosted on websites such as WordPress.

Mobile Websites versus Apps

What's the difference between a mobile website and an app? Jason Summerfield of Human Service Solutions breaks down the differences simply:[23] Mobile websites are browser-based HTML pages that are linked together and are accessed over the Internet. They are designed for smaller, handheld devices that are touchscreen, such a tablets or phones. They are scalable and are built with a responsive Web design. **Apps** are actual **applications**—hence the name—that are downloaded and installed on your mobile device. Apps are now *browser-dependent*. They pull data and content from the Internet, but a user can be on an app without an Internet connection.

Livestreaming

Receiving or sharing live video or audio of an event over the Internet is considered **Livestreaming**. Live events are an opportunity to engage with an audience by sharing what's happening in real time. Livestreaming can happen over social networking sites such as LinkedIn Live, Facebook Live, YouTube Live, and Instagram Live or through apps such as Live Stream, YouNow, or Stream.

News Aggregators versus Content Aggregators

As you learned earlier in the chapter, *news aggregators* are Web applications that pull news stories from different Internet sites into a single location that the user can view at their leisure. Similarly, **content aggregators** are websites that collect content focused on a specific topic in one place.[24] Although not considered social media per se, news aggregators and content aggregators can be part of a social media strategy. Examples of aggregators include Google News, Reddit, Fark, Hacker News, News360, Flipboard, and Feedly.

Email Marketing

Email marketing is not a form of social media; however, through e-marketing campaigns practitioners can drive engagement to a company's social media channels. This form of content distribution involves the use of email marketing to promote products and or services to a target audience. Newsletters, fundraising efforts, company updates, and coupons can be sent via email to a brand's target audience. Some of the most widely used email marketing platforms include MyEmma, MailChimp, and Constant Contact. These platforms can connect to an organization's social media channels, making it easy for consumers to share news, discounts, and other information with their connections.

Bots

According to Zignal Labs, a media analytics company, **bots** are profiles on social media platforms powered by machine learning that are programmed to produce messages, follow other accounts, reply to users, and share content.[25] **Machine learning** is the process of developing computer programs that access data to learn and mimic the habits of humans.[26] The original intent of a bot was to automate simplistic tasks such as customer service efforts. Bots can be confusing because they are developed to mimic human activities on social platforms, but they are not considered a form of social media. In recent years, the ethics of using bots have come under scrutiny, because they are often utilized to spread misinformation rapidly. Twitter is the social networking site that has been impacted the most by bots.

Relational/Societal/Self: When Trolls Take Control

The framework with which each of us approaches social media is varied. Most often, when initially learning how to utilize social media to connect with your target audience, there must be a change in mindset. Quite often students demonstrate their know-how by pointing to their personal social media accounts and highlight usage. However, we will challenge readers to move away from the self- or "me/I"-centered consumption of social media to a relational-or societal-focused approach.

Think about It: Describe how social media impacts you. Describe how social media impacts society. Give examples of how the two might intersect and what that means personally as well as professionally.

CHAPTER WRAP-UP

After reading this chapter, it's easy to see why distinguishing among social media, social networking sites, apps, websites, blogs, and forums can be difficult, as these tools and platforms often overlap. As the social media landscape continues to evolve, what will remain constant is the idea that social media was created as a way for people to interact with one another.

CRITICAL-THINKING QUESTIONS

1. Based on the definitions included in the chapter, explain social media in your own words.

2. What are the similarities of and differences between social media and social networking sites?

3. What role does the Social Media Pyramid play in understanding the various elements of social media?

4. Describe each tier of the Social Media Pyramid and illustrate it with an example from the Internet.

5. What is participatory media? In your answer include an example of participatory media happening in the social sphere.

6. Have you taken part in any participatory media activities? Why or why not?

7. In which tier(s) of the Social Media Pyramid can livestreaming, apps, and content aggregators fall?

ACTIVITIES

1. Take inventory of the social media you consume. Develop a list of social networking sites you have heard of, and then circle the ones you have an account with. How many did you list? How many do you use?

2. Based on the list you developed, track your social media usage over one day. Take note of the time of day that you begin to take part in social media and when you stop using it. How often do you check the social networking sites you have accounts with? Do you visit the Internet? If so, what are you searching for? How many apps are you checking? Do you use news or content aggregators? Summarize your media consumption.

3. Using the Social Media Pyramid, choose a favorite product and identify which layers are being used to connect it with their target audience. Analyze the types of conversations happening at the top and bottom of the pyramid.

KEY CONCEPTS

Application (app)
Bots
Browser
Content aggregators
Email marketing
Generation Z (GenZ)
Instagram
Livestreaming
Machine learning
News aggregators
Passion connection sites
Snapchat
Social media
Social networking site (SNS)
Thought leaders
TikTok
Website
Video connection sites
Virtual communities

MEDIA SOURCES

Social Media Fact Sheet: www.pewinternet.org/fact-sheet/social-media.

Generation Z characteristics. Five infographics on the Gen Z lifestyle: https://www.visioncritical.com/blog/generation-z-infographics.

Marketing to GenZ: https://www.agencysparks.com/infographics2/marketing-to-generation-z.

The Difference between Facebook, Twitter, Linkedin, Google+, YouTube, and Pinterest: https://www.impactbnd.com/blog/the-difference-between-facebook-twitter-linkedin-google-youtube-pinterest.

Participatory Media: https://www.youtube.com/watch?v=4dbn77qBGCk.

The Dark Side of Social Media

WHEN SEEING ISN'T BELIEVING: DEEPFAKES AND THE WAR ON TRUTH

By Nina Brown, Esq.

LEARNING OBJECTIVES

2.1 Describe the negative aspects of social media communications and how they occur.

2.2 Identify the societal impact of "Dark Side" social media activities, including its impact surrounding trust and privacy.

2.3 Analyze the impact of the "Dark Side" of social media on the self and personal relationships.

The gold standard for truth has long been visual proof. *"I'll believe it when I see it." "I saw it with my own eyes!"* The connection between our eyes and brain is powerful, offering a certainty that what we have seen is real. Although we might expect video manipulation from Hollywood, we trust that most video content posted in our social media feeds, whether by friends or news organizations, serves as an authentic representation of reality. What happens when they are not?

In the newest battle of the war on truth, artificial intelligence software known as **deepfakes** makes it possible for anyone to create fake videos that look real. The technology allows for easy manipulation of audiovisual content to make it look as though people said and did things that never happened. Although video editing has been around for decades, the process used to be long and tedious, requiring large budgets and skilled artists.

Thanks to recent advances in computing power and speed, deepfake programs are freely available and are easy to use. All it takes is a computer and an Internet connection.[1]

For example, the free program FakeApp allows users to create realistic face swaps, where they can replace a person appearing in a video with someone else entirely.[2] The technology is also capable of voice duplication, making it simple to literally put words into someone's mouth. Although the results are not perfect, they are pretty convincing. As the technology continues to rapidly and constantly improve, it carries immense potential to be indistinguishable from real-life videos.

The prediction of the technology's rapid growth and improvement has raised concerns about the likelihood of its abuse. In fact, when deepfakes first emerged online, most uses involved creation and manipulation of pornographic video content. The faces of adult film stars were replaced with the faces of actresses and other women who did not consent to appear in the videos.[3] A convincing deepfake could also cause harm on a national or global level, such as disrupting democracy or threatening public safety. Consider, for example, a deepfake of a politician engaging in an illicit act before an election, generated to sway voters toward their opponent or a deepfake of a public official announcing that there had been an attack on US soil when no such act had taken place. Lawmakers and leaders of US intelligence agencies have already identified deepfakes as a significant global threat.

Like any new technology that could be used in nefarious ways, a natural response is to ban deepfakes altogether. But this strong reaction is unwarranted because the technology is not inherently problematic. Beneficial uses abound, such as providing vocal avatars to those without a voice, recreation of historical events, parody, entertainment, and more. Strong First Amendment protections for these positive uses complicate the regulation of deepfakes.

Of course, one important stakeholder in this technological arms race is social media. Without widespread distribution, deepfakes will have little impact. Their creators will likely rely on social platforms for dissemination, which are designed to share information to a large audience in real time. Although most social platforms' **terms of use** would prohibit sharing such harmful deepfakes, that will not stop the deepfake from actually being shared. The content might ultimately be removed for violation of the platform's terms of use, but that will happen only after the content has been flagged (likely by another user) and the platform determines removal is appropriate. By this point, the video may have already spread enough to generate an impact.

The only way social platforms could stop a deepfake from being shared at the outset would be to employ a detection algorithm and block anything flagged as a deepfake. There are two roadblocks to this solution. First, although efforts are underway, such a detection tool does not yet exist (and is likely years away).[4] Second, because it is impossible for an algorithm to make the necessary judgment calls to distinguish between protected (satire, parody, vocal avatars, etc.) and problematic applications of deepfakes, an additional step in the review process would be necessary for any platform that wanted to block only harmful or illegal applications of the technology. This step would require human content moderation, which would be cumbersome, expensive, and ongoing.

Importantly, this is not something the government can require social platforms to do. Laws requiring removal of all deepfakes would run afoul of these companies' own First Amendment rights.[5] And a separate powerful law, Section 230 of the Communication Decency Act, immunizes platforms from most harms caused by content posted by its users.[6] The threat of deepfakes is compounded by this unchecked power of social media.

Like all new technologies, the pressure is on to find a solution that accounts for the fact that the technology—and likely the way it is used—will continue to evolve. In the meantime, we must accept that seeing isn't always believing. Consider the following:

- Two types of harmful deepfakes—nonconsensual pornography and political disruption—were mentioned earlier. What other harms can you imagine arising from a deepfake video?
- Social platforms have no legal obligation to remove deepfakes. What ethical obligations exist, if any?
- Compounding the threat of deepfakes is the fact that adults in the United States have trouble identifying whether information they encounter on social media is trustworthy. What are some ways social platforms could address this challenge, particularly considering deepfake content?
- Because of the costs associated with filtering unwanted deepfakes, it is possible that a social platform would choose to ban all deepfakes from its service—whether or not they are legally problematic. Is this a desirable outcome?

Although it is widely accepted that social media has many useful and helpful qualities, serving as a communication channel and tool for personal and business use, there are also those who argue that it comes at a cost to us as consumers of the media. From the spread of Internet hoaxes like Slender Man,[7] the Momo Challenge,[8] the Cinnamon Challenge,[9] and the Tide POD Challenge,[10] to more benevolent ones including the Wakanda Forever (#MBaku) Challenge[11] and the #WhatTheFluff Challenge,[12] the power of "virality" in posts cannot be ignored. This chapter examines the power of social media's darker aspects over the health of relationships, society, and self.

THE DARK SIDE DEFINED

Because of its widespread use throughout the world, the "bright side" of social media has received a great deal of attention over the last decade. Only recently have we really begun to explore what is often referred to as its "dark side." Because social media has completely transformed how individuals create, share, and consume all types of data, both large and small, this negative dimension deserves closer examination.

In October 2018, at a company-wide town hall meeting, employees of Facebook were encouraged to speak about the workplace culture of the company.

Following the broadcast of this town hall, former Facebook employees took to other social media platforms to air grievances about the company and its culture. Among those complaints, CNBC reported the following:

- More than a dozen former Facebook employees detailed how the company's leadership and its performance review system have created a culture in which any dissent is discouraged;
- Facebook's stack ranking performance review system drives employees to push out products and features that drive user engagement without fully considering potential long-term negative impacts on user experience or privacy;
- In one of the more damning claims, internal reliance on peer reviews creates an underlying pressure for Facebook employees to forge friendships with colleagues for the sake of career advancement.[13]

During a speech at a Stanford Business School event, Chamath Palihapitiya, a former Facebook executive, stated that he regretted that some of the tools he helped create "are ripping apart the social fabric of how society works."[14] His remarks came on the heels of those of Facebook's founding president—now conscientious objector—Sean Parker, just a week or so after Parker criticized Facebook for finding ways to "exploit a vulnerability in human psychology" in creating a "social-validation feedback loop."[15] Not dark enough for you? Palihapitiya also said,

> "imagine when you take that to the extreme where bad actors can now manipulate large swaths of people to do anything you want. It's just a really, really bad state of affairs. You have no civil discourse, no cooperation; misinformation, mistruth."[16,17]

Although always present in social media, this chaos has seemingly come to a head in the last few years. Think about Russia's election posts during the 2016 US presidential election;[18] the Brexit vote in the United Kingdom; and social justice issues including Black Lives Matter, the #MeToo movement, and the "ethnic cleansing" of Myanmar's Rohingya group.[19] Each of these movements centers on social media and involves the **amplification** of fake news,[20] concepts that will be discussed further in this and later chapters.

To better understand the functional building blocks of social media and how individuals, communities, and organizations use social media platforms, researchers Jan H. Kietzmann, Kristopher Hermkens, Ian P. McCarthy, and Bruno S. Silvestre developed the first honeycomb model (see Figure 2.1).[21]

- **Sharing**—"The extent to which users exchange, distribute and receive information."
- **Presence**—"The extent to which users know if others are available."
- **Relationships**—"The extent to which users relate to each other."
- **Identity**—"The extent to which users reveal themselves."
- **Conversations**—"The extent to which users communicate with each other."
- **Reputation**—"The extent to which users know the social standing of others and content."
- **Groups**—"The extent to which users are ordered or form communities."

This model was later added to by Christian V. Baccarella and Tim Wagner in collaboration with the original authors, Jan H. Kietzmann and Ian P. McCarthy, in an attempt to identify dark side–oriented social media theories. The revised model introduced a functional and multidimensional framework that reveals the darker aspects like excessive, aggressive, and/or inaccurate engagement (see Figure 2.1).[22] This research describes the complex features that social media users experience and what drives users to prefer one medium with a certain functionality over another.

The lens of these researchers' analysis is more or less focused, depending on the combinations of media and their functionality. By illustrating these as simplified building blocks or honeycombs, the motivations of social media users can be discovered, and higher-level explanations about activities thought to be "dark"—like **cyberbullying**, **trolling**, **fake news distribution**, and the like—can be offered. You will learn more about cyberbullying, trolling, and fake news distribution later in the chapter.

Although the honeycomb model can help identify and perhaps unveil risks associated with social media, much more work is needed to identify and create remedies or antidotes for this dark side of social media.[23,24] The longer we live with social media and the more we discover about it, the more urgent the need to address the changing aspects of the social sphere will become.

Who's to blame for the rise in the dark side of social media and its inherent risks? The short answer to this question is, we are. Well, it's us and the **TL; DR (too long; didn't read)** attitude of social media consumers along with the social media platform policies constructed for account creation. Take for example, the 2018 Facebook data "crisis" involving third-party **Cambridge Analytica**, a political consulting firm, and their use of Facebook-mined data from more than 87 million users. You could argue that this wasn't a crisis at all. After all, every single consumer who has a Facebook account has given consent through Facebook's Terms of Use to grant access by third parties to their data. Oh, wait, you didn't *read* the terms of use before you clicked the little box saying yes, please give me my account? Although more than two-thirds of US adults obtain their news from social media (with Facebook leading the way at 45 percent of news consumed; see Figure 2.2[25]), it turns out that most people

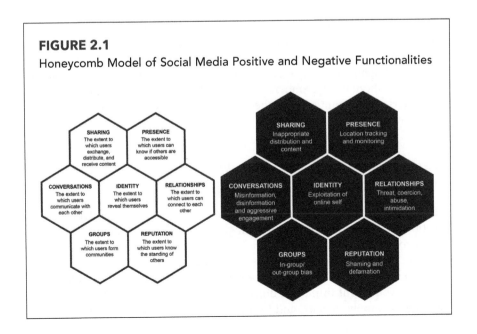

FIGURE 2.1

Honeycomb Model of Social Media Positive and Negative Functionalities

FIGURE 2.2

Pew social media graphics. (A) About two-thirds of Americans get news on social media, but most social media news consumers expect news they see there to be inaccurate. (B) Social media sites as pathways to news.

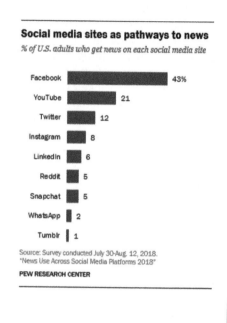

About two-thirds of Americans get news on social media

% of U.S. adults who get news on social media ...

Often 20%
Never 32%
Sometimes 27%
Hardly ever 21%

68% ever get news on social media

But most social media news consumers expect news there to be inaccurate

% of social media news consumers who say they expect the news they see on social media to be ...

Largely inaccurate	Largely accurate
57%	42

Note: No answer responses not shown.
Source: Survey conducted July 30-Aug. 12, 2018.
"News Use Across Social Media Platforms 2018"

PEW RESEARCH CENTER

Social media sites as pathways to news

% of U.S. adults who get news on each social media site

Facebook	43%
YouTube	21
Twitter	12
Instagram	8
LinkedIn	6
Reddit	5
Snapchat	5
WhatsApp	2
Tumblr	1

Source: Survey conducted July 30-Aug. 12, 2018.
"News Use Across Social Media Platforms 2018"

PEW RESEARCH CENTER

did not fully understand their relationship with Facebook and third-party advertisers. As a result, 2.2 billion users who did not read Facebook's terms or consider the ramifications of their personal browsing or data histories to be at personal risk were left exposed and manipulated.

At the time of Mark Zuckerberg's Senate hearing about Cambridge Analytica, even democratically elected representatives of the US government, forty-four of whom were members of the Judiciary and Commerce, Science, and Transportation committees at the time, didn't truly understand how social media worked.[26]

TRUST, PRIVACY, MEDIA, AND THE IMPACT ON SOCIETY DECEPTION

If those enforcing the law do not fully comprehend the basic tenets of the platforms, what should we do? You might be surprised at just how many laws apply to social media. Table 2.1 presents some North American and EU laws that are directly related to social media behavior.

Unless you are an attorney or perhaps a social media legal scholar in the making, you might think you don't have to understand how the laws shown in Table 2.1 apply to you—and for the most part you may be right. However,

TABLE 2.1 North American and EU legislation related to social media behavior.

Anti-SLAPP[a]	US state law that provides protection against Strategic Lawsuits Against Public Participation (SLAPP). SLAPP laws are intended to prevent litigation filed for purpose of censoring, intimidating, or silencing parties illegally.
Americans with Disabilities Act (ADA)[b]	US federal law that prohibits discrimination based on disability. This pertains to anything on a website or an application from images to language, access to navigation.
Canada's Anti-Spam Legislation[c] (CASL)	Deters damaging and deceptive forms of spam (unsolicited bulk messages) occurring in Canada. Email tactics and list making fall into this legislative purview.
Canada's Copyright Modernization Act[d]	Implements the rights and protections under the World Intellectual Property Organization (WIPO) Internet treaties and addresses various challenges and opportunities to copyright owners posed by the Internet and digital media.
Communications Decency Act[e] (CDA)	US federal law that regulates indecency and obscenity on/in cyberspace. Section 230 provides a safe harbor for third-party providers who are not construed as publishers of their users' content.
Computer Fraud and Abuse Act (CFAA), 18 U.S.C. § 1030 *et seq.*[f]	US federal law that projects the common law tort of real property trespass into the virtual realm of computers.
Copyright Act[g]	US law that sets out exclusionary rights for works of authorship.
Children's Online Privacy Protection Act[h] (COPPA)	US federal law and Federal Trade Commission regulations that regulate online collection of personal information of persons under 13 years of age.
Digital Millennium Copyright Act[i] (DMCA)	Part of US copyright law, the DMCA limits liability to service providers even if they have actual knowledge of infringing activity.
Electronic Communications Privacy Act (ECPA), 18 U.S.C. § 2511[j]	US federal law that prohibits interception of "any wire, oral, or electronic communication."
Electronic Funds Transfer Act (EFTA)[k]	US federal law that establishes responsibilities of participants of electronic funds transfers and dictates rights and liabilities of consumers.
Family Medical Leave Act (FMLA)[l]	US federal law that requires certain employers to provide employees with unpaid leave for qualified family and medical reasons. Posts can and have been used against those claiming FMLA for injury or illness, yet not following this conduct in their lives and posting online. Not using FMLA for its intended purpose.

[a] Media Law Resource Center. "Anti-SLAPP Statutes and Commentary." Media Law Resource Center. http://www.medialaw.org/topics-page/anti-slapp#startOfPageId3494.
[b] United States Government. "The Current ADA Regulations." United States Government. https://www.ada.gov/2010_regs.htm.
[c] Office of the Privacy Commissioner of Canada. "Canada's Anti-Spam Legislation." Office of the Privacy Commissioner of Canada. Last modified December 14, 2018. https://www.priv.gc.ca/en/privacy-topics/privacy-laws-in-canada/the-personal-information-protection-and-electronic-documents-act-pipeda/r_o_p/canadas-anti-spam-legislation.
[d] Government of Canada. "Copyright Modernization Act." Government of Canada. Last modified June 29, 2012. https://laws-lois.justice.gc.ca/eng/annualstatutes/2012_20/fulltext.html.
[e] Electronic Frontier Foundation. "Section 230 of the Communications Decency Act." Electronic Frontier Foundation. https://www.eff.org/issues/cda230.
[f] Computer Fraud and Abuse Act ("CFAA"), 18 U.S.C. § 1030 *et seq.* (1984).
[g] The Copyright Act of 1976 Pub.L. 94–553 (1976).
[h] Children's Online Privacy Protection Act (COPPA) 15 U.S.C. §§ 6501–6506 (1998).
[i] Digital Millennium Copyright Act (DMCA) 17 U.S.C. §§ 101, 104, 104A, 108, 112, 114, 117, 701 17 U.S.C. §§ 512, 1201–1205, 1301–1332; 28 U.S.C. § 4001 (1998).
[j] Electronic Communications Privacy Act (ECPA), 18 U.S.C. § 2511 (1986).
[k] Electronic Fund Transfer Act (EFTA) 12 U.S.C. ch. 3 § 226 *et seq.* 15 U.S.C. ch. 41 § 1601 *et seq.* 15 U.S.C. ch. 41 § 1693 *et seq.* (1978).
[l] Family and Medical Leave Act of 1993 (FMLA) Pub.L. 103–113 (1993).

Federal Trade Commission (FTC) Act, 15 U.S.C §§ 41–58[m]	US law that authorizes the FTC to investigate and curb unfair trade policies.
General Data Protection Regulation (GDPR)[n]	A European Union law on data regulation with no US equivalent that requires US websites to comply if they are doing business with international clientele or end users that reside in the EU.
Lanham Act, 15 U.S.C. § 1051[o]	US federal law that provides protection for trademarks and service marks.
National Labor Relations Act[p]	US federal law that guarantees rights of employees to participate and engage in concerted activity for better conditions in the workplace.
SPEECH Act of 2010, 28 U.S.C. §§ 4101–4105[q]	US federal law that makes foreign libel judgments unenforceable in US courts, unless those judgments comply with the First Amendment.
Stored Communications Act (SCA)[r]	Part of ECPA, it prohibits unauthorized access of stored wire and electronic communications and records that are intended to be private.
Patent Act[s]	US federal law provides patent holders with a temporary right to exclude.
18 U.S.C. § 875[t]	US law that makes it a federal crime to transmit in interstate or foreign commerce a threat to kidnap or injure a person, or to threaten property or one's reputation with an extortion component.

[m] Federal Trade Commission ("FTC") Act, 15 U.S.C §§ 41–58 (2006).
[n] Burgess, Matt. "What Is GDPR? The Summary Guide to GDPR Compliance in the UK." *Wired.* Last modified January 19, 2019. https://www.wired.co.uk/article/what-is-gdpr-uk-eu-legislation-compliance-summary-fines-2018.
[o] Trademark Act of 1946 aka Lanham Act, 15 U.S.C. § 1051 (1946, 1976).
[p] The National Labor Relations Act of 1935 (49 Stat. 449) 29 U.S.C. § 151–169 (1935).
[q] Speech Act of 2010, 28 U.S.C. §§ 4101–4105 (2010).
[r] Stored Communications Act Pub.L. 99–508 (1986).
[s] The Patent Act of 1790 1 Stat. 109 (1790).[t] Interstate Communication and Threats Code 18 U.S.C. § 875 (1940).

a number of topics are relevant to the everyday (or every few minutes) social media user, including privacy; trust and influence; fake news; and bullying, harassment, trolling, and hate speech.

Privacy

With the Cambridge Analytica scandal, Facebook users were given a behind-the-curtain peek at how Facebook categorizes each user through the Facebook ad preferences page.[27] About half of users say that they are not comfortable when they see this categorization data, and more than 25 percent claim that the site's classification does not accurately represent them. However, a majority of users (59 percent) say that these categories reflect their real-life interests.[28] Even more shocking, 74 percent of US adults surveyed by the Pew Research Group had no idea that Facebook maintained a list of their interests and traits to use for their algorithm in targeting advertisements (see Figure 2.3).[29]

Most commercial sites—not just social media platforms—collect a variety of data about their users' habits. This data allows marketers to target ads more precisely, in the hope that tailored, highly targeted messaging is more compelling and thus more likely to result in the purchase of a product or service. The accuracy of these collection methods is determined by algorithms. The data may be input by the consumer through filling out a form or through viewing their browsing history, and the link between user and algorithm impacts the notion of privacy over time.[30] The algorithms filter, rank, and organize the data that are served up, based on relevance and a defined set of criteria in order to achieve a specific goal.[31]

As the number of active users per month on social media platforms has grown, so too has the need for algorithms in order to maintain high relevance.

FIGURE 2.3

Seventy-four percent of Facebook users did not know that the company catalogued their interests and traits and about half are not comfortable being categorized.

Many Facebook users say they do not know the platform classifies their interests, and roughly half are not comfortable with being categorized

% of U.S. adult Facebook users who say ____ after being directed to view their Facebook 'ad preferences' page

74%   They **did not know** Facebook maintained this list of their interests and traits

51%   They are **not comfortable** with Facebook compiling this information

27%   The listings **do not very or at all accurately represent** them

Source: Survey of Facebook users conducted Sept. 4-Oct. 1, 2018. "Facebook Algorithms and Personal Data"

PEW RESEARCH CENTER

The idea is to keep content fresh and engaging. To do this, algorithms need data that they can use. As you may have already guessed, this is where privacy may seem to be invaded. Facebook, Twitter, Instagram, and Pinterest provide company and organization accounts the ability to **boost** posts—sometimes referred to as **pay-to-play** (advertising). This is simply an exchange of money for amplification of content to an existing user base. Targeting advertising based on your private information specifically and strategically allows you to view content at the whim of the advertiser.

Trust and Influence

The public has mixed feelings about the computer algorithms that decide what to serve them via social media channels and other digital platforms, from e-commerce to entertainment.[32] The popularity of social media as a news gathering and sharing tool also raises many questions regarding trust. What type of news and news sites can you trust? In addition, the notion of social media **influencers** and their popular influence has long been a topic of conversation in social media research, but only recently has it been examined through a lens of trustworthiness.[33,34,35,36,37,38] Both computer algorithms and social media influencers impact public trust of digital platforms.

According to an article in the *International Journal of Information Management*, "The main function of a social media platform is to develop and maintain mutual relationships through effective online communication."[39] Interpersonal relationships thrive in an environment of trust; although there are many problems—or barriers to trust—within virtual communication, people need to establish minimum levels of trust in order to have meaningful interactions. Building trust is of critical importance to establishing effective social media relationships.[40] Social media is a participatory experience in which relationships are established through a series of online interactions.[41] As a result, valuable information spreads at a rate much faster than is possible with traditional media. Its ability to reach virality at rates not typically seen with traditional media is likely a result of trust.[42,43] (See the In Theory feature.)

In online social media-sharing communities, the success of social interactions for content sharing and dissemination among completely unknown users depends on "trust." Therefore, providing a satisfactory trust model to evaluate the quality of content and to recommend personalized trustworthy content providers is vital for a successful online social media-sharing community. Current research on trust prediction strongly relies on a web of trust, which is directly collected from users.[44]

IN THEORY | The Trust Cognitive Onion Model in Social Media Communications

Xusen Cheng, Shixuan Fu, and Gert Jan de Vreede developed a hybrid model in an attempt to explain how trust works in social media. The *trust cognitive onion model* (see Figure A) is a mashup of Eden's **cognitive mapping model**,[45] which serves as a mental map or model serving as the ability for an individual to code, store, and recall information, and Tor J. Larsen, Fred Niederman, Moez Limayem, and Joyce Chan's causal model for the analysis of the role of **Unified Model-**

ing Language (UML) in software engineering intended to provide standard visualization of system designs.[46] As a result of their research on trust in the social media platform **WeChat**, Cheng, Fu, and Jan de Vreede threw out the traditional model modes listed in the methods mentioned earlier and created new layers from the trust relationship in social media, formulating a model that is easy to both use and understand.[47]

From this model you can see how trust factors in social

media start to develop into the following factors for decision making: information quality, shared preferences, familiarity, privacy, chatting topic, convenience, and time-saving.[48] These factors provide insight into the how and why of trust in and influence of social media for non–e-commerce transactions, broadening the scope and understanding of "interpersonal relationships, group communication and mass media broadcast in the context of social media communication."[49]

Continued

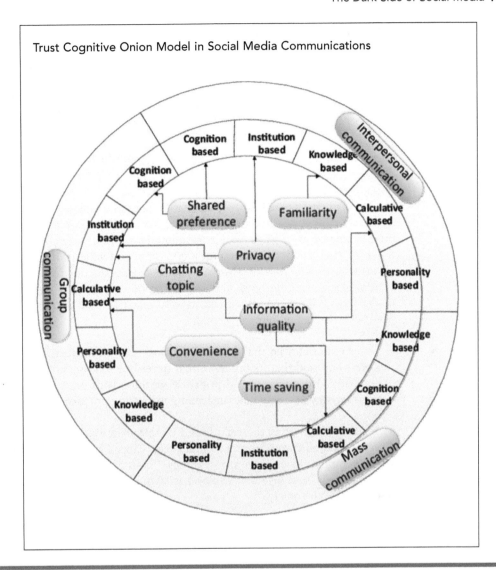

Trust Cognitive Onion Model in Social Media Communications

Another study focused on five different validated measures—integrity, competence, benevolence, concern, and identification—to investigate the impact of gender, age, and amount of time spent on social media on the perception of trust. The results indicated that trust is essential in online engagement, especially among women and younger users who have higher expectations for integrity, trust in others, and empathy as a path to goodwill.[50]

Influence and trust are directly related. Just as you might value a recommendation from a friend on which car to purchase or what restaurants to avoid, influencers have stepped into the communications spotlight as the new "trusted friend." Many influencers have paid sponsorships (aka advertising), which impact how consumers perceive brands.[51] The Federal Trade Commission (FTC) has guidelines for how influencers should disclose their relationships with brands in an effort to improve trust scores and quality indices of advertised products.[52,53] Although these are guidelines—not regulations—and were introduced simply to improve disclosures in social media endorsements, a few civil cases have served as precedents[54] concerning the use of endorsements and testimonials in advertising (see Section 5 of the FTC Act (15 U.S.C. 45)).[55] Originators of the guide claim that it was intended to provide the basis for voluntary compliance by advertisers and endorsers, but its critics say it has "no teeth" as it is not policed and is enforced haphazardly.[56]

As service providers, influencers rely on their audiences for advocacy. Successful influencers are commonly associated with high levels of *trust, commitment,* and *authenticity.*[57] Some studies even indicate that influencers hold nearly as much or more influence as friends with regard to purchasing power.[58] This influence has the potential to be used to subvert or undermine other causes in a deliberate and deviant manner.[59] To combat this, global brand Unilever, which has brands including Dove, Lipton Tea, Axe, and Ben & Jerry's, has called on the practitioners in public relations, marketing, and advertising to stop working with influencers who do not reveal that they receive money or other compensation for goods that appear in their social media feeds. Unilever has laid out steps to distance itself and all its brands from social media influencer accounts:

> Unilever announced that it would not work with influencers who buy followers and said that its brands would never buy followers of its own. The company also said it would prioritize working with partners to increase transparency and eradicate misleading marketing practices.[60]

To date, Unilever is the only brand of this magnitude that has publicly divested relationships with paid influencers. Chief Marketing Officer Keith Weed is looking to improve transparency "in an era of fake news and toxic online content" and says that Unilever is trying to "rebuild trust back in our systems and our society."[61]

Disinformation

You are what you read … and then share. A Pew Research Center study following the 2016 US presidential election showed that 64 percent of US adults think that fake news stories cause a "great deal of confusion," and 23 percent actually admitted to sharing a fabricated story themselves—sometimes by mistake, but sometimes intentionally![62]

> The manipulation of public opinion over social media platforms has emerged as a critical threat to public life. Around the world, a range of government agencies and political parties are exploiting social media platforms to spread junk news and disinformation, exercise censorship and control, and undermine trust in the media, public institutions, and science. At a time when news consumption is increasingly digital, artificial intelligence, big data analytics, and "blackbox" algorithms are being leveraged to challenge truth and trust: the cornerstones of our democratic society.[63]

Social media can be used as a tool for online **propaganda**,[64] intentional manipulation of public opinion. Online propaganda is a process or product that usually goes by the name **fake news**. Its tactics include amplification of hate speech; creation of false or harmful content; creation and use of fake accounts to manipulate public opinion; illegal data harvesting; spread of misinformation on social platforms; use of bots; and utilization of clickbait content to increase virality. The list goes on and on. **Disinformation** is a broad concept that goes far beyond the notion of fake news; it includes all forms of false, inaccurate, or misleading information designed, presented, and promoted to intentionally cause public harm or for profit.[65]

> Social media manipulation is big business. Since 2010, political parties and governments have spent more than half a billion dollars on the research, development, and implementation of psychological operations and public opinion manipulation over social media. In a few countries this includes efforts to counter extremism, but in most countries, this involves the spread of junk news and misinformation during elections, military crises, and complex humanitarian disasters.[66]

Such intentional acts seek to influence global society, but acts to harm and misinform are not limited to society-wide efforts. The social sphere has made it possible to infiltrate individual networks and target groups with nefarious content and actions as well.

Cyberbullying, Trolling, and Hate Speech

According to a Pew Research study, "A majority (59 percent) of US teens have been bullied or harassed online, and a similar share says it's a major problem for people their age."[67] The very first studies[68,69] into cyberbullying adapted the Olweus definition of bullying, which states: "a person is bullied when he or she is exposed, repeatedly and over time, to negative actions on the part of one or more other persons, and he or she has difficulty defending himself or herself"[70] and applied it to the digital space by maintaining that this type of bullying was done via electronic means of communication, including social media, texting, websites, and the like.

> Certain characteristics distinguish cyberbullying from interpersonal bullying, including (a) the potential for an infinite audience; (b) an altered balance of power between the bully and the victim, rendering the victim unable to effectively defend himself or herself against the bullying behaviors; (c) an inability for the bully to observe the immediate reaction of the victim; (d) the absence of space and time constraints on bullying; and (e) the perception of anonymity on the part of the bully.[71,72]

Findings from Allison Ann Payne and Kirsten Hutzell show that "interpersonal bullying victimization is far more prevalent than cyberbullying victimization. Results also illustrate differences in the relationships between demographics and bullying victimization" (see Figure 2.4).[73] Finally, they found that students who are a victim of either form of bullying are more likely to engage in school avoidance behaviors. These articles demonstrate the urgent need for programs to reduce the consequences of cyberbullying.

Though much of the research related to cyberbullying is focused on children, a Pew Research Center survey of adults in the United States found

FIGURE 2.4

Cyberbullying. A majority of teens have been the target of cyberbullying, with name-calling and rumor-spreading being the most common forms of harassment.

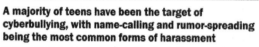

A majority of teens have been the target of cyberbullying, with name-calling and rumor-spreading being the most common forms of harassment

% of U.S. teens who say they have experienced ___ online or on their cellphone

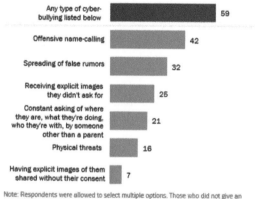

Note: Respondents were allowed to select multiple options. Those who did not give an answer or gave other response are not shown.
Source: Survey conducted March 7–April 10, 2018.
"A Majority of Teens Have Experienced Some Form of Cyberbullying"

PEW RESEARCH CENTER

that age and gender differences existed in "receiving nonconsensual explicit images" and that women ages eighteen through twenty-nine are especially targeted with this behavior.[74]

A familiar social media term is *troll* or *trolling*. This doesn't refer to the dolls or the movie featuring adorable little creatures with colorful hair. Internet **trolls** focus on provoking other users by instigating negative and sometimes harmful dialogues; such activity is referred to as trolling. Imagine that you've posted a selfie to your Instagram account, only to have complete strangers suddenly hijack your post and begin posting negative comments about your appearance. Your once mood-boosting selfie now has a negative connotation that likely will cause you to delete it. These often-anonymous bottom feeders of the Internet target not only individuals but big brands, entertainers, politicians, athletes, and industries as well. The nature of the content can vary from light-hearted ribbing during a sporting event to the spread of misinformation and, at the extreme, **hate speech**, which includes "abusive or threatening speech or writing that expresses prejudice against a particular group, especially on the basis of race, religion, or sexual orientation"[75] and incitement of violence (see the Relational/Societal/Self feature).

What role should social media play in protecting people from harassment, cyberbullying, and/or hate speech? This is a confusing and oftentimes disappointing area of concern in society today. An attack on two mosques in Chirstchurch, New Zealand, which was streamed live on Facebook, made international news. The video was shared millions of times before being removed by Facebook and other online platforms. For some, the lack of prompt action by social media platforms exemplified all that is wrong with social media.

Elizabeth Dwoskin of *The Washington Post*, who was interviewed by Judy Woodruff of PBS immediately following the shooting, said, "social media companies, often, they say, it's like, another day, another failure. This isn't the first murder that's been streamed live on Facebook or uploaded onto YouTube, but it was the one most designed to go viral, because the shooter was livestreaming himself while appearing to niche online communities that aggressively reposted it."[77]

Max Boot, a *Washington Post* columnist, wrote that "terrorism is inconceivable without mass media"[78] and that the need for fighting the spread of propaganda online needs to be prioritized worldwide. Despite existing checks and balances,[79] many people have figured out ways around them by tricking programming that is specifically built to deter online harassment

Relational/Societal/Self: When Trolls Take Control

In 2017, Kids Plus Pediatrics in Pittsburgh found themselves embroiled in a strategic trolling campaign by anti-vaccination advocates after posting a video on Facebook encouraging parents to vaccinate their children against the human papilloma virus (HPV). In an article for *The Washington Post* published on March 21, 2019, Lena Sun wrote that the post received 10,000 negative comments posted by approximately 800 individuals in just over one week, including threats, misinformation about vaccinations, and conspiracy rhetoric pointed at medical professionals and the government. The initial response to the trolling included the blocking of hundreds of users. Then the practice was able to con-nect with someone inside the closed Facebook group spearheading the attack who provided them with information needed to anticipate the type of content and where it would be posted. In the hopes of preempting another strike to their social platforms and wanting to better understand the group dynamics behind the event, Kids Care Plus partnered with researchers at the University of Pittsburgh. The findings of the study reinforced the need for organizations to practice proactive communication strategies, target audiences with accurate content, and use additional tactics to mitigate the spread of misinformation on social channels.[76]

Social media events like what happened to Kids Plus can be detrimental to an organization or brand, affecting their reputation and bottom line; however, when the attacks are vitriolic and aimed at undermining trust in healthcare information and providers, they have the potential to become fatal. The digital space has removed geographic obstacles, making connecting with like-minded persons as simple as a click of the mouse.

Think about It: Do you think that blocking commenters is the best response for the organization? Why or why not? What other proactive measures could be taken by Kids Plus Pediatrics to prevent something like this from happening again?

and/or hate speech on social media platforms through manipulation of search or application programing interfaces (API) to change the features of data in and on an operating system, application, or any other kind of service online.[80,81,82]

Google (the owner of YouTube) and Facebook have spent years attempting to prohibit problematic videos from appearing to the public via their sites, often employing the use of artificial intelligence (AI). Still in development, AI could block violent and graphic content before it reached the end user. However, expectations may be too high at present.[83] This leads us back to our original question of responsibility and ownership: Will governments begin to regulate how social media oversees content?[84] For much of the world, the answer to this question is yet to be determined.

PSYCHOLOGICAL AND PHYSIOLOGICAL IMPACTS OF SOCIAL MEDIA

The increasing amounts of time spent by adults and children on social media have shown a negative impact on our psychology and physiology. Social media use has been attributed to increased stress, decreased self-esteem, depression, anxiety, and a variety of other maladies, such as sleep disruption. Most people spend more time on social media than reading or exercising![85] We should all just quit, right? If it were only that easy.

Among the most intriguing features of social media exposure is the linkage of **social media fatigue**, a condition that refers to user tendency to remove themselves from social media when they are feeling overwhelmed or unsafe, and high anxiety with the concepts of **fear of missing out (FOMO)**[86] and **fear of living offline (FOLO)**.[87] Despite social media user reports of high levels of anxiety, their never-ending quest to not miss out on anything compels them to keep using it, increasing their social media fatigue and anxiety, and the cycle goes on and on.[88] A 2018 study revealed that compulsive social media use positively predicted fatigue.[89] If this sounds like addiction to you, you're on to something.[90] Another study revealed the prevalence of addiction-like symptoms in relationship to use of social media sites; this creates a "tug of war" between social self-regulation and the habit of social media use.[91]

Studies have found that use of social media can have negative effects on individuals with depression.[92,93] Depressed adolescents' social media use included behaviors such as comparing themselves to others in an idealistic light, the sharing of risky behavior, the posting of negative or harmful content, and negative verbal interactions with others.[94] These traits have aligned with other behavioral health studies in which excessive use of the Internet and social media have been associated with behavioral addiction.[95]

Although it seems as though we have every reason to side with behavioral science on this one, studies also show that you will probably never quit social media. Much research has been conducted about Facebook use, specifically. Since the platform was introduced in 2004, it seems like Facebook has created the magic mix to keep you as a monthly—or more likely daily—active user. A UK study concluded that "the perceived need to be online may result in compulsive use of SNSs (social networking sites), which in extreme cases may result in symptoms and consequences traditionally associated with substance-related addictions."[96]

Distraction

So how bad is it really? With all the previous talk about addiction, depression, anxiety, and other negative implications of social media use, how much time does the average person spend on social media? The short answer is a lot. Research from Digital Information World indicates that the average person spends 142 minutes per day on social media, including social networking and messaging platforms (see Figure 2.5).[97] More than two hours of a daily distraction is a pretty hefty number, especially considering that we only spend about six hours per day sleeping![98]

The study by Digital Information World shows that there may be saturation in social media consumption. Researchers have hypothesized that advanced awareness about the negative impact of screen time may be impacting this plateau, but it is too soon to tell.[99]

Facebook still dominates the social media industry, claiming that more than 85 percent of the world's Internet users are members (excluding China) (see Figure 2.6). However, YouTube, Facebook Messenger, WhatsApp (owned by Facebook), Instagram (also owned by Facebook), and Twitter are close behind and gaining ground.[100]

Among young people (17 and under), 95 percent of teens have access to a smartphone, and 45 percent say they are online "almost constantly." They have

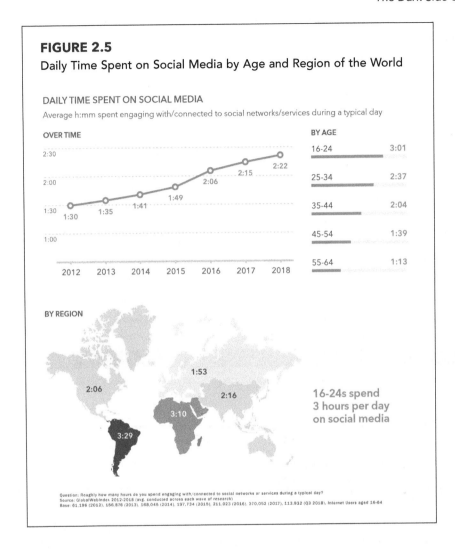

FIGURE 2.5

Daily Time Spent on Social Media by Age and Region of the World

shifted from Facebook to more photo- and video-centric social media like YouTube, Instagram, and Snap.[101]

Usage statistics aside, studies on distraction still send a loud and clear message that social media usage has negative effects, negatively affecting task performance and negatively affecting happiness.[102] The question is, now that we know about the negative impact, what are we going to do about it?

Social Disenfranchisement

The notion of the social media nonuser who may actually be prevented from social media use because of lack of desire for social engagement (not functional or otherwise developmental) issues (like disability or cognition) has been studied less extensively. Xinru Page, Pamela Wisniewski, Bart P. Knijnenburg, and Moses Namara found that even social media nonusers faced social consequences both on and off social media.[103] This disenfranchised group of people, though decreasing as society becomes increasingly connected, are "left behind and even ostracized,"[104] showing a dark side even to social media nonuse.

FIGURE 2.6
Top 15 Most Popular Social Networks

Top Social Media Apps Worldwide for January 2020 by Downloads — SensorTower

	Overall Downloads		App Store Downloads		Google Play Downloads
1	TikTok	1	TikTok	1	TikTok
2	Facebook	2	Instagram	2	Facebook
3	Instagram	3	Facebook	3	Instagram
4	Likee	4	Kuaishou	4	Likee
5	Snapchat	5	Snapchat	5	Snapchat
6	Helo	6	Twitter	6	Helo
7	Twitter	7	Wesee	7	VMate
8	Kuaishou	8	Pinterest	8	Twitter
9	Pinterest	9	Vigo Video	9	Pinterest
10	VMate	10	WeChat	10	Kuaishou

Note: Does not include downloads from third-party Android stores in China or other regions.

SensorTower Data That Drives App Growth   sensortower.com

CHAPTER WRAP-UP

Social media offers many opportunities, but there is obviously a malicious aspect to the same tools that offer us the benefits of convenience, speed, ease, and connectivity. With reports of cyberbullying, anxiety, depression, deep fakes, the spread of misinformation, and addiction on the rise, it is important to ask yourself whether social platforms are causing more harm than good.

CRITICAL-THINKING QUESTIONS

1. Now that you have read this chapter, offer your own perspective on the "dark side" of social media.

2. Have you ever thought of "quitting" social media? Why or why not? Do you think you could do it? What would be the challenges? The benefits?

3. Do you ever experience FOMO or FOLO?

4. Over your lifetime, would you say that your experience with social media has been positive or negative? Explain your answer.

5. Have you ever experienced or witnessed cyberbullying? How should it be/was it addressed?

6. Does privacy exist anymore? Will it exist in the future? How does your behavior now shape your social media privacy?

ACTIVITIES

1. Check your smartphone settings to see how much time you spend in/on your apps. What takes up the majority of your time? How much and what percentage of your time is spent on social media apps? Were you surprised by your findings? Would you change anything after quantifying your behavior on social media? If so, what's your strategy? Compare your results and strategy with a partner and then with your class as a whole.

2. Now that you have a stronger understanding of the dark side of social media, choose a concept discussed in this chapter and explain why you believe it should be remedied, and explain how to do so. Consider actions that can be taken by service providers as well as government legislation.

3. According to Nielson, US adults spend more than eleven hours per day online and interacting on social media.[105] Give up social media for one day. Throughout that day, jot down the feelings you experience every time you have the urge to check your social media. Are you anxious? More relaxed? Do you feel more or less pressure? Are you freer to be in the moment? How long do you think you could go without social media?

KEY CONCEPTS

Amplification
Boost
Cambridge Analytica
Cognitive mapping model
Cyberbullying
Deepfakes
Disinformation
Fake news
Fake news distribution
Fear of living offline (FOLO)
Fear of missing out (FOMO)
Hate speech
Influencer

Pay-to-play
Propaganda
Social media fatigue
Terms of use
TL; DR (too long; didn't read)
Troll
Trolling
Unified modeling language (UML)
WeChat

MEDIA SOURCES

The Cruelty of Call-Out Culture: How not to do social change. https://www.nytimes.com/2019/01/14/opinion/call-out-social-justice.html?rref=collection%2Ftimestopic%2FCyberbullying&action=click&contentCollection=timestopics&region=stream&module=stream_unit&version=latest&contentPlacement=1&pgtype=collection.

Confronting "Alternative Facts": A Twenty-First-Century Incredibility Chasm. https://www.commondreams.org/views/2019/01/10/confronting-alternative-facts-twenty-first-century-incredibility-chasm.

60+ Fascinating Smartphone Apps Usage Statistics for 2019: https://www.digitalinformationworld.com/2019/03/amazing-mobile-apps-usage-facts-infographic.html.

2018 Reform of EU data protection rules: ec.europa.eu/commission/priorities/justice-and-fundamental-rights/data-protection/2018-reform-eu-data-protection-rules_en.

FindLaw for Legal Professionals. Guide to Social Media Articles: https://technology.findlaw.com/modern-law-practice/social-media.html.

Benefits of Social Media

SOCIAL SAVES JIMMY

LEARNING OBJECTIVES

3.1 Explain the benefits of social media usage in personal and professional situations.

3.2 Apply existing models of communication to the social sphere.

3.3 Identify the ethical ramifications of social media behaviors.

This social media story is not one that you have read about. It's not one that graced the headlines of the *New York Times*; it did not, in fact, go viral or lead to world peace, though a recap did land in the Huffington Post. This is the story of Jimmy—a limping, old, senile, overweight black lab and master backyard escape artist. One evening through Google hangouts a message pinged my phone: "OMFG—JIMMY IS GONE. HELP ME FIND HIM?" It was late at night, he's a black dog—sure, how hard could that be? Although some folks might be a "feet on the street" kind of person, the likelihood of finding a jet-black dog in the middle of a jet-black night would be best served with as many eyeballs as possible. This news spread quickly via social sharing from both personal and local business pages—Facebook, Twitter, Nextdoor, through local dog lover groups, the Humane Society, and the Love of Fido to local neighborhood groups.

At the same time we were searching feverishly, Jimmy had already been found in the parking lot of a local dive bar (this is so Jimmy) without his collar (that was found later hooked to the piece of wood he rammed out to escape his backyard oasis), so there was no way for the finders to align with the seekers—except through social media! The couple who found Jimmy deployed a social media strategy of "do you know whose dog this is" via social media channels on Facebook, Instagram, and Twitter. Though I live in a fairly large city in the Midwest, it didn't take too long for the finders and the seekers to intersect on a Facebook group through a tertiary friend connection. Jimmy's great big adventure lasted just three hours due to the intervention of social media and the interconnectivity of community that is built as a result of networking through a variety of social media. Our relationship with technology is a complicated one, but it can be used for good on both macro and micro levels.

As you learned in Chapter 2, social media does have a darker side. That said, it also comes with a multitude of benefits. From reconnecting with old friends and finding new ones to improving social and business outcomes, social media is a cheap, fast, and reliable tool to facilitate relationships of all kinds. Chapter 3 focuses on its benefits as a communication tool through the lenses of well-being in relationships, society, and self, spending time examining the lighter, brighter, and more positive side of social media.

Social media must be beneficial or we wouldn't invest the amount of time we do staring at our smartphones or calling out into thin air, "Alexa," "Hey, Google," or "Siri" for search assistance. We have all been trained. Use of social media has become a habit. Before social media, we may not have known about the "perfect hamburger"[1] or have been able to "keep up" with the Kardashians,[2] but we would have missed out on the following:

- Miracles performed during crises via YouCaring pages and Facebook,[3,4]
- Crowdsourcing of a constitution in Iceland,[5]
- The 95-year-old World War II veteran in New Zealand who was so moved by the tragedy in Christchurch that he took four busloads of people to attend a solidarity march against racism in Auckland.[6]

Few of us read printed newspapers or watch the news on TV anymore. Instead, we view stories, often in real time, on our social media timelines.

Even the 2019 "Internet minute" (see Figure 3.1) is dominated by social media: 2.1 million snaps are created; 87,500 people tweet; 1.4 million swipe on Tinder; 41.6 million instant messages are sent via WhatsApp and Facebook Messenger; and 347,222 images are scrolled through and "loved" in Instagram.[7] But outside of killing time, what are the benefits of social media to relationships, society, and self?

RELATIONAL BENEFITS OF SOCIAL MEDIA USE

Many studies have shown correlations between social ties/interpersonal relationships (including the number and quality of intimate relationships) and happiness, health, longevity, and well-being.[8,9,10] Others have shown that lack of social relationships or social isolation creates "toxic" results.[11] By

FIGURE 3.1
Aggregate data of the online activity of billions of people globally. This is what an Internet minute looks like.

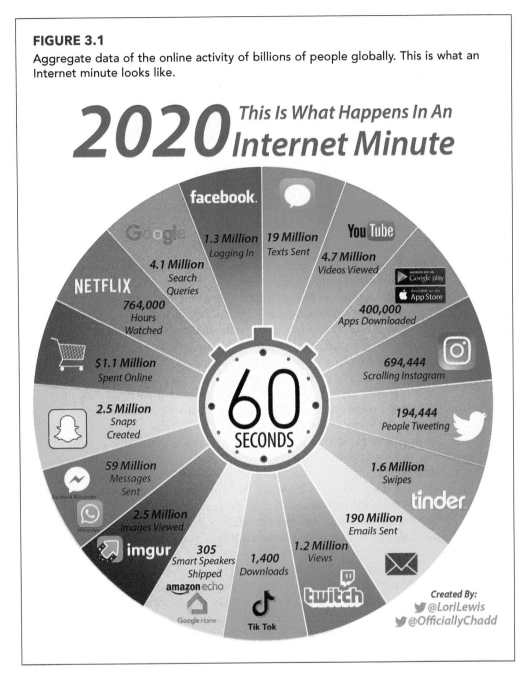

eliminating the need for geographic proximity, social media can shape many aspects of relationships, creating a more accessible, connected world for those with an Internet connection.

Researching Interpersonal Relationships

Virtual community researchers,[12] organizers,[13] and—of course—advertisers and marketers[14,15] have been very interested in how interpersonal relationships on social media can explain everything from trust and participation to influence. Honglei Li and Kun Change Lee researched participation in

virtual communities (VC) by incorporating comprehensive theoretical frameworks from social psychology (the Triandis interpersonal behavior model)[16] and communication studies (fundamental interpersonal relationship orientation).[17,18,19] VCs are "groups of people, who may or may not meet one another face to face, who exchange words and ideas through the mediation of digital networks."[20] In order for interpersonal needs to be met (either online or offline), a relationship must be satisfied at three levels: inclusion, control, and affection. Their conclusions show that traditionally offline frameworks can create a basis for interpretation of online interpersonal behavior.[21] Specific mediums may come and go, but behavior and motivation are rooted in all human experiences.[22,23]

The Influence of Networking on Social Connection, Social Support, and Social Capital

Years before the birth of Facebook, computer networks were defined and considered as inherently social networks[24] because they linked people to other people and to sources of knowledge. The strength of a computer network was often used to magnify and measure social capital, a concept predating all types of digital media, that refers to an individual's networks and contacts related to conversion into economic capital.[25] More specifically, social capital can be noted as "a concept in social science that involves the potential of individuals to secure benefits and invent solutions to problems through membership in social networks. Social capital revolves around three dimensions: interconnected networks of relationships between individuals and groups (social ties or social participation), levels of trust that characterize these ties, and resources or benefits that are both gained and transferred by virtue of social ties and social participation."[26] This definition is better supported in business and management literature than in the social media literature.[27] However, creating the connection is simple: Networking (both online and offline) provides the *social connections* and *social support* that can lead to the development of *social capital*. For the purposes of this discussion, we consider **social capital** in an online context to be captured from embedded resources in social networks.[28]

There has been a great deal of research exploring the idea of **social connection**, which is the "experience of feeling close and connected to others. It involves feeling loved, cared for, and valued, and forms the basis of interpersonal relationships."[29] Researchers Jenna L. Clark, Sara B. Algoe, and Melanie C. Green investigated the extensive body of research on social network sites. Their work suggests that a single theoretical approach can reconcile conflicting results. According to the **interpersonal connection behaviors framework**, social network sites benefit end users when they are used to make connections, but harm them when things like isolation and direct social comparison are experienced.[30,31,32,33,34,35] Similar to other studies, Clark, Algoe, and Green's findings are correlational; the interpersonal connection behaviors framework "plausibly explains positive associations between use of social network sites and well-being."[36]

Like behavior and motivation, the concept of **social support**, a resource that results from development of a network,[37,38] has also gained attention from social media researchers.[39,40] In reviewing motivation theories and models across different types of social media, Sanghee Oh and Sue Yeon Syn demonstrated an extension to the previous studies: People go to different social media for different reasons that are based on their need for social support and connection.[41]

Extensive literature has surfaced on the relationship between social capital[42] and social media.[43] Research has shown how social networks, both online and offline, influence how social media is associated with social capital and how much social capital is possible to achieve through the use of social networks.[44,45] In an effort to differentiate social network structures from social media features, Weixu Lu and Keith Hampton studied the relationship between structure and "various activities on Facebook for one type of resource: informal social support in the form of companionship, emotional support, and tangible aid." They found that social capital both on- and offline contributed positively to user experiences.[46]

Online networks rely on both structures and user-defined purpose in order to grow social connections, increase social support, and provide social capital. Flexibility in the application of theory and frameworks assists researchers in applying meaning to user-based experiences.

User-Generated Content for Influence and Decision Making

You did it! You bought the new iPhone after seeing it on your friend's Instagram story. Congratulations! You're among the one in four people who has bought a product after seeing it featured in **user-generated content (UGC)**. Do consumers take relatable content seriously? Across vertical markets, studies have shown that 49 percent of people are more likely to purchase a product when endorsed by a real person, and 76 percent of eighteen- to twenty-four year-olds surveyed[47] trust UGC over other forms of content because it is considered to be "more honest." UGC is considered earned media, which is referred to as "publicity gained through promotional efforts other than paid media advertising, which refers to publicity gained through advertising, or owned media, which refers to branding."[48] This and other research performed by Olapic, a marketing software platform built to assist brands collect, use, and distribute user-generated content, also shows that age can influence how a person experiences social media content and makes decisions based on it.[49]

User-generated content builds trust[50] and drives decision making[51] for everything from which doctor you might want to see to what restaurant you go to on a first date. More and more frequently, brands are using UGC for direct advertising to all generations.[52,53] A recent consumer trust survey revealed that consumers prefer images of other consumers seven times more than traditional advertising tactics, with more than 76 percent of respondents concluding that UGC is "more honest."[54] So if we are engaged in UGC, we are all social media influencers. That opens us all up as targets for earned media and paid placement, activities that can take place on or through social media as well as more traditional mass media channels like television or radio.

In addition to trusting UGC more, people are using it in an effort to help their friends make good decisions. Seventy-five percent of those surveyed by Olapic have uploaded a photo hashtagging a brand; of those, 40 percent say that the main reason for doing so is to share purchases with friends.[55] Because this study also showed that respondents perceive earned media as the most honest form of content, a result backed up by a comprehensive review of the literature, UGC is an affordable way for brands, organizations, and people to win over trust and drive decision making. In a review of empirical evidence, author Johannes Knoll reviewed fifty-one studies that examine advertising in social media, concluding the following:

> UGC is as an important factor in social media advertising that influences recipients' attitudes and perceptions in conjunction with the original advertising messages. Depending on the positive or negative content of the UGC, advertising effects can be enhanced or diminished. Relationships between UGC originators and recipients seem to moderate this process, as recipients are mostly influenced when they share social relationships with the originators of the content. Although a minority of users actively engages in creating UGC, a much larger number of people may be influenced through the friendship networks of these users. This highlights the potential impact of user-to-user interactions in social media advertising.[56]

Such studies further exemplify the importance of network, social connection, social support, and social capital mentioned earlier in the chapter as a benefit to social media activities that can allow for better decision making regardless of the medium.

SOCIETAL BENEFITS OF SOCIAL MEDIA USE

Chapter 2 discussed many of the downfalls of the consumption of social media and subsequent sharing in ways that aren't very beneficial to society. Incidents of media bias, fake news, hoax sharing, and the like were revealed to highlight the negative influence of social media on our personal lives. For both consumers of and researchers in social media, it's easy to get caught up in the bad stuff. We are often building the bridge as we walk on it, diagnosing our experiences based largely on lack of precedent in analyzing exposure to this relatively new type of media. But what about the good stuff that's happening? This section addresses the benefits of social media to our society as a whole.

Social Media: Research, Discovery, Sharing, and Knowledge Management

If you're a traditional student reading this book for a college class, chances are you don't recall a time before social media. You probably have always been able to type a question into Google and have information available to you almost immediately. Thinking about a time that pre-dates Internet-mediated communication is hard for most people to wrap their heads around. Every day, we rely on a complicated structure for decision making that is often aided by technology. As studies have shown, we value recommendations of our peers over those of advertising techniques; we often seek social media to conduct our decision-making research. In performing such research, we discover information and then share to inform what we've learned. During this process we are managing knowledge similar to that conducted by a database, only we do it through our social networks. Information goes into social networks by populating preferences and profiles and comes out in the form of recommendations, news feeds, and analytics.

Transparency, sentiment, conjoining of a physical network with a social one, and the speed of social media all enable faster diffusion[57] of information over networks.[58] This **diffusion**, or social media contagion,[59] so to speak, takes information and moves it quickly through networks to help us make better decisions or react more appropriately in moments of crisis,[60,61,62] to aid or avoid disasters,[63,64,65,66] to finding missing persons or solve crimes via **websleuthing**,[67] and to share significant events via livestreaming.[68,69] In all of these instances, first-person accounts of news often come from ordinary citizens or, simply, social media users rather than reporters. The idea of **citizen journalism** is just beginning to develop its own set of positives and negatives associated with its practices and expectations.[70,71,72,73] This leaves the social media user to decide for themselves about **newsgathering**,[74] which refers to "the process of researching news items, especially those for broadcast or publication."[75] This places *thought leaders* (see Chapter 1), particularly those with high social capital, in very influential positions[76]; disinformation can be spread as we wait for detection of fake news to catch up.[77] Although this concept might seem better suited to Chapter 2 as a social media negative, it demonstrates our unique opportunities to act as our own filter,[78] customize our own content experience, and create our own footprint in social media. As discussed in earlier chapters, we now have access to more information than at any other time in history to make decisions and mitigate risk, which is definitely a benefit.

Stakeholder Communications

With all of this information at our fingertips, brands can communicate directly with us on social media platforms, making one of the best-known communication theory models, the 1948 Shannon and Weaver[79] model of knowledge transfer (see Figure 3.2), hyper relevant. This model consists "of five elements: an information source, which produces a message; a transmitter, which encodes the message into signals; a channel, to which signals are adapted for

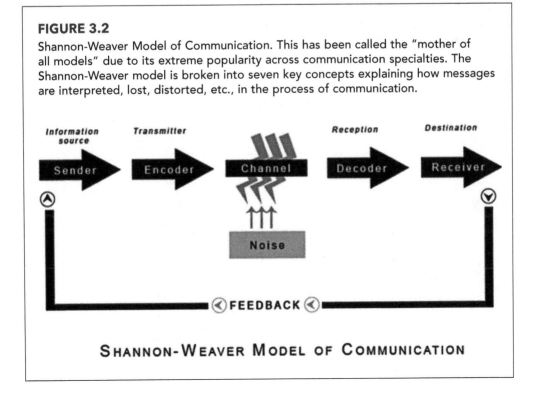

FIGURE 3.2
Shannon-Weaver Model of Communication. This has been called the "mother of all models" due to its extreme popularity across communication specialties. The Shannon-Weaver model is broken into seven key concepts explaining how messages are interpreted, lost, distorted, etc., in the process of communication.

Information source → Sender

Transmitter → Encoder

Channel

Noise

Reception → Decoder

Destination → Receiver

FEEDBACK

SHANNON-WEAVER MODEL OF COMMUNICATION

transmission; a receiver, which decodes (reconstructs) the message from the signal; and a destination, where the message arrives. A sixth element, noise, is a dysfunctional factor: any interference with the message traveling along the channel which may lead to the signal received being different from that sent."[80] From the standpoint of transmission of one-way communication, this is the equivalent of a brand shouting its unique value proposition (UVP) at you.

Following the Shannon-Weaver model, simply broadcasting content on social media leads to low reach of the intended audience and low referral traffic, so that a brand's message is never acted upon as intended. This model limits communication from brand to stakeholder or perhaps stakeholder to brand. It doesn't take into account any feedback or two-way communication between brands and stakeholders. However, social media has demonstrated that the idea of **engagement** with the brand, measuring public shares, likes, and comments, invites a two-way, more "social" method of communication in which information is exchanged, the feedback loop is closed, and the process is completed with multiple interactions between stakeholders and brands. This modeling looks a lot more like the Westley and MacLean model of communication (see Figure 3.3)[81] or the De Fleur model of communication (see Figure 3.4). In these two models, feedback and device media are taken into consideration from the perspective of the shareholder. They also contain **linear feedback** as a method of engagement with the recipient. One of the important aspects of the De Fleur communication model[82] in the context of social media is how the audience is targeted in the two-way communication process. Social media is the epitome of two-way communication. Unfiltered communication between an organization and its consumers can happen on the social sphere across multiple social media channels.

FIGURE 3.3

Westley & MacLean Model of Communication. A theory of mass communication that analyzes the communication between source and receiver, indicated as A and B, and other components.

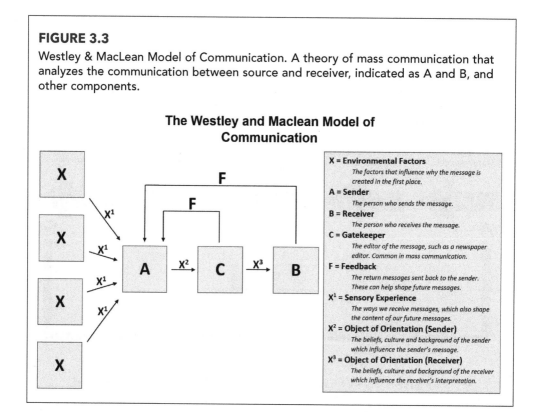

The Westley and Maclean Model of Communication

X = Environmental Factors
  The factors that influence why the message is created in the first place.
A = Sender
  The person who sends the message.
B = Receiver
  The person who receives the message.
C = Gatekeeper
  The editor of the message, such as a newspaper editor. Common in mass communication.
F = Feedback
  The return messages sent back to the sender. These can help shape future messages.
X^1 = Sensory Experience
  The ways we receive messages, which also shape the content of our future messages.
X^2 = Object of Orientation (Sender)
  The beliefs, culture and background of the sender which influence the sender's message.
X^3 = Object of Orientation (Receiver)
  The beliefs, culture and background of the receiver which influence the receiver's interpretation.

FIGURE 3.4

De Fleur Model of Communication. This model consists of a two-way process where the receiver becomes the sender in providing feedback and, by receiving feedback, the sender then becomes the receiver.

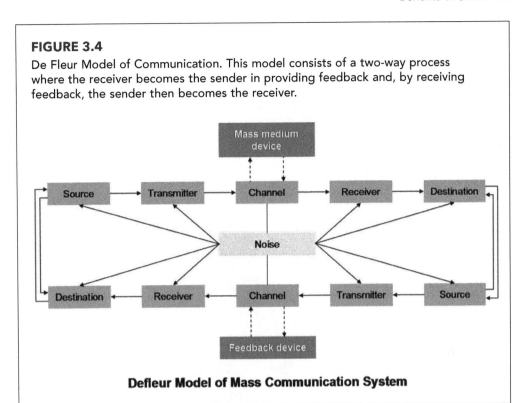

Defleur Model of Mass Communication System

For example, Swedish retail giant H&M created an advertisement[83] featuring a Black boy wearing a hooded sweatshirt that read "coolest monkey in the jungle" (see Photo 3A). The racial undertones of the ad ignited a widespread backlash on social media. After receiving overwhelmingly negative feedback, H&M announced the removal of the sweatshirt from their product line. Similarly, Gucci faced criticism and backlash from social media users over their blackface sweater (see Chapter 5).[84] These are just two examples of two-way communication on social media in which feedback notified or informed brands of their direction in the marketplace.

Social media platforms like Twitter and Facebook have become the first places people go to for customer support, product inquiries, or just to say thank you to businesses. However, in today's instant communication climate, if a brand doesn't reply, people are ready to bite back in the form of negative communication and/or publicity online. Even though social media is such a new tool, legacy models can continue to be used to provide insight into offline and online communication.

Big Data, Machine Learning, and Artificial Intelligence in Social Media

As the adoption of social media applications becomes habitual, massive amounts of data are created as a result of normal usage, integration, and all of the other daily activities associated with these applications. These enormous quantities of data are commonly referred to as **big data**. Although more than 90 percent of all available online data has been created in the last two years, the idea of big data has been around since 2005, when it was launched by

PHOTO 3A
H&M Monkey of the Jungle Sweatshirt

O'Reilly Media. However, the phrase as we now understand and apply it post–Web 2.0, which moved the Internet from static pages to dynamic and helped birth social media as we know it today, has come to mean so much more.[85]

A paper written by Norijhan Abdul Chani, Suraya Hamid, Ibrahim Abaker Targio Hashem, and Ejaz Ahmed provided a thorough discussion of the applications of social media big data analytics by "highlighting the state-of-the-art techniques, methods, and the quality attributes of various studies."[86] They also discussed present and future research challenges for analyzing big data, such as varying data quality, data locality, velocity of processing, data availability, and natural language processing, all of which can be difficult for computers to understand.

Though social media data are still being analyzed using traditional data-mining and machine-learning techniques, resulting in improved business decisions driven by mountains of marketing research,[87] more efficient techniques will be needed in the future to handle the increasing body of data being collected as a result of social media use.[88] **Artificial intelligence (AI)** and data mining will be required to collect and analyze the ever-increasing volume of information.[89] Most approaches to big data analysis are steeped in the use of *machine learning*, a growing field of artificial intelligence that uses classification, clustering,[90] and deep learning[91,92] to detect data patterns (see Chapter 1). These patterns are used for a variety of purposes, both commercial and personal, as big data on its own is practically useless without transformation into insight.[93]

As an end user of a number of social media apps, you are contributing to the body of big data. You are also a consumer of the results of big data efforts, benefiting from others as you benefit them. Later chapters explore the use and meaning of social media analytics for use in business and social constructs.

Psychological Benefits of Social Media Use

Research has found that social networks based on social support and connectedness are associated with a greater sense of well-being.[94,95] It should stand to reason, then, that moving these networks online has the ability to expand the social support available within an individual's network. On whether social media use contributes positively to "well-being," the research is actually mixed.

Where should we start? Social media research can be exhausting or even overwhelming. One of the upsides and downsides of social media research or discovery is that it is not contained within a single discipline; it often takes up residence in all of the disciplines it touches. When seeking models, frameworks, best practices, or creative ideas, don't be afraid to wander outside a discipline and take a walk in another to find inspiration.

In a study that examined when and why people **microblog** (e.g., Tweet or share status updates via a timeline, such as in the Facebook model), authors Eva Buechel and Jonah Berger found that "part of microblogging's appeal lies in its undirected nature. Allowing users to send undirected communication to multiple others."[96] This study asserted that the practice of microblogging allows users to reach out when they need social support "without having to bother anyone in particular."[97] This addresses the common criticism of social media networks reducing or replacing interpersonal interactions by "demonstrating how online social networks can foster connections for people who otherwise feel apprehensive about sharing."[98] Social networks actually encourage communication for those who may suffer from social anxiety or social apprehension and would otherwise not seek out face-to-face engagement for purposes of self-help or concern. It effectively builds a support community for them.

Results from another study suggested that "Facebook use may provide the opportunity to develop and maintain social connectedness in the online environment" and that "Facebook connectedness is associated with lower depression and anxiety and greater satisfaction of life."[99] Researcher Emily Weinstein describes social media as a "see-saw" that inflicts both positive and negative effects in well-being on adolescents.[100] Research team Orie Berezan, Anjala S. Krishen, Shaurya Agarwal, and Pushkin Kachroo maintain that the meaning of happiness ideals shift as age and lifespan increase and have concluded that social media provides different cognitive response per generation.[101] A paper examining the role of Facebook and its impact on life satisfaction in teen users suggested both positive and negative associations, but emphasized that recall bias plagues this field; the frequency and levels of activity are prolific and difficult to identify. This study concluded that the type of activity was a determining variable; active participation (chatting, posting, etc.) positively impacted teens, and passive following (scrolling through others' timelines and accounts) had an adverse impact on satisfaction.[102]

Social media and connectedness scholars Chorng-Shyong Ong, Shu-Chen Chang, and Shwn-Meei Lee were among the first researchers to apply psychological happiness theories to explore emotional and satisfaction issues when using the Web. They concluded that there are six factors based on theories

Relational/Societal/Self: FOMO versus FOLO versus JOMO

The *fear of missing out (FOMO)* and the *fear of living offline (FOLO)* (see Chapter 2) may have met their match in **JOMO**, the joy of missing out. In contrast to FOMO (a potential factor associated with problematic social media use) and FOLO (a feeling of being left out if not connected online), JOMO is the booster shot or immunization to FOMO. We think that the concept is best summarized by this poem from Michael Leunig:[106]

"Oh the joy of missing out.
When the world begins to shout
And rush towards that shining thing;
The latest bit of mental bling—
Trying to have it, see it, do it,
You simply know you won't go through it;
The anxious clamoring and need
This restless hungry thing to feed.
Instead, you feel the loveliness;
The pleasure of your emptiness.
You spurn the treasure on the shelf
In favor of your peaceful self;
Without regret, without a doubt.
Oh the joy of missing out."

Think about It: Have you ever experienced FOMO? FOLO? JOMO? Explain your answer.

of happiness, website satisfaction, and website emotion: informative support, website service reliability, connection, self-growth, website satisfaction, and emotional relaxation.[103] Their work provided a crossover into social media research, because they "not only accounted for website-performance-related features, but also specific social and leisure website features."[104] Their insights are particularly valuable given that research concerning the positive aspects of social media use is not as common as studies about its negative aspects[105] (see the Relational/Societal/Self feature).

ETHICAL, MORAL, AND SOCIAL RESPONSIBILITY: COMBATTING SOCIAL MEDIA'S "DARK SIDE"

Admittedly, after reading Chapter 2, using the "good" to combat the "bad" in social media may sound like an exercise in futility. When you compare the literature that highlights digital drama; livestreamed crimes; unintended consequences for consumers, businesses, and brands; and questions regarding privacy and mental health, it certainly doesn't feel like the benefits of social media outweigh the dark parts. So how do you combat the dark side? We asked ourselves that same question and came up with a few recommendations to consider when participating in social media:

1. **Know how the tools work.** Ignorance is no longer a plausible defense. Understand that anything you write anywhere can have consequences in this digital age. Understanding how the platforms work and where the information could land can keep you from making poor decisions.

2. **Be aware of your social, geopolitical, and industry environments.** Whether you are participating personally or working with a client, being well read never goes out of style. Avoid an ill-timed post or @ mention by staying on top of current events. This can keep your seemingly well-intended and downright hilarious joke from being the next embarrassing meme or corporate bankruptcy story. Virality is cool, but it can also be very, very bad.

3. **Evaluate before posting.** Consumer activism has become intertwined with brand values. Social media gives people and brands the ability to become online activists immediately. Although seemingly well intended, such activism has long-term and sometimes unintended consequences. Before posting a comment or review, evaluate carefully its place in digital history; the Internet is your actual permanent record.

4. **Use social media wisely.** Social media overuse, overconsumption, and addiction are real. As you learned in Chapter 2, there can be long-term consequences to "too much" social media. Set limits on your personal consumption habits. Whether a literal timer or acute awareness of a set of personal guidelines, self-awareness helps keep social media a benefit and not a total time suck or emotional burden that needs to be unloaded later.

5. **Decide what is private and then act accordingly.** This is closely related to item number 1. Having an understanding about what happens to the data you put in clarifies what comes out and is shared with platform owners and advertisers. Choose the appropriate amount or type of information that you wish to disclose, knowing that any or all of it can be used to help the bottom line of a business that may not be helping you.

6. **Understand the data so you can USE it.** If you are one of those people who thinks "wow—this is so fascinating!" immerse yourself in analytics. A thorough understanding of consumer wants, needs, behavior, and history allows a stronger focus on audiences and segmentation, a powerful skill to have in any career in today's digital world. The ability to transform data into insights (aka strategy) is also important.

7. **Ask questions and self-regulate.** In Chapter 2 you learned lots of rules, regulations, and guidelines, but none of them told you how to not be a jerk online. Following the law is obviously important, but self-regulation is just as important. A lawyer's goal might be "avoid litigation," but the goal for a social media practitioner sounds a little like that of a physician: First, do no harm. In a work setting, self-regulatory guides help create the culture of digital media practices. On a personal level, although you are not likely to have an immediate impact on the business practices of social media companies, you can compile and adhere to your own digital constitution, making it a beacon lighting up the "dark side."

8. **Consider your data collection behavior.** According to an old-school model of data collection, you need to grab everything AND the kitchen sink, too! A future-focused data collection method is to collect only what you need to formulate strategy and mitigate the risk to your audience. This is a win-win that scores well with both future customers and karma. Make sure you understand the sensitivities of data and address them ethically. Delivering data-driven strategies requires ongoing attention to understanding new privacy concerns that emerge with new platforms and capacities.

9. **Don't add to the drama.** Instead, educate your audience. This tip might not help keep your aunt from sharing fake news, but it will help the rest of your audience if you are able to Shut It Down. Avoid reposting content that is false, misleading, or ill constructed. Remember, you are what you read, and then share. Your digital reputation is at stake.

10. **Take a hard line on the negative side of social media.** "Haters gonna hate" was a really funny tagline until we took it too far and became a society that tears one another apart on social media behind our computer screens. Social media has evolved from a feel-good "get the gang together" medium into one that has the potential to tear society apart, fostering bullying, trolling, and all types of toxic, violent, and hateful speech. It's nearly impossible to escape it, but you can counteract it by being better than the trolls, better than the bullies, and better than the propagators of hate and fearmongering. You simply must be better. In addition, report instances of digital drama to the platforms when you see them.

CHAPTER WRAP-UP

The relationship of social media to well-being is not clear-cut. It's complicated. Because mixed research results and a litany of variables make getting a holistic picture of the benefits of social media use in every age group very difficult, discovering the benefits of social media proves to be a much more difficult task than you might think. Much research can be found regarding the dark or negative impacts of social media, but there is less available on its brighter, more positive aspects. Isolating pure social media positives when not imprinted on, say, business, medicine, or politics are hard to come by, but multidisciplinary research provides an opportunity for researchers and individuals like you to monitor and report the positive impacts of social media and create the environment for a kinder, gentler, more positive social media world.

CRITICAL-THINKING QUESTIONS

1. After reading Chapters 2 and Chapters 3, do you think the good outweighs the bad in social media? If not, why do you think we continue to give social media our time and attention? If so, how do you think you can be a better conduit for social media good?

2. How are your own interpersonal relationships impacted by social media? Given what you have learned here, discuss the future of your online behavior.

3. Social media data are already being used to fuel artificial intelligence and machine learning. So, what's the next thing? What's the next step in our relationship with social media data?

4. How and why do you use social media? Are there positives or is it just a tool for procrastination? Do you feel that social media usage has resulted in any drawbacks in your personal or professional life?

5. What else would you add to our list of tips to combat the dark side of social media? Do you engage in any current behavior that helps dispel the ill impacts of social media?

ACTIVITIES

1. Personal social media audit: Set an alarm on your phone for the same time every day. When the alarm goes off, document how you feel and how much you estimate you have used social media platforms since the last alarm in a journal (physical or electronic). (You could also download an app or use the built-in tracker on your device to track this information.) After a period of fourteen days, examine your journal and analyze your results: (a) Did the deliberate tracking of your own personal data make a difference in your perception of social media? (b) Did it add to or detract from your overall satisfaction with your lifestyle? (c) Discuss your results with a trusted friend. What were their insights? (d) How might you improve any negative feelings over time? (e) Did this self-study impact how you feel about social media? Explain your answer

2. This chapter cited two examples of poor decisions made by two companies—H&M and Gucci. Conduct a simple search on the Internet to find other companies that have made poor choices, and discuss how they responded.

3. Read the following article: *Krispy Kreme, Panera Bread owner learns of family's Nazi ties; Albert Reimann Sr. and his son, Albert Reimann Jr., used forced laborers under the Nazis during World War II to work in their industrial chemicals company.* Discuss whether or not the Reimann family's handling of the issue was appropriate. https://nbcnews.to/2FFgs53.

KEY CONCEPTS

Artificial intelligence (AI)
Big data
Citizen journalism
Diffusion
Engagement
Interpersonal connection behaviors framework

Linear feedback
Microblog
Newsgathering
Social capital
Social connection
Social support
User-generated content (UGC)
Virtual communities (VC)
Websleuthing

MEDIA SOURCES

The Online Journalism Blog: https://onlinejournalismblog.com.

The Pew Research Center: https://www.pewresearch.org/topics/social-media.

The American Psychological Association: https://www.apa.org/members/content/social-media-research.

Psychology Today Blog: https://www.psychologytoday.com/us/blog/evidence-based-living/201903/the-complex-links-between-social-media-and-mental-health.

Social Media Research Foundation: https://www.smrfoundation.org.

COMMUNICATION CONTEXTS FOR SOCIAL MEDIA

PART — 2

Mass Media to Niche Media

A COMMUNITY BUILT FROM THE INTERNET UP

LEARNING OBJECTIVES

4.1 Outline the evolution of media over time.

4.2 Articulate basic theories associated with mass media.

4.3 Identify the purpose of mass and niche media in the current landscape and provide examples of each.

4.4 Compare the ways in which traditional, digital, and emerging media impact audiences.

Thriving in our complicated digital ecosystem is tough! Just ask anyone who decided to try to become a "lifestyle blogger" or "influencer" in the last decade. In attempting to diversify revenue, organizations often seek out niche media to combine business and consumer-facing audiences in order to maintain a well-rounded and successful media mix. From woodworking to investing, political commentary to fancy socks, a specialized segment exists. Take Food52 for example, founded in 2011 by Amanda Hesser and Merrill Stubbs. Its funding includes $13 million in crowdsourcing over four rounds of asks. Food seems like a really broad category, right? Not for Food52. They have spent more than a decade developing content and products specifically for the home chef. The company earns much of its revenue through e-commerce, selling anything from small-batch organic chocolate subscriptions to top-of-the-line cookware, "perfect" wineglasses, user-generated and populated cookbooks to eco-friendly kitchen towels, and generic pantry staples. They frequently feature their cult-like followers on their social media feeds and print materials. Recently Food52 dove head-first into video and launched its own cooking channel on the ad-heavy platform XumoTV as an added revenue stream, proving there is no category that niche media can't overcome with great content delivered to a smartphone and community built from the Internet up.

Mass media impacts our daily lives whether we acknowledge its presence or not. Think about this. When you made the decision to attend the college or university that assigned you this textbook, how did you share the news with others? Did you hire the town crier? Was it featured on the local news? Probably not. More likely, you went directly to your smartphone and shared the news with the world by posting on your favorite social media platform. This chapter explores the evolution of media from mass media to niche media and then analyzes the effects of these changes on audiences within the social sphere. Finally, we compare the ways in which traditional, digital, and emerging media reach their audiences in informative, engaging, and effective ways.

THE EVOLUTION OF MASS MEDIA

So, what exactly is mass media? Scholars "have largely ignored the task of constructing a definition of 'mass media' or 'mass communication,'"[1] and the task has not become any easier in a "new" media environment that includes social and digital media. Even more troubling, or perhaps freeing to some scholars, is that the terms *mass media* and *mass communication* have been used interchangeably for decades,[2] causing confusion even among those who are "in the know." In the simplest of terms, **mass media** are the channels through which communication is intended to reach large groups of people. Its messages are designed to be disseminated to wide and diverse audiences quickly with the purposes of informing, connecting, and influencing people.

The most often-discussed mass media channels are television, print, and radio, also referred to as **traditional media.** However, books, film, and many aspects of digital media are also considered mass media channels. Looking way back in time, we see that societies, including ancient Egypt and its hieroglyphs, have understood the importance of sharing messages with the public for centuries. As literacy increased and technological advances occurred, the channels improved. Arguably the most important mass media inventions to date, in order of appearance, are the printing press, radio, television, computer, mobile phone, and the World Wide Web.

Mass media works in a number of ways to keep societies functioning. At the most basic level, mass media communications inform, educate, and entertain us. Messages disseminated via mass media also contribute to the formation of public opinion and can influence individuals' thoughts, actions, and behaviors.[3]

Information Dissemination

Mass media informs the public of events, happenings, and ideas. An excellent example of this function is news. Whether communicated via television, radio, newspaper, or a website, news outlets let the public know what is going on in our communities, the nation, and the world. You might tune in to find

PHOTO 4A
The History of Mass Media

A BRIEF HISTORY OF
MASS MEDIA

PRE-INDUSTRIAL AGE
1041 Movable Printing in China
1440 Printing Press
Johannes Gutenberg
1447 First Printed Ad Appears

INDUSTRIAL AGE
1774 Electric Telegraph
Georges Louis Lesage
1829 Typewriter
W. S. Burt
1876 Telephone
Alexander Graham Bell
1876 Phonograph
Thomas Edison
1894 Radio
Guglielmo Marconi

EARLY 1900s
First Commercial Radio Broadcast 1920
KDKA Pittsburgh
First News Magazine, *TIME* 1923
First TV Transmission 1927
Philo Farnsworth

ELECTRONIC AGE: 1930s-80s
1940s Antenna TV and Early Cable
1950s A TV in Every Living Room
1960s Rise of FM Radio
1963 Audio Cassettes Introduced
1972 Email Developed
Ray Tomlinson
1973 First Mobile Phones
John Mitchell and Martin Cooper
1975 VCRs Introduced
1975 Microsoft Founded
Bill Gates and Paul Allen
1976 Apple Computers Founded
Steve Jobs

CABLE TV & EARLY COMPUTING: 1980s
First Online Newspaper 1980
Columbus Dispatch
Microsoft Windows is Launched 1985
First Commercial Email Service 1986
MCI Mail

NEW MEDIA: 1990s-TODAY
1991 World Wide Web Launched
Sir Timothy John-Berners Lee
1995 Microsoft Internet Explorer
1997 DVDs replace VHS
2001 First Instant Message Service
ICQ
2002 Satellite Radio Launched
XM Radio

SOCIAL MEDIA CRAZE: 2000s

Facebook 2004 — *Mark Zuckerberg*
YouTube 2005 — *Steve Chen, Chad Hurley, Jawed Karim*
Twitter 2006 — *Jack Dorsey, Noah Glass, Biz Stone & Evan William*
Tumblr 2007 — *David Karp*
WhatsApp 2009 — *Brian Acton, Jan Koum*
Instagram 2010 — *Kevin Systrom*
Snapchat 2011 — *Reggie Brown, Bobby Murphy & Evan Spiegel*
TikTok 2016 — *Zhang Yiming*

out something as simple as what the weather will be so you know to grab your umbrella on the way out the door. Or it might provide facts regarding overseas trade negotiations that may impact the domestic cost of goods. The fact that this information is transmitted to all persons with access to that specific communication channel establishes a baseline of information from which individuals may begin to form opinions and connect with others to engage in dialogue about a particular subject.

Watchdoggin'

One of the most important roles of mass media is to act as a **watchdog**. Because a nation's macro values, beliefs, and actions are defined by *elites*, those persons deemed to hold the greatest power within the society, specifically governments, it makes sense to have an entity that keeps them in check. Some examples of how the media carries out this role include fact-checking, reporting on public meetings, and investigative journalism. Of course, the ability of the media to keep information balanced varies, based on a nation's political system and its notion of a free press. In many countries around the world, where the mass media is controlled by the government, their role is to share information that

FIGURE 4.1
Mass Media Forms

is in-line with the current administration.[4] Reporters Without Borders (RWB) is a nongovernmental organization that serves the public interest through their global advocacy in support of freedom of information. They consider that freedom is vital to the human condition.[5] The organization provides an annual report called the "World Press Freedom Index," which ranks 180 countries based on their level of freedom of the media (see Figure 4.1).

Entertainment

Entertainment is a performance that provides a certain pleasure to people. Mass media fulfills the function to entertain us. It allows us to escape the drudgery of the day by tuning into the latest television or streaming series, a hot new Hollywood film, or a great book, reducing tension to a degree. Print media like magazines and newspapers offer stories, comics, and investigative pieces to inform and entertain an audience. Role models from the mass media shape culture through attitude and behavior changes in the general public.[6] Leisure and technological change will determine how much of a hold entertainment continues to achieve over the public via mass media.

MASS MEDIA THEORY

Mass communications and mass media have been and continue to be heavily researched. Over the years, a multitude of theories of media effects and media content have been explored and reexplored, so delving into every theory is outside the scope of this text. That said, it will be helpful to keep in mind a handful of mass media theories as you work your way through this text, including gatekeeping, agenda setting, and the conflict and feminist perspectives.

Gatekeeping: Mass Media Chooses for Us

Let's face it, there are thousands of messages that could be served up fresh every day. So why do we see what we see on television or read what we read online? The answer is that mass media acts as a **gatekeeper**. According to prominent media scholars Pamela Shoemaker and Tim Vos, their gatekeeping model (see Figure 4.2) is the process by which all possible messages are packaged in a mass media friendly way, and the quantity of information is reduced to an amount the masses can manage.[7]

There are gatekeepers everywhere and at all levels within any organization. The story that you are reading in a print magazine or checking out online had many approvals before the final article made it through to the end user. The author, editor, publisher, and photographer all had roles in selecting what messages you received and how you received them. How do they make these decisions? It's complicated. What we see on the news is often reflective of the routines and values of the media organization, and often depends on whatever information is available at the time.[8]

Gatekeeping is very much the case in Western, democratic societies, but it does not hold true around the world. There are nations, such as those identified by Reporters Without Borders, in which the government or group in power is the sole gatekeeper, resulting in limited access to information by the public.

FIGURE 4.2
RWB World Press Freedom Map

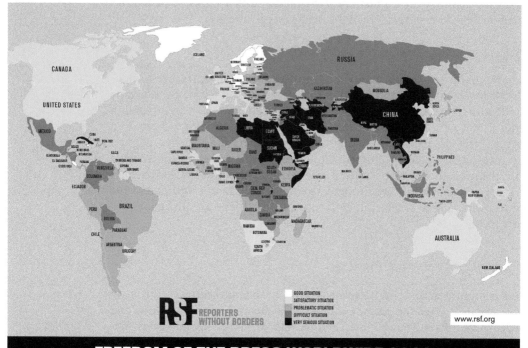

FREEDOM OF THE PRESS WORLDWIDE 2020

Mass Media Sets the Agenda

One of the most powerful roles of mass media is its ability to tell us what ideas to think about and what level of importance to attach to them. Often discussed in scholarly circles, the **agenda-setting** function of mass media is a theory that originated in 1922 by Walter Lipmann in his book *Public Opinion*. Over the years other scholars continued to refine the theory. Then in 1972 researchers Max McCombs and Donald Shaw formally developed the theory to what is commonly used today.[9] Research for their Chapel Hill study revealed a strong correlation between what the news media reported as the most important election issue and what Chapel Hill, North Carolina, voters considered the most important issue, suggesting that the media "sets the agenda" for the public—telling us not *what* to think but what to think *about*.

Agenda setting is not limited to traditional media. Most social platforms provide a section labeled something like *trending*. Trending implies that an inordinate number of users are clicking, reading, and sharing this content. Once it has reached a predetermined threshold of interest, the platform labels it, telling you what is important to learn about on that day at that moment. Trending occurs at multiple levels, from national trends down to your own zip code.

Because mass media is geared toward a general audience of consumers, its roles in the formation of public opinion and the maintenance of democracy by inspiring public discourse[10] make it a significant force in our society and an excellent communication tool.

Mass Media and Culture: The Conflict and Feminist Perspectives

Mass media both reflects and creates culture, the umbrella term for social norms, knowledge, beliefs, customs, etc., as we know it. Mass media is able to project the same messaging to large numbers of people at one time, suggesting and reinforcing cultural norms and belief systems. An excellent example is the portrayal of families on television over time. *The Donna Reed Show*, which aired in primetime in the late 1950s and early 1960s, depicted a nuclear family. The mom was a homemaker; the dad was a doctor whose role was to provide financially for the family; and there were two kids (a boy and a girl), a dog, and the quintessential white picket fence. All of this reflected and reinforced the notion of family at that time. Today we see same-sex parents raising children; women as the breadwinners while their spouses rear the children; and single mothers like Lorelai on *Gilmore Girls*, who raised her daughter Rory while working and eventually running her own business.

There are two perspectives worth mentioning in contemplating the creation of culture in media—the **conflict perspective** and the **feminist perspective**. Conflict theorists approach the study of mass media through the lens of those in control. The conflict perspective suggests that mass media underrepresents the US working class, especially people of color. Instead, it shows the norms of the white upper-middle class, who control it. Conflict theorists note that members of the working class and persons of color are often shown in criminal roles and other negative roles, which continues the cycle of accepted stereotyping.

The feminist perspective calls out the prevalence of the idealization of females in the media as young and svelte, and light-skinned if not white. This represents the culture's accepted standards for female beauty, which reinforces stereotypes and misrepresents actuality in favor of dominant ideologies.[11]

Mass media is present in our lives every day, from the television shows we watch or stream, the news outlets we count on in print or online, the social media we consume and/or contribute to, and even the billboards we see every day. These channels help us understand who and what are important to think about and help us craft our fashion choices and decide what we might like to eat. Most importantly, mass media brings people together to engage in conversations that help us form opinions about topics and people that—ideally—benefit the common good.

MASS MEDIA AND THE SOCIAL SPHERE

For a long time, mass media was a one-way communication tool. It shared information with the public, but there were limited options for the audience to respond outside of their own personal networks. Audiences were, for the most part, passive. Sure, you could pen a letter to the editor that might or might not get printed, or send a complaint or your opinion on a story to your local news station about their coverage of a particular topic, but these options didn't often result in discussion and dialogue. The digital space has made it possible for the audience to be active participants in mass media. The ability to share a point of view through comments on articles or via social platforms has taken the audience's ability to connect to a whole new level.

As noted in Chapter 1, the digital space is participatory. It has provided the ability to start conversations about what is important to us as individuals in society in real time using text, a gif, or a meme to get our point across. These interactions have transformed mass media from one-way to two-way communication.

As a participatory audience, we now have the opportunity to become citizen journalists, making us to some extent both gatekeepers and agenda setters. As discussed in Chapters 2 and 3, these interactions can be beneficial or a cause for concern; regardless, though, they put some messaging power back in the hands of the people and jumpstart conversations about events and ideas that are worthy of discussion. In addition, the nature of the social media environment adds a level of "watchdog" power, as users can fact-check and monitor not just the media but the people who are doing newsworthy things, including the elites who are in control.

Niche Media

The word *niche* refers to a distinct subset of a larger group. Over time, media has exploded with **niche media** channels that are hyper-focused on consumers' viewing, listening, reading, and social interests. The rise of cable television saw the development of television stations that are committed to specific content of interest; science fiction fans can tune into Syfy, foodies can watch the Food Network and the Cooking Channel, and those who like music have MTV, VH1, and Country Music Television (CMT). These changes to the mass media landscape posed challenges and created opportunities for anyone seeking to connect with audiences.

Niche Social Media Platforms

The Internet has made it possible to create online spaces for nearly any kind of niche interest, in turn providing a wealth of opportunities to communicate with people who share those interests. At one time there was even an entire social network dedicated entirely to connecting fans of David Hasselhoff!

Are you into knitting? If not, perhaps you know someone who is. Ravelry. com describes itself as "a place for knitters, crocheters, designers, spinners, weavers and dyers to keep track of their yarn, tools, project and pattern information, and look to others for ideas and inspiration. The content here is all user-driven; we as a community make the site what it is."[12] The Ravelry.com online community brings together textile handicraft enthusiasts to share tips and patterns, and to build relationships. It is funded primarily through—you guessed it—yarn-related advertising. And what a great opportunity for those advertisers—they are connected to a network of nearly one million yarn users!

Although thousands of users view and engage content of all varieties on larger, more general platforms like BuzzFeed, companies can benefit greatly from these hyper-focused niche networks filled with people who have a demonstrated interest and engagement with the platform content. Assuming that you have done all of the appropriate research to identify your target audience, investing the time and money to develop a presence on a niche site has the capacity to convert more prospects to customers than spreading a broad message on a general platform.

Niche platforms allow the opportunity to form deeper connections through more intentional, relevant content strategies that respect the audience's existing knowledge. There is also the opportunity to increase credibility by becoming a **thought leader**, a person or organization viewed as an expert on a topic with opinions and beliefs that may influence others. As a bonus for small or new businesses trying to break into a market, the entry cost for niche social media is typically much lower than attempting to enter the mass media space.

Influencers

Mass media channels often feature advertising using celebrity endorsements whose broad level of fame and general appeal reach large numbers of people. Based on the celebrity's involvement, these people may be enticed into learning more about a product or making a purchase. Consumer decision making is influenced by the popularity of the celebrity and what they represent. The celebrity may even give the consumer a feeling of commonality with someone famous and feed the aspiration that one day, we too, can be celebrities if we follow their lead.[13]

But celebrity is only one type of **influencer** (see Figure 4.3). Social media has opened the door to **influencer marketing**, connecting companies with very specific target audiences. Celebrities continue to be sought after for endorsing brands in the social sphere, but regular, everyday people are also being identified as influencers in that space. Like celebrities, these *social media influencers* are widely known within their niche. However, they differ in that they are renowned for their expertise and seen as a trusted source of information. This makes them ideal connections for brands seeking to reach a specific target audience. For more on the relationship between an influencer and one such audience, see Figure 4.3 and Box 4.1.

CONVERGENCE AND THE SOCIAL SPHERE

So, the birth of the Internet and social media has created a magnificent opportunity for people to access and create content about nearly any topic

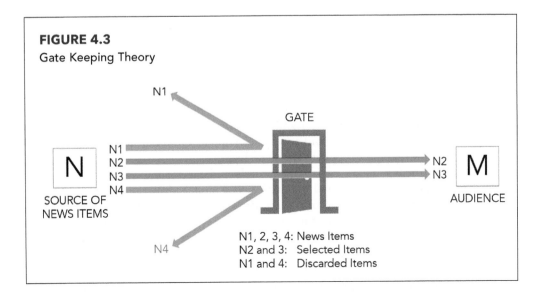

FIGURE 4.3
Gate Keeping Theory

GATE

N1

N1
N2
N3
N4

N

SOURCE OF
NEWS ITEMS

N2
N3

M

AUDIENCE

N4

N1, 2, 3, 4: News Items
N2 and 3: Selected Items
N1 and 4: Discarded Items

Box 4.1: BearfootTheory.com

Adventuring has a wildly popular niche following. Research has confirmed that millennials in particular are seeking to spend their money on experiences rather than "stuff."[14] Travel adventure blog Bearfoot Theory considers itself "the leading outdoor adventure and travel blog for the everyday explorer, where founder Kristen Bor helps readers discover new destinations, conquer their fears, and get their hands on the latest and greatest outdoor gear."[15] Kristen didn't set out to be an influencer—she just wanted to improve the existing adventuring community by creating a hub; thus, the blog BearfootTheory.com was created for those interested in learning more about outdoor adventuring,

like hiking and van life, and registering for guided adventures led by Kristen herself. The site is complemented by Facebook, Instagram, Pinterest, Twitter, and YouTube accounts that share impactful and engaging content with more than 1.7 million visitors each year.[16] Bearfoot Theory averages monthly affiliate sales in excess of $75,000, demonstrating the power of investing in niche social media.[17] Other outdoor companies specializing in consumer goods—including REI Co-op, The North Face, and even van conversion company Sprinter—reap the benefits of an audience that is seeking the best products for their current and future adventures. Bearfoot Theory is also attractive to the tour-

ism industry; Kristen travels the United States in her converted Sprinter van and highlights her adventures in real time through Instagram live, stories, and other platform tools, creating awareness of and driving adventurers to new locations. Visit California and Visit Idaho are just two of the organizations that have chosen to partner with Kristen's brand.

Think about It: Check out Kristen's social media sites. What's appealing about them to both her followers and the brands that support her through advertising on her platforms?

---

you can imagine and provides the opportunity to focus on a topic through niche media options. Along with these seemingly limitless opportunities come some challenges and benefits, for both those disseminating content and those receiving it.

Media Fragmentation

With so many options for the public to obtain information, interact, and be entertained, audiences are becoming increasingly fragmented. Back in the day, traditional mass media channels including just three major television networks and hometown and national newspapers were the primary ways to share information and advertise. With such limited choices, organizations knew that their messages would be heard.

Today's media environment finds audiences splitting their time across multiple platforms, and the number of channels continues to grow. The one-size-fits-all approach to message transmission has pretty much disappeared. Now, people who purchase streaming subscriptions to Netflix and Hulu can eliminate advertisements altogether. Newspaper journalism has transitioned from print to online formats that include *paywalls* (restricted access to content via a purchase or paid subscription). In addition, the multitude of electronic options for getting news from sources other than mainstays like *The New York*

Times (websites, apps, etc.) has grown exponentially. Audiences are relying more and more on Web sources for news, entertainment, and information; along the way, they are finding sites that cater more specifically to their own values and belief systems.

It was once possible to get results by taking out an ad in the local paper or selling a product on one of three television networks; sticking with one channel is just not as successful today. Brands and others trying to get the word out are faced with the challenge of finding their audience within a saturated and noisy media environment.

Information and News

In many ways, the proliferation of news sources has been a wonderful thing. The public now has multiple ways to check facts and learn about differing points of view. In theory, this access should improve our ability to have meaningful discussions with one another and our ability to form uber-informed opinions. But this isn't always the case.

One of the most significant developments is that media has become like a Las Vegas buffet—we have too many choices. When you consider all of the information options—including niche media and personalized social media networks where developers utilize algorithms to serve up ideal content—there just isn't enough time to explore them all. In this space it is easy to become trapped in an **echo chamber**, where your own opinions are reinforced by others without introducing new or conflicting content into the mix, which limits public discourse and can lead to extremes.

This is most evident in the realm of politics. Traditionally, mass media has been a place to tune in and hear nonpartisan reporting of facts about a situation or candidate, giving everyone equal access to the vital information necessary to form opinions and make decisions. Cable news networks and partisan online sources can limit the audience's ability to access accurate, full-picture information. In some cases, audience members have made the conscious decision to only engage with content that is in line with their ideals.

The Effect on Brands

The fragmentation of the media market has led to big changes in the ways that brands reach their audiences. Companies have had to rethink their approach to advertising and marketing as they attempt to reach their target audience in an effective and engaging way while maintaining a reasonable budget. The key to success is understanding your audience and leveraging traditional and social media aligned with their needs. Chapter 5 will dig more deeply into

Relational/Societal/Self: What If Mass Media Did Not Exist?

Now that you have a better understanding of today's media landscape, its evolution, its role, and the impact of social media, imagine that mass media doesn't exist and that all you have are your social platforms. That's right—imagine counting on just your social network to tell you what's going on around the world through shared posts and their first-, second-, or third-hand accounts.

Think about It: Our friends are all great, but this really scares us. Does this scare you? Why or why not?

the strategic and business aspects of competing in an ever-changing media landscape, but before you jump ahead, consider what life would be like if there were no such thing as social media or mass media (see the Relational/Societal/Self feature).

CHAPTER WRAP-UP

The media landscape is quite complex. It offers important opportunities from creating dialogue and shaping public opinion to providing brands with platforms to develop awareness and sell their products. Social media disrupted the mass media landscape. It has transformed a formerly passive audience into one with the opportunity to actively participate in the conversation. Audience members can now even become influencers, taking on the role of information disseminators by telling their networks, the media, and businesses what is important to be thinking about.

CRITICAL-THINKING QUESTIONS

1. How are the conflict and feminist perspectives evident in the social sphere?

2. In what ways has social media disrupted the media landscape?

3. What are the consequences of echo chambers? How do they affect individuals and the greater society?

4. Will social media eventually replace mass media? Why or why not?

ACTIVITIES

1. Take an inventory of the media you consume and categorize each medium as mass or niche. Based on the list you created, which form of media do you believe has the greatest impact on your life and why?

2. Construct your own personal theory of the media, explaining who (if anyone) controls it and how that is evident in the culture.

3. Identify one celebrity influencer and one social media influencer. Compare their networks and the companies with products/services they promote; make note of both similarities and differences.

4. Lindsay Rothfeld, Mashable contributor, contends that there is a niche market for just about anyone or anything. "From vinyl pressing shops to 'barcades,' and roller derby supplies to pizza cones, there's an infinite number of unique business concepts that are taking the U.S. market by storm."[18] Conduct an Internet search; find some niche businesses. Evaluate them based on their connections to their target audience. How are they using media to share their products, services, or passions? Do they have advertisements on their social platforms?

KEY CONCEPTS

Agenda-setting
Conflict perspective
Echo chamber
Feminist perspective
Gatekeeper
Influencer
Influencer marketing
Mass media
Niche media
Thought leader
Traditional media
Watchdog

MEDIA SOURCES

Reporters without Borders: https://rsf.org/en.

Top 20 Hollywood Blogs, Websites, and Influencers in 2020: https://blog.feedspot.com/hollywood_blogs.

More on Gatekeeping: https://www.oxfordbibliographies.com/view/document/obo-9780199756841/obo-9780199756841-0011.xml.

CHAPTER 5

Business and Strategic Communications

WARBY PARKER FOR SOCIAL GOOD

LEARNING OBJECTIVES

5.1 Identify the impact of social media on business and strategic communications.

5.2 Describe the role of social media in building a brand.

5.3 Analyze how organizations use social media to engage in corporate social responsibility (CSR) initiatives.

5.4 Explain the role of social media in an integrated communications strategy.

Warby Parker sells affordable prescription eyeglasses that consumers can try on at home for free. Like Toms Shoes, Warby Parker employs the 1-for-1 model: Buy a pair of glasses, give a pair of glasses. Partnering with a variety of groups worldwide to give the gift of sight, to date they have given away more than 4 million pairs of glasses to people in need.[1] The company is melding their business values with their strategic objectives. Along with Toms and Warby Parker, Patagonia and Nike are just some of the brands leading the way in recognizing the role and impact of strategic communications on their overall business.

As future communications practitioners, know that the old saying still rings true: Actions speak louder than words. What a brand does—or fails to do—speaks volumes about the company, the products and services they offer, and—most importantly—their reputation.[2] Dave Kerpen, founder and CEO of Likeable Local, a social media software company, suggests that brands align their strategic goals with corporate social responsibility, strategic communications, and business endeavors.[3]

THE BUSINESS AUDIENCE

Businesses have seen dramatic changes as digital and social media have infiltrated strategic planning across the globe. Brands have been given a stronger voice, allowing organizations to connect more efficiently with internal and external **stakeholders**, those persons integral to an organization's existence, including employees, consumers, and—when appropriate—shareholders. Simultaneously, technological advancements are allowing audiences to interact with brands on a whole new level. This has created heightened stakeholder expectations. It has also transferred power to users as they become the watchdogs, holding organizations and even governments accountable in a very public forum.

Just a few short years ago, the world's population was estimated to be 7.676 billion. Of those, 3.484 billion people, or 45 percent, are active social media users.[4] In addition, billions of people (3.256 billion)[5] use mobile technologies to access social media as their primary resource for information, communication, and entertainment. Smartphones and the apps that go with them allow not only telephone calls and text messages (via **short message service**, or **SMS**) but access to news outlets and streaming media as well.

Organizations must communicate with multiple audiences to achieve their business goals. They communicate with customers to persuade them to use their products or services and to expedite customer service. They communicate with employees to ensure that teams are engaged and understand their tasks and corporate endeavors. In addition, many companies communicate with shareholders to provide them with necessary information to justify continued support through financial investment. In all these cases, the proliferation of social media has forced businesses to rethink their communication strategies to keep up with the growing expectations of their audience, balancing the need to promote the company with the need to build meaningful connections.

Consumers spend approximately 2 hours and 16 minutes across 8.9 social media channels per day.[6] In the social sphere, eyes are always on a company, just waiting to engage in and share comments about both the remarkable and the awful surrounding their experiences with a brand. For companies to build lasting, meaningful relationships, this exchange of open two-way communication is essential. There's no doubt about it—social media keeps brands on their toes. And there's no reason to think it will be slowing down anytime soon. From managing corporate identity to scanning the business environment for crises and competition, the digital space has changed the way organizations strategically communicate with their publics.

THE IMPACT OF SOCIAL MEDIA ON BRANDS

Can you think of a company that *doesn't* have a social media presence? It's difficult to imagine because social media has become such an important tool for companies to leverage for branding, public relations, advertising, and marketing. The plethora of options for engaging people with text, images, audio, and video have enhanced the ways in which organizations tell their stories, inform audiences, and sell their wares. It is necessary for businesses to meet the audience where they are at. With so many people relying on mobile technology as their direct connection to the world, having a social presence is really a must for all businesses. This transition has impacted the business world in a number of different ways.

Talk to Me!

Perhaps the most significant impact social media has had on organizations is the ability to create an environment in which businesses and brands can engage directly and have a dialogue with their audiences. As discussed in Chapter 4, companies historically practiced one-way communication, which did not provide such an opportunity. Think about it—the one-way method made financial sense in the presocial media world, as the cost of engaging each audience member individually would have been prohibitive, especially for very large organizations. Social media has presented a cost-efficient means of engaging in two-way symmetrical communication with audiences, enabling the development of "high-quality, long-term relationships." Not only are such relationships a foundational aspect of trust building, but they are likely to mitigate risk and even increase revenue as the organization gains a clearer vision of the needs of its audience[7] (see the In Theory feature).

IN THEORY | Stakeholder Theory

In addition to providing a direct line of contact between stakeholders and organizations, social media provide a multitude of data that help those organizations better understand the needs of their stakeholders. Management scholar R. Edward Freeman came up with the term **stakeholder theory** to describe the role of an organization as creating value for stakeholders within the confines of that organization's goals and beliefs without compromising its intent. In essence, organizations should seek to align their purpose with the needs and interests of their audiences. Using data, including real-time conversations on social platforms, organizations have their finger on the pulse of the types of content, corporate values, and corporate initiatives that are meeting audience needs. If they find that audiences are not responding, the nature of social media interactions lends itself to effective and expedient changes of course in an effort to better align company and customer.

Think about It: Freeman's theory suggests that a company should attempt to satisfy all stakeholders to be successful. These stakeholders include people such as employees, customers, community members, competitors, vendors, contractors, and shareholders.

Do you agree? How can one company satisfy all of these stakeholders and what role does a public relations practitioner play?

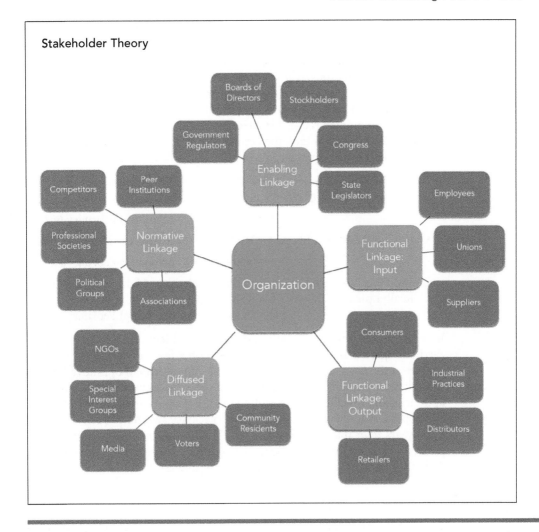

Stakeholder Theory

Transparency and Trust Building

Whether looking to purchase a new product or considering switching employers, we live in a world that is full of options. This multitude of choices translates to a very competitive market. How is a business supposed to attract and hold onto customers, grow revenue, and retain great employees? It comes down to trust. Trust leads to loyalty for both internal and external stakeholders.

Websites provide an outlet for **owned media** (content created by and for the organization) such as corporate biographies, the company website, earnings reports, and blog posts. These types of collateral material provide businesses the opportunity to share insights with stakeholders. Their use is one way that an organization can provide clear information about who they are, what they do, and how they do it. The shared content available on social media has allowed stakeholders to dig deeper through observing and interacting not only with the brand itself but with others who have had experiences with it. This provides both company and stakeholder the opportunity to collect the full spectrum of positive and negative comments and concerns.

Social media has created more savvy consumers and raised the expected level of transparency, which is a vital aspect of trust building. Corporate social media channels allow stakeholders to hold organizations accountable. If content on a brand's social channels contradicts what the company claims to stand for or actions on the part of a company are questionable, audiences can respond with their concerns. For example, when Gucci created and sold a sweater that embodied racist "blackface" culture, the social community swiftly and without reservation took the company to task (see Figure 5.1).

Twitter users were quoted as saying:[8]

So this is what we're doing now @gucci A #BlackFace sweater ????? First Prada, now you? 😵 😵 😵 pic.twitter.com/PdQJcGIXNG

— SinnamonS ♥ (@SinnamonS) February 6, 2019

GUCCI IS CANCELLED ALL 2019 🙅 🧕 ♂ pic.twitter.com/YtGKdKZwqX

— 4amtravo (@TravieJx21) February 7, 2019

Today Gucci released their Balaclava Knit Top. Sigh. Really @Gucci? Really? pic.twitter.com/ETWKFhHVEB

— Keisha Ka'oir (@MikeishaDache) February 6, 2019

In a 2016 interview with Interbrand, Gucci president and CEO Marco Bizzarri was quoted as saying, "At Gucci, we have a few, very simple key values that are at the heart of our organization: the empowerment of innovation and risk taking, a sense of responsibility and respect, an appreciation for diversity and inclusion, excellence in execution, and, last but not least, cultivating joy and happiness in the way we work."[9] The blackface sweater debacle happened three years *after* that interview. Although Gucci did release an apology and pulled the sweater off the market, some customers lost trust in the company. And, the last thing a brand needs is an erosion of trust.

The Need for Speed

The social universe never sleeps, and information is passed along at lightning speed through comments, shares, and other interactions. From media outlets breaking news and sacrificing accuracy for the notoriety of being first to consumers expecting resolution of customer service issues in mere moments, companies are rethinking their response strategies to questions, complaints, and crises like the Gucci sweater debacle. Organizations must be ready to engage with their audiences and "manage the moments." Chapter 6 will delve more deeply into the use of social media during a crisis, but it is important to note here that speed is especially relevant in times of calamity. On the one hand, if a company waits too long to respond, it risks the situation becoming more complex. On the other, waiting a bit to see where the conversation goes can help identify the most relevant points for a response, ensuring that the company is meeting its audience's needs.

Customer Service

Thousands of people take to social media platforms to voice their dissatisfaction with organizations and/or their products. Social media managers are now tasked with scanning the digital environment for kudos and complaints alike. The speed with which complaints are addressed can have a major impact on a brand's reputation. Answer too fast, and your audience comes to expect immediate attention; if you're too slow, you risk the consumer getting upset

FIGURE 5.1

Gucci Website Selling the Balaclava Knit Top Black

gucci
@gucci

Follow

Gucci deeply apologizes for the offense caused by the wool balaclava jumper.
We consider diversity to be a fundamental value to be fully upheld, respected, and at the forefront of every decision we make.
Full statement below.

GUCCI

Gucci deeply apologizes for the offense caused by the wool balaclava jumper. We can confirm that the item has been immediately removed from our online store and all physical stores.

We consider diversity to be a fundamental value to be fully upheld, respected, and at the forefront of every decision we make. We are fully committed to increasing diversity throughout our organization and turning this incident into a powerful learning moment for the Gucci team and beyond.

10:08 PM - 6 Feb 2019

and sharing multiple negative posts that may be viewed and reshared both within and outside their networks.

At a time not that long ago, if you had an issue with a company's product or service you had two choices: (1) Call a 1-800 number to lodge a concern, or (2) write a letter (or eventually an email). The real-time nature of social media has turned corporate social platforms into a vehicle for customer service inquiries. Companies can no longer hide from unhappy customers. As just mentioned, those customers are very happy to post their concerns publicly. Companies have had to rethink their approach to customer service and develop ways to have these conversations publicly while keeping in mind that negative comments can be viewed by many, many people on the platform. Rectifying service issues and making customers feel like their issue is being resolved effectively and within an appropriate timeframe can be a challenge in this public space, but the reputation of the company is on the line.

In some cases, companies have leveraged the connected and cost-efficient nature of social media and created customer service–focused accounts on platforms like Twitter. Accounts like Hyatt Hotel's Twitter account (@HyattConcierge) work to manage customer concerns and enquiries by answering questions and resolving issues in real time.

Changing Department Structure

For a long time, separate corporate departments handled marketing, advertising, and public relations. This led to a **silo effect**, in which departments function independently of one another instead of collaborating as they work toward shared goals. Although independent of one another (like separate grain silos for oats, corn, and wheat), the separate departments attempted to tell a consistent story and strived to meet overall business goals. Social media platforms lend themselves to a more collaborative approach. Organizations benefit from breaking down the silos, allowing departments to work together to coordinate integrated strategic campaigns that leverage the "power of social media" as a complement to more traditional channels.

Because the social sphere has become such an important component of communications and marketing, over time, more and more organizations have hired social media managers and coordinators responsible for working with other departments to develop strategy and execute it. Having dedicated social media staff allows an organization to have experts with a deep understanding of the capabilities of the various platforms and the insights that can be gleaned from them. A critical skill for an effective social media program involves interpreting data accurately and translating it into action. Committing and scheduling staff to "be the voice" on social platforms ensures that users receive timely interactions. Social media managers also perform an **issues management** function, scanning the social landscape consistently and watching for emerging problems that may affect the organization.

Internal Communications

Employees are arguably the most important stakeholder group for any organization. They can be an organization's biggest fans or its loudest critics. Much of this relies on the ability of a company to communicate with staff members clearly and transparently, and to make them feel valued. Like customers, internal stakeholders have become accustomed to personal, transparent, two-way communication from brands, which has resulted in higher expectations for communications in the workplace. Excellent employee communications not only provide the information needed to perform their roles, but also enhance **employee engagement**, the feeling of connectedness among employees, and between employees and employer. "When people feel like they belong at work, they are more productive, motivated, engaged and 3.5 times more likely to contribute to their fullest potential."[10] This can have a great impact on the bottom line.

Challenges to workplace communication include the tremendous number of messages that are communicated and the lack of available channels to provide feedback and inspire dialogue. Email remains a primary channel for employee communications, and its use continues to grow. The average number of business emails sent and received per day, per person is approximately 129.[11] With email read rates averaging around 42.1 percent, it is apparent that there is something lacking in the content and perhaps the channel.[12] Irrelevant information and the impersonal nature of internal emails are often to blame. Today's employees expect their employers to talk *with* them, not *at* them, an important shift in the paradigm.

Although technological advances like email have made the transfer of information more efficient, it has reduced interaction between coworkers. This has contributed to the previously mentioned silo effect. A *Harvard Business Review* survey found that 40 percent of employees feel isolated in the workplace, making effective communication across the board even more important to employee retention.[13] Understanding your employee audience and how best to communicate with them is important for employee engagement. Disconnects between organizations and employees lead to cynicism and low morale. This affects the company's bottom line through drops in productivity and, inevitably, loss of profit. So, what is a company to do?

Social and digital media have improved strategic, targeted communication in the workplace, providing an effective suite that complements traditional methods, meets the revised expectations of internal stakeholders, and supports employee engagement efforts. Employees are already using social media in personal communications to share ideas, collaborate, and have conversations. **Enterprise social networks (ESNs)**, including products such as Yammer (Microsoft), Chatter, Jive, Slack, @Workplace by Facebook (see Figure 5.2), along with internally produced proprietary systems, allow organizations to connect employees and connect to them in a similar way. In some cases replacing the corporate **intranet**, a private network once used to communicate and share company information and resources among employees, ESNs make important content easily accessible by employees regardless of location and provide opportunities for company-wide interactivity and collaboration. This can be especially beneficial to large organizations and those with employees who are spread out geographically. Through their ability to build trust among employees, these platforms improve team communication, expedite decision making and problem solving, increase collaboration, and inspire creativity, among other benefits.

In a study exploring the connection between an organization's use of social media and employee engagement, researchers Michelle Ewing, Linjuan Rita Men, and Julie O'Neill found that companies that implemented ESNs experienced higher employee engagement and collaboration.[14] Incorporating corporate social media into the internal communications mix promotes open and transparent communication; connects colleagues with one another and with the organization; and provides a platform for employee recognition.

As with any communications tool, some people will be active users, and some will not. That said, the research continues to support the implementation of social networks and Web-based functions as an essential part of strategic internal communications.

Employee Advocacy

Engaging employees in a strong employee advocacy program involving social media can build brand awareness and trust. **Employee advocacy**, the promotion of an organization by its employees, benefits the bottom line of any organization while increasing employee engagement. Employee-generated content can result in an audience increase of 567 percent, and employee advocacy programs have the capacity to increase revenue 26 percent year by year.[15] Edelman's 2019 Trust Barometer found that consumers pay attention to what employees have to say about their employers; 78 percent of respondents reported that the way employees are treated by their company is a top indicator of organization trustworthiness and that employees are highly credible sources for brand information and experiences.[16] Leveraging employees' voices also has the capacity to increase sales and help companies recruit great talent. The truth is that many employees are already sharing their workplace experiences in the social sphere. It is a natural progression for companies to

FIGURE 5.2

List of Top 12 Most Popular Enterprise Social Networking Software

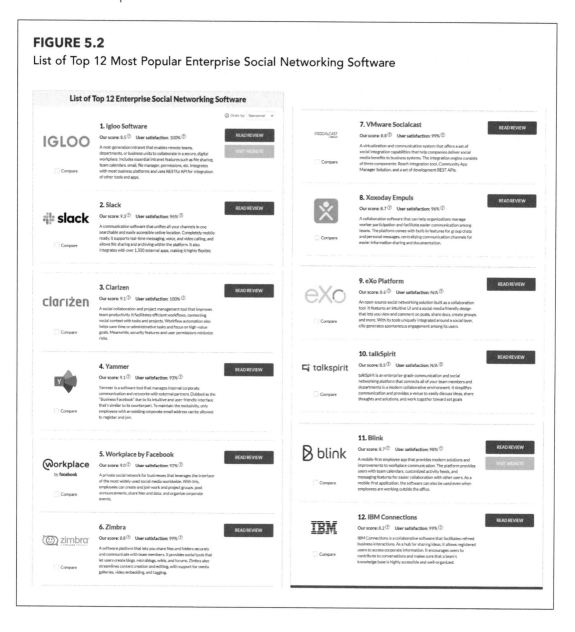

capitalize on this behavior to enhance their reputations and brand awareness. L'Oréal, an international leader in the cosmetics industry, has made employee advocacy a part of their strategy for nearly a decade by maximizing the use of social media to build connections and foster relationships (see Box 5.1).

Branding and Brand Management

Social media provides an ideal environment for interacting with audiences and building relationships. Its freedom of communication also necessitates a strategic approach to **brand management**, the activity of handling the promotion of a particular brand. Susan Fournier and Jill Avery describe the environment as "open source branding" that encourages "participatory, collaborative, and socially-linked behaviors" in which consumers "serve as creators and disseminators

Box 5.1: #LifeAtLoreal

#LifeAtLoreal began as a way for the corporate communications team to get an idea of the types of events and activities that were going on in L'Oreal offices across the United States. It grew into one of the largest and most successful employee engagement and advocacy campaigns at the company. L'Oreal—which is headquartered in France, is active in 150 countries, and employs 86,000 people[17]—soon realized that the hashtag could also be leveraged as a tool for international employee engagement and to meet recruitment goals. To encourage employee buy-in, L'Oréal provided incentives in the form of prize contests. Building on the successful connections made using #LifeAtLoreal, the company implemented #LorealCommunity on Instagram for employees to share images of workplace experiences. The initiative was a tremendous success, resulting in more than 200,000 impressions on Instagram and reaching more passive job candidates.[18] L'Oréal understands the power of the employee voice and continues to implement the strategy. The most recent hashtag, #WeAreLoreal, focuses on connecting employees around the globe, fostering corporate culture, and showcasing employee experiences for prospective hires.

Think about It: #LifeAtLoreal is a huge hit; how would you build something like this from scratch at a company such as Burt's Bees? Describe the steps involved.

of branded content."[19] Shared, user-generated brand content may be in line with or contradict **brand image**, the way that the brand is perceived by its audience.

The complex nature of brand management aside, social media is an excellent tool for companies to reinforce their **brand identity**, how the organization intends the brand to be perceived. Strategic and consistent cross-channel content that resonates with its intended audience can advance business goals. Freaker USA is an example of a company that has created a strong brand identity. The company is located in Wilmington, NC. From the name of the company alone, you are probably already starting to develop some perceptions about it. The company sells one-size-fits-everything beverage koozies called—what else—Freakers. A visit to the company website is full of bright colors, quirky photographs, and fun. The "About" section, titled "Storytime," describes the company as "the global leader of preventing moist handshakes and sweaty beverages with high quality American-made products. They aren't just selling you their fit-everything product, they're giving you an invitation to their party—a starter kit for a new lifestyle."[20] This unique personality and personal touch is consistent across all of Freaker USA's marketing and communications channels (see Photo 5A), including their social media. Every email sent by the company is personalized, and every order is accompanied by a postcard with an on-brand, personalized humorous message signed by "The Freaker Team." The company's social media platforms are an eclectic mix of product information: photos of founder Zach, the Freaker Team, and their friends; behind-the-scenes video of the factory where the product is made; and accounts of their efforts to be active in the community and to make change happen through advocacy of social and political policies and causes.

Freaker USA's social media accounts are a clear reflection of their personality. They use their social channels to provide product updates that are fun and engaging, handle customer service issues, and importantly, are vocal about company involvement in community events and identify their stance on social and political issues.

PHOTO 5A
Image of the Freaker USA team shows an eclectic mix of the company's unique personality. This helps achieve brand consistency.

CORPORATE SOCIAL RESPONSIBILITY

A recent study by public relations firm CONE Communications found that 94 percent of Generation Z, 87 percent of Millennials, and 86 percent of the general population believe that businesses should work to address social and environmental issues.[21] In addition, the study showed that when an organization supports these issues, consumers come away with a more positive company image and are more likely to trust the brand and be loyal to it.[22] **Corporate social responsibility (CSR)** is an organization's commitment to doing business in a socially responsible way. In other words, the organization is operating ethically and with the betterment of society in mind. Some well-known examples of brands with strong CSR programs include the LEGO® Group and Adidas AG (see Figure 5.3).

FIGURE 5.3
The Adidas Sustainability Strategy identifies six strategic priorities to address the issues and challenges of the spaces where sport is made.

WE TAKE RESPONSIBILITY FOR THE ENTIRE LIFE CYCLE OF SPORT:
IN ALL SPACES WHERE SPORT IS ⊢— MADE → SOLD → PLAYED

PRODUCT

1 WE VALUE WATER

2 WE INNOVATE MATERIALS AND PROCESSES

3 WE CONSERVE ENERGY

PEOPLE

1 WE EMPOWER PEOPLE

2 WE IMPROVE HEALTH

3 WE INSPIRE ACTION

Increasing Goodwill

CSR initiatives have the capacity to enhance brand reputation, increase profits, strengthen brand loyalty, and improve employee engagement.[23] CSR also may provide a bank of **goodwill** when a crisis strikes; it can foster employee engagement as colleagues rally around the organization's appropriate response. Some believe that goodwill is an intangible asset that represents nonphysical items that add to a company's value. In some cases, a company's CSR strategy can even impact consumers' perception of product performance.[24] In short, CSR continues to be an important aspect of doing business. Companies with strong CSR programs have the potential to be very successful, especially when audiences are aware of their efforts.[25]

To develop awareness, organizations use traditional methods of communication, such as broadcast and print advertising, to tell their story and demonstrate the good they are doing. Some corporate websites have entire sections dedicated to sharing and reporting their efforts. By making consumer engagement possible, social media has become a prime tool for sharing a company's values and commitment. At the end of the day, research tells us that consumers and employees like doing business with organizations that are good corporate citizens and hold values like their own.

The LEGO® Group does an excellent job transitioning their CSR messaging to various social platforms (see Figure 5.4). What's more, they recognize that their audience includes adults and children, and they engage both through a strategic mix of traditional and digital channels. The LEGO® Group has a very sophisticated CSR program and uses their website to clearly state the 5 W's of their commitment to being good stewards, ensures transparency through clear access to their policies and reporting,[26] and also offers opportunities to join the company in their efforts.

FIGURE 5.4
LEGO® Responsibility Page

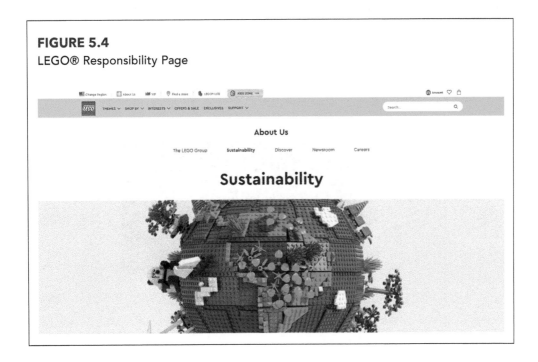

In 2019, the LEGO® Group partnered with Pride in London to host an interactive station at a Pride in London event celebrating all things LGBTQ during London's Pride Month. Announcing this partnership via Twitter, the company encouraged families to visit the play area, where children could customize a Lego person to participate in the march (see Figure 5.5).[27]

LGBTQ-focused conversations occurred on the brand's social platforms. In addition, posts about Pride in London drove traffic to the event, creating an opportunity for both children and adults to engage in play that supports the LEGO® Group's commitment to acceptance and inclusion. Such **corporate social advocacy** is a part of CSR practiced by companies to advance social agendas.

It's one thing to support a social agenda, but what about companies that take a stand? **Corporate social activism** refers to companies that choose to take a public stance on a social or political issue. Ben & Jerry's is for sure at the top of this game through campaigns like 2016's "Empower Mint," which sought to draw attention to barriers to voting and voter ID laws. In November 2018, the company presented a flavor called "Pecan Resist" that advocated for standing in unity with minority groups that came under attack from the president. In fact, they even have a corporate activism manager on staff who manages their corporate support for issues such as democracy, racial justice, climate justice, LGBTQIA equality, refugees, fair trade, and GMO labeling.[28] With this campaign and their public support of Black Lives Matter and climate justice, Ben & Jerry's continues to leverage their corporate values in their communications—including social media—to inspire conversations and prompt action to advance their progressive political views. "When the whole company is values-aligned, corporate activism really works. The people who believe what we believe are extremely loyal to our business, and they buy a lot of ice cream."[29]

FIGURE 5.5
LEGO® London Pride Tweet helped drive traffic to the march.

Although CSR can be a wonderful tool for building relationships with audiences, keep in mind that companies sometimes do not follow through on their promises or act in ways that conflict with the values they've promoted. As we've already discussed, the social sphere makes it increasingly difficult for organizations to "hide" from the public. Their efforts at corporate social responsibility are subject to the same scrutiny. Companies may share their diversity and inclusion campaigns or try to build corporate value through their commitment to the environment, but sometimes the corporate messaging is in direct opposition to these values. Such a misstep can spread across social platforms like wildfire, garnering attention not only from users and customers but the media and competitors as well, which can lead to a crisis of grand proportions.

Before engaging in any CSR initiatives, organizations should do their research. Their initiatives must be aligned not only with their corporate values, but with the values of their stakeholders as well. Only then should they seek to share and engage audiences in transparent and rewarding ways.

Stakeholder and shareholder expectations about CSR initiatives are increasingly more apparent, so much so that stakeholders and shareholders may become activists, challenging organizations in an attempt to control a brand's CSR narrative. It is often said that stakeholders can vote with their dollars in terms of purchasing power and online activism. For example, consider the worldwide social media phenomenon when Colin Kaepernick took a knee to stand up for injustices he saw in the world. This sent some Nike stakeholders into such a rage that they burned their Nike apparel and shoes, and then posted about it on social media to go on record with their dismay.

The same type of reaction by shareholders is called **shareholder activism**, and such shareholders are sometimes referred to as *activist investors*.[30] In a widely cited foundational paper, Admati, Pfleiderer, and Zechner[31] showed that activist investors have an incentive to sell most of their shares and to monitor very little. However, in recent years, this idea has become weaponized to some degree. Strategic private investors and hedge funds sometimes use shareholder activism campaigns to enact consumer voice. They could use their influence, voice, and loyalty to impact social gains and regulate a specific industry. In some cases, this has created fairer business practices and redress for consumers,[32] demonstrating the growing importance, both internally and externally, of CSR alignment with your audience.

Data Is Key

Businesses are data driven and use insights collected through nearly every click of a link or tap of an app. Each digital interaction provides information about a consumer's demographics and psychographics, helping brands formulate their messages and eventually becoming the advertisements we see while interacting online. In fact, The Digital Hyve, a full-service digital marketing agency located in Syracuse, NY (and the fifth fastest-growing marketing agency in the nation, according to *Inc.*), employs "digital psychologists." Their job is to "identify the behavior, interests and psychographics of the target audience for the most engaging ads in the most relevant places."[33] Our digital footprint is out there for organizations to mine, analyze, and leverage in their quest to develop integrated marketing and communications strategies that achieve business goals.

LET'S GET STRATEGIC

Now that we've painted this very complex picture of the media landscape, imagine yourself in a future career as a marketing, advertising, or other communications professional. How do you put all of this together to ensure that your organization or client is meeting its business goals? The answer has two parts: Identify your target audience(s) and then develop integrated communications plans using a mix of traditional mass media and social media platforms. In order to compete and truly resonate with your audience, you must leverage multiple forms of media so that the use of each channel complements the others. Introduced by Gini Dietrich, the **PESO model** quickly became a leading guide for marketing and communications strategy across industries. PESO is an acronym for four types of media—paid, earned, shared, and owned—and includes both mass and niche media channels (see Figure 5.6).[34]

Casper ("The Sleep Company"), which initially built their business on innovating the way that people buy mattresses, has since expanded their product offerings to include everything a person needs to "join the well-rested."[35] The company, which boasted revenues of nearly $400 million in 2018, has established an international presence by mastering the strategic integrated campaign. Casper's customer commitment to a good sleep uses sustainably manufactured items and a lighthearted sense of humor, which is clear in their cross-channel strategy. Casper's agency describes the brand voice as a "quirky

FIGURE 5.6

The PESO model, developed by Gini Dietrich, illustrates how to incorporate paid media, earned media, shared media, and owned media with strategic public relations and social media.

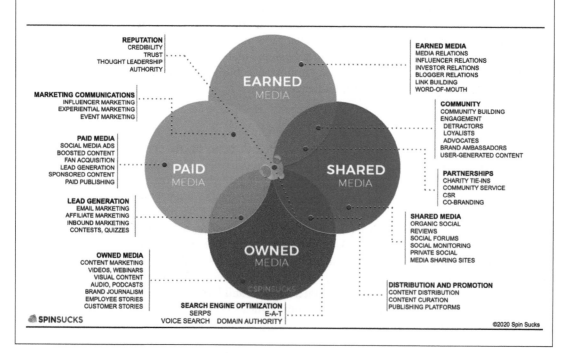

and lovable personality with which customers were eager to engage."[36] Here's Casper's PESO strategy:

- *PAID:* Casper ads appear on television, in print, on billboards, and on social media.
- *EARNED:* Casper's earned print, online, and broadcast media include *Architectural Digest*, Bustle, "The TODAY Show," and multiple blogs.
- *SHARED:* Casper's social media presence includes Facebook, Twitter, Instagram, LinkedIn, Pinterest, and YouTube (where they offer The Casper Sleep Channel, which plays bedtime stories!).
- *OWNED:* Casper's website and blog "Pillow Talk" provide consumer information and thought leadership content pertaining to their expertise ... sleep!

Casper's use of cross-channel content marketing resonates with consumers and investors alike. Each channel shares Casper's story in a consistent voice, providing customers with the information and engagement they need to build a relationship with the company and trust Casper as their go-to sleep and sleep accessory expert (see the Relational/Societal/Self feature).

Relational/Societal/Self: Social Media and the College Application Process

Prior to applying and surely before accepting an offer, you must have done your research to learn everything about your preferred college(s). After all, continuing your education is a big deal, involving commitments of time and (often) finances. You likely started online with the school's website, carefully combing through pages of academic content and extra-curricular or athletics information to be sure that what they offered fit your dreams and to get a feeling for the campus scene. Following that initial research, you probably used a search engine to find general reviews, including current students' reviews of the school and faculty, and explored their social media accounts to get a better feel for the school's personality and how you might fit in. As humans we have an innate desire to make choices that fulfill our needs and help advance our goals.

Think about It: How are the values of organizations and individuals similar? How do they differ? What, in your personal journey, did you discover about the college you now attend during your research process?

CHAPTER WRAP-UP

Stakeholder expectations and social media have changed the ways in which businesses develop their communications strategies and have affected how marketing, advertising, and public relations tell stories. Audiences seek to be engaged in two-way communication with organizations and to be assured that their feedback will be heard and acted upon. Through interactive cross-channel efforts that are transparent and engaging, organizations have the opportunity to share their brand stories and build deeper relationships with their internal and external audiences.

CRITICAL-THINKING QUESTIONS

1. Based on what you read in this chapter, what do you believe are the top three action steps an organization should consider before adding social media to their integrated communications plan, and why?

2. How would you encourage employees to integrate enterprise social networks into their daily communications? Consider the pros and cons for an employee. Why should they become a brand advocate?

3. Discuss the differences between corporate social responsibility, corporate social advocacy, and corporate social activism. Which do you believe is most effective, and why?

4. How should a company manage an employee who is sharing content that is not aligned with brand identity?

ACTIVITIES

1. Interview a friend or family member about the ways that their employer communicates with them. Ask which channel is the most effective, and why. How might this person's demographics and psychographics impact their response?

2. Locate the social media accounts for the last three items, meals, or services you purchased and start a discussion about your experience—good or bad. Take note of the time it took the company to respond and how it made you feel when they did. Did it meet your expectations? Explain your answer.

3. Check out the following article outlining Warby Parker's business and strategic goals: http://bit.ly/CSRWarbyParker. What works, and why? How is the company embodying what you have learned in this chapter? Now imagine that you are a marketing and communications executive for Warby Parker. Based on what you have learned in this chapter, review their social presence and provide three recommendations to enhance their strategy.

KEY CONCEPTS

Brand identity
Brand image
Brand management
Corporate social activism
Corporate social advocacy
Corporate social responsibility (CSR)

Employee advocacy
Employee engagement
Enterprise social network (ESN)
Goodwill
Intranet
Issues management
Owned media
PESO model
Shareholder activism
Short message service (SMS)
Silo effect
Stakeholder
Stakeholder theory

MEDIA SOURCES

International Association of Business Communicators: https://www.iabc.com.

SpinSucks: Professional Development for PR and Marketing Pros: https://spinsucks.com.

Public Relations Society of America: https://www.prsa.org.

American Marketing Association: https://www.ama.org.

Advertising Federation: https://www.aaf.org.

Association for Business Communication: https://www.businesscommunication.org.

American Communication Association: www.americancomm.org.

Association for Women in Communication: www.womcom.org.

Global Alliance for Public Relations and Communication Management: www.globalalliancepr.org.

International Communication Association: https://www.icahdq.org.

International Public Relations Association: https://www.ipra.org.

Social Media Association: http://socialmediaassoc.com.

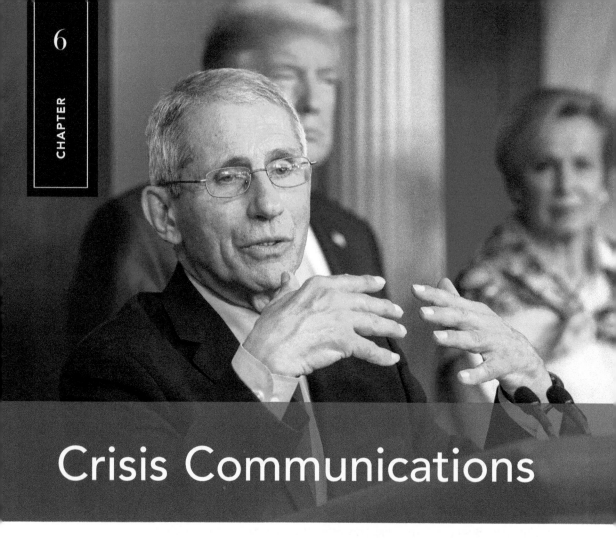

Crisis Communications

EFFECTIVE COMMUNICATION DURING COVID-19

LEARNING OBJECTIVES

6.1 Explain how crisis communications management is performed in the twenty-first century.

6.2 Identify the stages and best practices of crisis management.

6.3 Compare the various models and theories related to crisis communications management.

Effective communication is critical during any crisis. However, the historic COVID-19 pandemic outbreak in the United States and throughout the world illustrated the need for even more effective communication. In the United States when the Centers for Disease Control and Prevention (CDC) along with the White House sent mixed messages early on, it made it difficult for the public to know what to listen to and who to trust. The ways in which leaders address the public matter, particularly during times of catastrophe. As you will see in this chapter, when corresponding during a crisis is done well, people's anticipations, fears, and anxiety may decrease, and their likelihood to hear important messaging may increase.

PHOTO 6A

David Carroll (center) in his video, "United Breaks Guitars"

In the now-infamous and classic textbook case of how *not* to handle a crisis, the "United Breaks Guitars" video featured Dave Carroll responding to United Airlines' refusal to reimburse him $1,200 for a broken guitar. The video racked up an astonishing 19,465,950 views,[1] turned into a trio of music videos and then a book, and now funds a new public-speaking career for Dave Carroll of Dave Carroll Music, showing that social media has become the great equalizer for the common man or woman stuck in economy class. Shortly after "United Breaks Guitars" went live, columnist Chris Ayres of the UK's *Times Online* wrote that "within four days of the song going online, the gathering thunderclouds of bad PR caused United Airlines' stock price to suffer a mid-flight stall, and it plunged by 10 percent, costing shareholders $180 million. Which, incidentally, would have bought Carroll more than 51,000 replacement guitars."[2]

Year after year, despite having access to the most expensive and advanced social media monitoring software available in the free world, United and other airlines continue to have some of the worst social calamities. And it seems that they have not learned from their mistakes. Fast-forward to Boeing in 2019. Following two horrific crashes, one with Lion Air and the other with Ethiopian Airlines that collectively killed over 300 people, Boeing's 737 Max was grounded by air traffic authorities worldwide. Boeing has been working on the software that runs these airplanes since these accidents occurred in 2019. However, as this book goes to press, the issue has gone unresolved. Boeing finds itself in a captive situation, as the media continue to create stories about its history of unanswered complaints and the production of the airplane in general. But the worst critics have taken to social media, which led the *Wall Street Journal* to run several pieces regarding the power of social media. In one of them, boldly titled "Did Twitter Help Ground the Boeing 737 MAX,"[3] author John D. Stoll examines the notion that corporations no longer have the upper hand in "controlling" a crisis. As social media has moved into the hands of the public via smartphones, it has wreaked havoc for brand experts. In just one week following the initial announcement from the company, nearly one million tweets were posted about Boeing's 737, most of them negative in nature. Following this Twitter storm, Boeing lost approximately 15 percent in market value by the end of the week.[4] A **Twitter storm**, also known as a *tweet storm*, is defined by the *Oxford English Dictionary* as "A period characterized by a sudden increase in the number of posts made on the social media application Twitter about a particular issue, event, etc., especially one that is controversial in nature."[5]

Relational/Societal/Self: Seeing Detroit

The population of the city of Detroit, Michigan, is 85 percent Black. So, when Dan Gilbert, billionaire and owner of real estate services firm Bedrock, launched the "See Detroit Like We Do" campaign, fierce backlash ensued. A campaign poster featured white citizens almost exclusively, in stark contrast to the people who actually live in the city. Detroiters immediately turned to Twitter and Instagram using the hashtag #SeeDetroitLike-WeDo, "arguing that the ad promoted gentrification, made Black people invisible, and generally underlined their skepticism of Gilbert's intentions for downtown."[6]

Read the tweets: http://bit .ly/SeeDetroit. Gilbert apologized, but not before the social sphere had their say.

Think about It: After viewing the campaign, what are your initial thoughts? How do you personally feel about #SeeDetroitLikeWeDo? What could the impact be on society?

With this type of negative publicity, it's no wonder that airlines have beefed up their social media game. But is it enough? For another example of the power of social media, see the Relational/Societal/Self feature.

CRISIS COMMUNICATIONS MANAGEMENT

Like most ideas in communications, it stands to reason that defining what a crisis is depends on a large number of variables. According to renowned crisis researcher and author W. Timothy Coombs,[7] a *crisis* is a negative circumstance involving an organization and its stakeholders, such as employees, customers, and investors. Coombs warns that "issues emerging online can be more unpredictable, taking dramatic turns and multiplying more quickly than issues that emerge offline."[8] In 1990, with the introduction of the World Wide Web, new communications evolved, yet the definition of crisis communications stayed the same. It just involved greater speed, communication across more mediums, and—according to some—greater risk. Although digital tools can help solve issues as they arise, frequently they cause crises due to their ease of use and speed of dissemination. To break it down even further, researcher Kathleen Fearn-Banks[9] differentiates between the management of a crisis and the communications during a crisis as follows:

Crisis management. A *process* of strategic planning for a crisis or negative turning point that removes some of the risk and uncertainty from the negative occurrence, allowing the organization to be in greater control of its own destiny.

Crisis communications. The *dialogue* between the organization and its public prior to, during, and after the negative occurrence that details strategies and tactics designed to minimize damage to the organization's image.

Fearns-Banks says that effective crisis management includes crisis communication, which can alleviate or eliminate the crisis. In addition, it can also give the organization a more positive reputation than before the crisis and can restore trust.[10] Crisis communication often includes public relations in the mix to reach specific audiences targeted by the strategies employed in the crisis management process.

Since 2001, Edelman Intelligence (a division of global communications marketing firm Edelman) has produced the Trust Barometer, a global survey and measurement of trust across the world (see Figure 6.1). Its humble beginnings of surveying 1,300 people in five countries has grown to a response rate/sample of more than 33,000 people worldwide.[11] Each year Edelman Intelligence unveils the theme of the Trust Barometer Report, which is usually related to a current state of affairs in the socio-political environment worldwide. Results are shared with business professionals around the world to improve trust globally.

In its 2016 report, "The State of Trust," Edelman Intelligence reported that the level of trust in all institutions had reached its highest level since the Great Recession. Businesses received the largest trust increases among both "informed" members of the public and the general public.[12]

Unfortunately, this indicator was short lived. In 2017, the theme of the report changed to "Trust in Crisis." The general population trust across four key measured institutions—business, government, nongovernmental

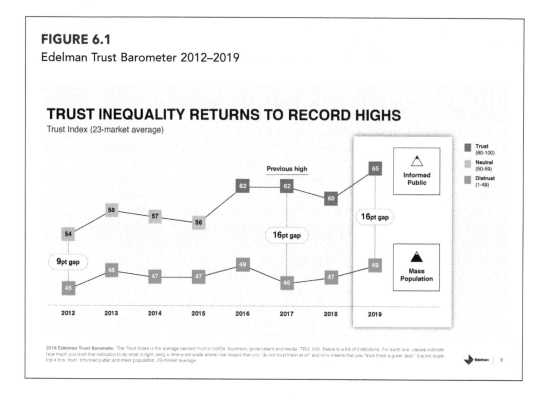

FIGURE 6.1

Edelman Trust Barometer 2012–2019

TRUST INEQUALITY RETURNS TO RECORD HIGHS
Trust Index (23-market average)

organizations (NGOs), and media—declined across the board, which had not been reported since the founding of the report twenty years earlier.[13]

In 2018, Edelman Intelligence reported no significant change from 2017, reporting that trust—particularly in the United States—saw the steepest decline. In contrast, China experienced a large gain in trust across all four institutions.

Also, in 2018, confusion about the credibility of news reporting became directly connected to the rather foggy idea of what platforms people consider to be part of "the media." Nearly half (48 percent) consider social media a part of "the media," and 25 percent feel that search engines fill that role. Journalism, which includes publishers and news organizations, came in at 89 percent.

> "Trust in journalism jumped five points while trust in platforms dipped two points. In addition, the credibility of 'a person like yourself'—often a source of news and information on social media—dipped to an all-time low in the study's history. Most likely, the falloff of trust in social and search, and of the credibility of peer communication, are contributing to the overall decline of trust in media."[14]

The 2019 report suggested that an "'urgent desire for change' could be driving a renewed interest in factfinding … with trust in social media laying in crisis (43 percent), especially in several developed regions that show enormous trust gaps between traditional and social media (U.S./Canada and Europe)."[15] People continue to have very low confidence that institutions like business, government, NGOs, and media will help them navigate through a tumultuous world, so they have turned to their employers to lead the way. You do not have to look far to discover the irony of one person's employer being another person's business, government, or NGO. However, employers have a tremendous opportunity to take the lead in cultivating stronger relationships, which could boost trust overall.

As shown by just a few years of results from the Edelman Trust Barometer, the quickly moving and always changing digital media in the age of digital communication have modified risks dramatically and challenged communicators' responses to threats. The definition of crisis may have stayed consistent with Coombs' model, but the way that communicators respond to crises or reputational threats has changed. That said, in all situations businesses must interpret or determine who is responsible for handling a crisis and how the issue will impact the stakeholder relationship with the brand or organization, in both the short term and the long term. Companies must consider issues from public safety to financial loss to reputation loss.

STAGES AND BEST PRACTICES OF CRISIS MANAGEMENT

The process of crisis management is meant to lessen the impacts on an organization or deliver fewer losses to the brand. Traditionally, most research has divided the process of crisis management into either three or five stages.[16,17,18] Regardless of whether an organization chooses to follow the three- or five-stage model, what is important is that there is a plan in place before a crisis hits.

The three stages are as follows (see Figure 6.2):[19,20]

1. **Pre-crisis**: prevention and preparation;

2. **Critical response**: actual response to the crisis;

3. **Post-crisis**: prevention of future crises and fulfilling commitments made during the response as well as recovery.

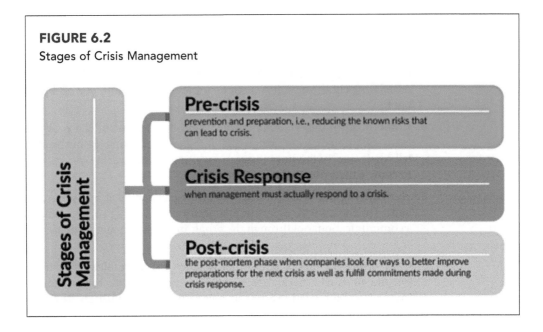

FIGURE 6.2
Stages of Crisis Management

Stages of Crisis Management

Pre-crisis
prevention and preparation, i.e., reducing the known risks that can lead to crisis.

Crisis Response
when management must actually respond to a crisis.

Post-crisis
the post-mortem phase when companies look for ways to better improve preparations for the next crisis as well as fulfill commitments made during crisis response.

The five-stage model is as follows:[21,22]

1. **Detection**: This is the warning stage. Observing/looking for *prodromes*,[23] or warning signs, can aid in stage two;

2. **Prevention/Preparation**: Regular two-way communication with key publics when there are no active crisis scenarios is really the best way to prepare for a crisis. A company must do right and be prepared to tell the public that it is doing right to lay the foundation for a recovery (stage 4). Preparation can be as simple as preparing a process to be implemented at a time of crisis;

3. **Containment**: This stage includes efforts to limit the duration or impact of the crisis when it occurs;

4. **Recovery**: The effort to return the company to the same state or better includes reestablishment of public trust;

5. **Learning**: This final stage includes assessment and critical examination of what happened, discovery of what was lost/gained, and identification of how those in key roles reacted and performed. This learning is reflexive to stage one; it becomes a prodrome for future activities.

Although these models remain structurally sound, the addition of digital media is much like adding an Instagram filter to this process. When thinking of the negatives of social media in a crisis scenario, such as speed of information sharing, it's easy to flip these issues, allowing the unsung benefits of social media in the crisis space to emerge.[24]

1. **Real-time trend analysis**. It provides the ability to uncover industry trends in real time via **social listening**, or what we refer to as *environmental scanning*, when considering all variables in a business landscape.

2. **Competitive analysis**. You can get more comprehensive analysis of competitor markets by conducting social competitive analyses with tools that look at social performance across multiple platforms.

3. **Enhanced customer service**. Providing exceptional customer service in real time can dilute incoming social media issues if handled quickly and authentically.

4. **Lots of data**. Evidence, content, and future stories can be tracked and curated through high-profile and high-volume traffic online. Social proof works both ways: It can condemn and redeem both you and your publics.

5. **Brand positioning**. Positioning the brand during time of chaos can be managed immediately through digital channels, allowing the business to tell "their side" of the story instead of waiting days or weeks—or worse—to convey their point of view.

6. **Humanizing the brand**. It's easy to throw jabs online at a business. It's harder to engage with a person in a negative way. Using social media as a communication tool through the *people* in your company—not *as* your company—demonstrates civil engagement.

7. **Controlling the message**. In order to adapt to and resolve issues in an "on-the-go" world, elevating social media and dedicating top employees to crisis communications management can allow a business to regain control online.

To properly capitalize on these benefits, a brand must do their due diligence regarding social media. In addition, Christina Newberry and Sarah Dawley of social media management platform Hootsuite propose a practical guide for making it through a social media crisis:[25] "Corporations and other institutions are recognizing the 'new normal' of crisis management—some are adapting faster than others. In fact, some crisis experts estimate that fewer than half of all organizations have updated crisis plans that address potential digital issues."[26] Despite understanding the rate at which a crisis can spread through digital channels, organizations still struggle to prioritize and establish the formal plans necessary to respond in near real time. They believe that "crises are too random, unlikely or impossible to plan for,"[27] which is a mistake. For more on Hootsuite's plan, see Box 6.1.

Box 6.1: Hootsuite's 9 Social Media Crisis Management Tips for Business and Brand[28]

1. **Create a social media policy**. Although the details of your policy will vary, all social media policies should, at a minimum, discuss copyright guidelines, privacy guidelines, confidentiality guidelines, and brand voice guidelines.
2. **Secure your accounts**. Do not allow some of your most precious assets to be compromised. Limit access and have strong passwords in order to control who has access at all times.
3. **Use social listening to identify potential issues**. Spot an emerging issue on social media well before it turns into a crisis. Monitoring brand mentions can give you some advanced warning of a surge of social activity. But if you really want to keep an eye out for a potential social media crisis, you should be monitoring social sentiment; this usually requires some sort of social media tool and a subscription. Many providers will allow you to test out their tool at low cost or even no cost before you make a decision.
4. **Define what counts as a crisis at your organization**. My crisis is not necessarily your crisis. Some brands, especially big brands, are perpetually in crisis—they tend to be easy targets. People continually say terrible things online about people and brands, so understanding your normal can help you determine whether the level is above, at, or below the threshold of normal.
5. **Craft a crisis communications plan that is quick, company-wide, and medium-agnostic**. Acting fast is important. More than a quarter of crises spread internationally within just one hour. But it takes companies an average of twenty-one hours to defend themselves in any kind of meaningful way. That's nearly a full day for the crisis to make the rounds on the Web with no meaningful intervention from your team.
6. **Stop all regularly scheduled posts**. A prescheduled post that goes out during a social media crisis situation can make your brand appear ignorant and insensitive. During a crisis, it is essential that all communication be deliberate, planned, consistent, and—most importantly—appropriate to the matter at hand. This is not business as usual, so nothing on your social media outside of your current focus should be distributed. Deactivate any scheduled posts—period.
7. **Engage, but do not argue**. Issuing a statement via media release or a letter or video from a CEO might seem like the right thing to do offline, but online the game is different. Outgoing messaging only is the kiss of death; the public yearns for empathy, listening, and understanding in times of crisis. And keep it short. Avoid getting pulled into a long discussion of what went wrong. Instead, try to move the conversation to a more personal channel, like private messaging. You could also offer a phone number, email address, or other means of communicating outside social media.

8. **Communicate internally**. Keep everyone on the same page, maybe even in the same room. Turn trusted company employees into an amplification of your company messaging and allow them to share across personal platforms. Internal communications as a preventative measure saves external communications in practice.
9. **Learn from experience**. Take time to perform a postmortem of the crisis. Use the lessons learned to improve your crisis communication plan.

Think about It: Seeing a "practical plan" in action can sometimes help articulate a model or theory more clearly. How does this more practical approach from Hootsuite align with some of the models already discussed in this chapter? Which steps align with the stages from earlier in the chapter?

THEORIES ABOUT CRISIS COMMUNICATIONS MANAGEMENT

There are a few different theories related to crisis communications management. These include situational crisis communication theory, the social-mediated crisis communication model, and the integrated crisis communication model.

Situational Crisis Communication Theory (SCCT), formulated by W. Timothy Coombs,[29] explains how managers should manage crisis response in a strategic manner. SCCT matches crisis responsibility to the level of a reputational threat (see In Theory: Situational Crisis Communication Theory).

IN THEORY | Situational Crisis Communication Theory

An effective response to a crisis relies on appropriate assessment of the situation and its reputational threat. Coombs distinguishes among three different *clusters* of crisis events:

1. *Victim*: The organization itself is the victim of rumor, natural disaster, or reputational. This results in a *minor reputational threat*;
2. *Accident*: The organization leads to the crisis in an unintentional manner, such as product failure or accident. This is considered a *medium reputational threat*;
3. *Intentional*: The organization knowingly takes a risk in an inappropriate manner. This is a *major reputational threat*.

Other factors that can intensify a crisis include history (Are there similar crises in the company's past?) and prior relational reputation (How do they usually treat their stakeholders?). Depending on the answers to these questions, there are four main strategies to plan stakeholder replies:

1. *Rebuild*. Redemption of the organization's reputation relies on rebuilding relationships with stakeholders. In taking responsibility for a crisis and/or offering compensation, apology, etc., the brand attempts to "do right" by the individual or group impacted;
2. *Diminish*. Efforts focus on minimizing the amount of responsibility the organization has for the issue at hand;
3. *Deny*. Blame is reassigned away from the organization. This confronts the cause of the crisis instead of affirming it to avoid further escalation and is only effective if the organization is not at fault for the situation.

Continued

4. *Bolster.* Positioning of the organization as valuable to its stakeholders can be used to take advantage of a previously good reputation to increase stakeholder praise, dedication, and/or loyalty following a victim crisis.

Think about It: Using the COVID-19 pandemic, classify whether the pandemic was a minor, medium, or major reputational threat to the following organizations: Detroit Institute of Art (DIA), an online store, or your favorite local restaurant. Once you've classified the threat, decide which of the four strategies would be appropriate to address it.

Although SCCT is the most prominent theory in crisis communications and has many benefits, one of its shortcomings[30,31,32] is the idea of uniformity of impact on all publics through the reputational lens. Having attribution[33] as the only key variable in understanding the reputational threat does not align with the idea of advocacy in communications. Most notably, in public relations a majority of this type of communication would be held in corporate crisis scenarios. To be fair, SCCT was constructed at the dawn of social media. It has stood the test of time in crisis communications literature by folding in social media (see In Theory: Social-Mediated Crisis Communication Model).

IN THEORY | Social-Mediated Crisis Communication Model

The **social media crisis communication (SMCC) model** aids in the use of both traditional and social media in crisis management, response, and recovery of reputation post crisis. The model proposes that social media be used during crises for three purposes: issue relevance, information seeking/sharing, and emotional venting/support. In addition, the SMCC model argues that crisis communication form and source affect the success of organizational crisis response strategies (see Figure A).[34]

Think about It: Now that you've learned about the SMCC model, align it with the nine steps outlined in Box 6.1. Does the SMCC model make more sense now? Why or why not? How can you take this model and apply it in practice?

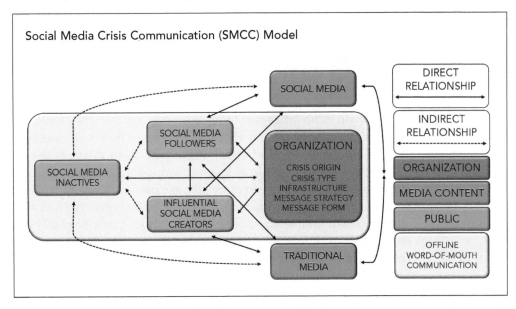

Integrating social media into the traditional framework of **crisis communication strategies (CCS)**, researchers Austin, Fisher, and Jin[35] set out to build on the SMCC model to understand how individuals (as opposed to companies) use social media to communicate in the event of an organizational crisis. Their research revealed that the use of traditional media by organizations is perceived as "more credible" than social media, so it is sought out less frequently by publics during crisis. However, this stands in direct contrast to findings from Bates and Callison,[36] which show that social media is perceived to be most credible, especially among those users considered "heavy" in terms of their day-to-day social media use.

Data analysis by Yang Cheng, a researcher from the Missouri School of Journalism,[37] demonstrates that incorporating social media strategies into the traditional framework enhances crisis communications strategies and reaches all stakeholders in ways that are meaningful to everyone. Although the idea of using social media to organize messaging during crisis is a sound one, the use of models requires a more integrated strategy to meet stakeholder and organizational goals in all crisis stages.

Because social media has become the "driving force in the bleeding edge of crisis communication,"[38] it is expected that—through synthesizing both traditional CCS and the updated SMCM research—this **integrated crisis communication (ICC)** model can be tested in future research and provide more theoretical and practical guidance about social-mediated crisis communication. Due to the rapid-fire response of the public, the dynamics of social media limit the time for thinking through a crisis response, especially in a trending situation. The worst time to start planning for a social media crisis is when you are in the middle of one. However, it is possible for time to be won back, especially in the preparation stage, as social media offers various opportunities to see a crisis coming through scanning and monitoring over time.[39] Frandsen and Johansen[40] of the National Research University Higher School of Economics, School of Integrated Communications, take this idea even further. They encourage crisis communication managers to look far beyond the organization in crisis or those impacted by the issue and to pay more attention to the micro voices offered by individual consumers or members of the general public.

CHAPTER WRAP-UP

Citizens are more influential today than ever before. They must be considered in crisis assessment efforts, regardless of the model used, as their use of various channels of social media puts them smack in the middle of strategy. An errant hashtag by one "wronged" consumer can be transformed into a social movement within minutes to hours as shown in the story in the chapter introduction. "United Breaks Guitars" shifted the stock price of United within hours of going live. Ignoring an individual with even a modest social following can have lasting and significant ramifications and can lead to deep regret. There is no shortage of cases of social media crisis communications on which to practice. This is an important area for future study that is likely to continue to change in upcoming years as social media channels continue to proliferate.

CRITICAL-THINKING QUESTIONS

1. Based on what you have just read, how has social media impacted crisis communication strategies and tactics?

2. Having lived through COVID-19, assess the communication efforts from your favorite brand, your university, or your state. Were they effective? Explain your reasoning, supporting your views with concepts found within the chapter.

3. Which theory do you believe is most effective in crisis communication, and why?

4. What are the best ways to evaluate risk in traditional media? In social media? Are your answers the same, or do they differ? Why?

ACTIVITIES

1. Review Coombs' three stages and Fearn-Banks' five stages of crisis management. Can you align the two models? Why is it important to consider both in a crisis scenario? Apply phases and stages to a modern crisis. If you only considered phases in formulating your strategy, what would you have missed that is covered by the stages model?

2. Conduct a quick Internet search of the top five brand crises over the past year. Based on what you read in the chapter, which brand managed their crisis best, and why? Which one(s) failed, and why?

3. Find a company that experienced a crisis in the past five years. Look up statements, press releases, and videos from the company spokesperson. Assess how well they did. Were their public outreach and communication efforts enough? Why or why not? How is the company doing now?

4. According to the US Department of Agriculture's Food Safety and Inspection Service (FSIS), in April 2020 Conagra Brands, Inc., the makers of Healthy Choice meals, recalled approximately 130,763 pounds of not-ready-to-eat chicken bowl products because the product might have contained extraneous material, specifically small rocks. If you were the social media director, how would you manage this crisis on the company social media pages? Read more about the recall: https://bit.ly/FoodRecallHealthyChoice and check out the company's social media pages.

KEY CONCEPTS

Crisis communication strategies (CCS)
Integrated crisis communication (ICC)
Situational Crisis Communication Theory (SCCT)
Social listening
Social media crisis communication (SMCC) model
Twitter storm

MEDIA SOURCES

MGM Reaches Vegas Settlement, but Money Can't Buy a Good Reputation: https://www.prnewsonline.com/category/topics/crisis-management.

Takeaways for Startup Communicators from WeWork's IPO Crisis: https://www.prnewsonline.com/wework-ipo-crisis-takeaways.

Five Examples of Crisis Communication and What You Can Learn from Them: https://blog.hubspot.com/service/crisis-communication-examples.

How to Be Ready When a Crisis Hits: https://blog.trendkite.com/trendkite-blog/2019-crisis-strategy-how-to-be-ready-when-a-crisis-hits.

Five things we learned about crisis management at the PR News 2019 Crisis Summit: https://www.newswhip.com/2019/03/crisis-management-pr-news.

Sports Communication

SPORTSCASTER MIKE TIRICO, NBC SPORTS

LEARNING OBJECTIVES

7.1 Identify the theories of mass communications that underpin sports communication.

7.2 Explain the impact of social media on various participants in the sports industry.

7.3 Describe e-sports and their relationship to sports communication and social media.

Mike Tirico's career as a national sports broadcaster spans thirty years. His first role was with ESPN, where he was well known for his National Football League (NFL) play-by-play broadcasts. In 2016, Tirico joined the team at NBC Sports. Throughout his career, Tirico has covered a myriad of sports including football, basketball, soccer, and golf, among others. We had the opportunity to talk with Mike about the impact social media has had on the sports industry. Here is what he had to say:[1]

"Social media has instigated some of the most significant changes I've encountered in our industry and has really heightened the sports experience for all audiences through its ability to connect.

From the perspective of sport journalism and broadcasting, our job has truly become 24/7. To provide the most relevant and current content to our audiences we are constantly reviewing team and player accounts as well as fan chatter—we need to be in the know to provide audiences with insights on the latest news and commentary.

We live in a time of the 'second screen generation,' where fans are watching the game and simultaneously reacting through social media. I think of it as an in-game town hall, where opinions and reactions from the audience are being shared and discussed in real time. It's not uncommon for production teams to have staff dedicated to scanning social media during games so that real-time content can be shared live during the broadcast, either on the screen or by the announcers to enhance the broadcast.

A great benefit of social media for fans is that it allows athletes to connect directly with fans on a personal level. These interactions can help build the brands of individual players and teams, which in turn aid in building loyalty to the franchises and players. One can argue the bonds built have a positive impact on revenues through ticket sales, and even be a benefit to advertisers when media broadcasts are going to deliver high viewership.

I use social media to inform my work each day. I share events and highlights that are important to me and my followers, and sometimes share my opinion about the latest happenings in the sports world. You'll also find me sharing some behind the scenes content, and of course, hyping my alma mater, Syracuse University - GO ORANGE!"

Mike Tiricio, American sportscaster working for NBC Sports

An "area of study that seeks to understand the relationship between communication processes and sport contexts"[2] at its most basic level, **sports communication** is communications within sport situations. Its study is a dynamic field, in part because of the sheer number of audiences and aspects of communications that have a role in the industry, including teams, leagues, athletes, brands, and fans, to name just a few. Social media has dramatically changed the ways in which sporting events are consumed. This chapter introduces the components and fundamental theories of sports communications and takes a high-level look at how sports communications have been impacted by social media's ability to connect and engage multiple audiences on a global scale.

THE COMMUNICATIONS PLAYING FIELD

At the micro and macro levels, sports communication is influenced by mass communications theories. From individual direct sports communications to its advertising, marketing, and public relations aspects, you will recognize many concepts already covered in this text. The use of sports communications today involves a variety of models and theories, including the Strategic Sports Communication Model.

Strategic Sports Communication Model

The **Strategic Sports Communication Model (SSCM)**[3] illustrates the sports communication process. The model identifies three components that explain the process (see Figure 7.1):

Component I: Personal and Organizational Communication in Sport. This represents communication happening at the micro level. Examples include interactions between athletes and coaches preceding and following a play, fan and spectator interactions, and conversations at the organizational level.

Component II: Mediated Communication in Sport. This includes watching a sporting event on television or live on a social media platform where the content you are seeing and hearing has been altered by an outside influence. In other words, through the production process, someone else has presented the content through their own filter, which may affect you differently than if you were experiencing it live in person.

Component III: Sport Communication Services and Support. This is comprised of the service side of the industry, which could be the advertising agency representing brands, purchasing advertising, or engaging in sponsorship deals with an athlete or sports team.

The SSCM is a comprehensive, big-picture view of the communications involved in sport that is not limited to participant interactions. Many levels of communication from micro to macro are represented here, including the marketing and advertising functions and sports broadcasting. This model makes it possible to see all of the ways in which social media impacts the industry of sport. See the In Theory feature for ways to apply this comprehensive model.

FIGURE 7.1
The Strategic Sports Communication Model (SSCM)

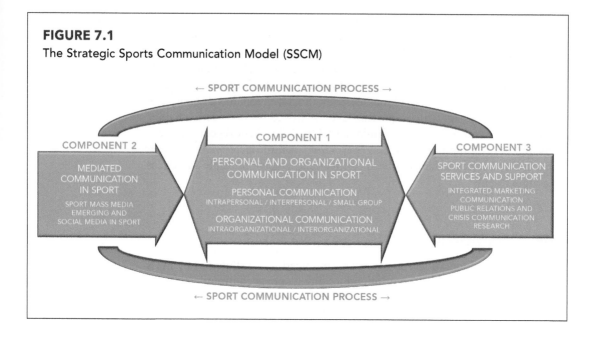

Mass Communications Theories and Sports Communication

Sports communication, which is represented in both mass and niche media, utilizes both traditional and social media. Concepts presented earlier in the text, including meaning creation, symbols, and fundamental theories of mass communications, also form the foundations for sports communications. Understanding them is important regardless of which component of the SSCM is being considered. In Chapter 4 you learned how mass communications theories including agenda setting and gatekeeping apply in the social sphere and how they affect what and how you think about events and ideas. These concepts are also applicable to sports communications.

IN THEORY | Applying the Strategic Sports Communication Model

Think about your most recent experience with a professional sporting event. It can be one that you attended in person or one you participated in using television/radio/social media. The various communications are relevant to different components of the SSCM model. For example, advertising on the boards around the arena in which you viewed the event belong in component III, services and support; and in-person conversations with the fans in your section belong in component I, personal and organizational communication.

Think about It: Assign each communication that you experienced during the sporting event to a component of the SSCM model and explain your rationale for doing so.

Let's use ESPN, a major purveyor of sporting content, as an example. ESPN is present in television, radio, and the digital space. The latter includes their website and social media platforms, through which they help mold the views of sports enthusiasts and professionals alike. Three of the most prevalent mass communication theories—gatekeeping, agenda setting, and framing—play a role in ESPN's sports communication.

- **Gatekeeping**: ESPN reporters, editors, producers, and managers decide what contests to air on their media channels and what stories to tell about athletic contests. They cannot show everything, so the gatekeepers choose for us. Sometimes it's soccer. Other times it's professional poker … or a spelling bee! Do you consider a spelling bee an athletic contest? We're not sure either, but we do know that ESPN sees value in airing the Scripps National Spelling Bee each year. Viewership of the finals has fluctuated between a 2015 peak of nearly 1 million viewers to a low of 547,000 viewers in 2017.[4]
- **Agenda Setting**: From a sports news perspective, ESPN chooses which sports highlights will be shared with the public via their broadcast and online platforms. These selections become the highlights that consumers are talking about, so ESPN is setting the agenda for discussions.
- **Framing**: Framing builds upon agenda setting; however, the concept of framing expands the research by focusing on the essence of the issues at hand rather than on a particular topic. Headlines appear on television during the SportsCenter broadcast, on the ESPN website, and on their social media platforms. Regardless of which or how many of them you consume, these headlines frame how ESPN believes we should feel about sports happenings.

The foundational theories of mass communications, which underpin what makes social media work as a tool to communicate, are present within industry segments as well.

NEW AVENUES FOR ENGAGEMENT

Social media has changed the ways in which we consume and interact with sports dramatically. Through livestreaming, events can be viewed, played, discussed, and enjoyed globally in real time. This allows our friends in Australia to follow along with the National Football League in the United States and for us to keep up with our favorite Australian footy teams (#BeMoreBulldog!) just as easily in real time. In addition to informing and influencing our ideas and perceptions of other cultures, from the perspective of business goals, this connectedness makes the world become the proverbial oyster for advertisers and marketers, especially those seeking to do business beyond their borders. We'll discuss revenue shortly. For the moment, let's consider how social media in sports communications connects people.

Social media has broken through the barriers between consumers and organizations and provided the opportunity for **two-way symmetrical communication**, one of the most balanced forms of communication between an organization and its public. This form of communication uses dialogue to confer with publics, resolve conflict, and promote mutual understanding and respect between the organization and its public(s). There was a time when the very idea of directly communicating with your favorite athlete or sports team involved letter writing or waiting to catch a glimpse following a game or match, but today's social media platforms have enabled fans and sports enthusiasts to have direct contact with their favorite athletes, teams, and supporting brands. Jeff Knauss, CEO of digital marketing agency The Digital Hyve, remarked to a group of students that he remembered writing a fan letter to NBA great Anfernee "Penny" Hardaway as a child; now, his children have the ability to connect directly with their favorite athletes through the power of social media. What's better than a signed photo of your favorite athlete? "A personal tweet," suggests Knauss.[5]

Multiple participants in the sports industry are affected by advancements in the social sphere: teams/leagues, athletes, fans, and sports broadcasters and journalists. The following sections provide brief overviews of the ways in which these participants experience the social sphere.

Sports Teams and Leagues

By sharing breaking news and information of interest, social media platforms provide individual teams and leagues with ways to communicate with fans and sports journalists and build their brands. With more than 60 million likes, LaLiga's Facebook page is a go-to resource for fans of men's professional soccer in Spain to get updates and view live action. Team Real Madrid boasts 111 million likes on Facebook and more than 33 million followers on Twitter, engaging their fans through fresh content and behind-the-scenes club action.[6,7,8] Brands are built and strengthened using social media.

In addition to getting the word out about news and happenings, social media provides a channel to supply shareable, behind-the-scenes moments. It is hard to forget the fun viral clips like the Orbit, the Houston Astros mascot who likes to break it down on the field to songs by artists like Beyoncé (see Figure 7.2).

FIGURE 7.2
Houston Astros Orbit Twitter page

Houston Astros Orbit ✓
@OrbitAstros

In an odd turn of events, it turns out @_ronaldguzman is a descent dancer.....
#InMyFeelingsChallenge

0:26 / 0:31

7:40 PM · Jul 28, 2018

♡ 1.4K   ♀ 320 people are Tweeting about this

Orbit is also known for impromptu dance-offs with fans and security guards and has even engaged opponents like Texas Rangers' first baseman Ronald Guzmán.[9]

Who knew a nun could throw a curveball? In August 2018 Sister Mary Jo Sobieck threw one of the greatest curveballs in opening-pitch history at a Chicago White Sox game (see Figure 7.3).[10] The clip was shared by multiple news and sports media outlets through social and traditional channels. ESPN nominated the clip for its "Best Viral Moment" category at the ESPY (Excellence in Sports Performance Yearly) Awards in 2019. It's these moments that bring people together with laughter, in awe, and sometimes in ways that touch our hearts.

In 2019 the St. Louis Blues, a member of the National Hockey League (NHL), won their first Stanley Cup. This amazing accomplishment was most certainly celebrated, but it was also complemented by the story of their support of superfan 11-year old Laila Anderson, who suffers from a rare autoimmune condition (see Figure 7.4). Players on the team, known for visiting sick children in their local hospital, met Anderson, who became a friend of the team and an inspiration on their journey to the championship.[11] The Blues shared Laila's story in an authentic way, ensuring that people around the world and the news media took notice. This relationship provided an opportunity for the team to partner with national bone marrow registry Be the Match to develop awareness about the organization and encourage people to see if they might "be the match" for someone like Lalia.[12] Not only did this use of social media provide a true human-interest

FIGURE 7.3
Mary Jo Sobieck throws out the ceremonial first pitch before the Kansas City Royals and the Chicago White Sox game on August 18, 2018.

story that captured the hearts of millions and the news media, but it also provided the brand with the opportunity to highlight their values and cultivate new fans of the NHL franchise.

Just like professional teams and leagues, collegiate athletics teams seeking to keep fans interested and recruit for the future have discovered the value of social media for branding and engagement. Clemson University focuses on engaging students, recruits, and fans through visual storytelling via their social channels. Jonathan Gantt, director of new and creative media, focuses on sharing stories through short videos and compelling graphics (see Figure 7.5).[13] Gantt notes that the Tigers' social media team is comprised of current students whose talents and understanding of the social sphere lend themselves to creating effective digital content. According to Joe Galbraith, Clemson's associate athletic director of communications, fans and recruits want behind-the-scenes info about what it's like to be a Clemson Tiger: "What's it like going to Media Day? Or going to class? Or hanging out in the locker room?"[14]

Athletes

Players also benefit from the direct connection to their fans and journalists. Through expressing their voices on individual platforms, athletes can share content and engage in direct conversations to build their brands and cultivate stronger relationships with audiences. To assist their players in reaching the younger and digital-savvy demographic, Major League Baseball (MLB) partnered with Greenfly, a platform that provides a central location for content storage and collaboration. This allows athletes easy access to images and videos that they can post directly to their platforms, helping both players and teams enhance their social presence and increase engagement with their audiences.[15]

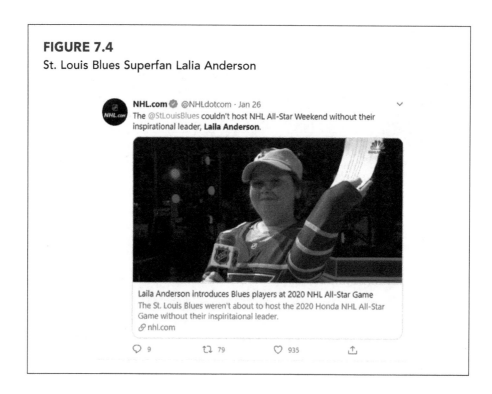

FIGURE 7.4

St. Louis Blues Superfan Lalia Anderson

NHL.com ✔ @NHLdotcom · Jan 26
The @StLouisBlues couldn't host NHL All-Star Weekend without their inspirational leader, **Laila Anderson**.

Laila Anderson introduces Blues players at 2020 NHL All-Star Game
The St. Louis Blues weren't about to host the 2020 Honda NHL All-Star Game without their inspiritaional leader.
🔗 nhl.com

♡ 9   ⟲ 79   ♡ 935   ⬆

FIGURE 7.5

Clemson Athletics uses Instagram's video abilities to provide brief video highlight reels that keep fans up to date and engaged with their teams.

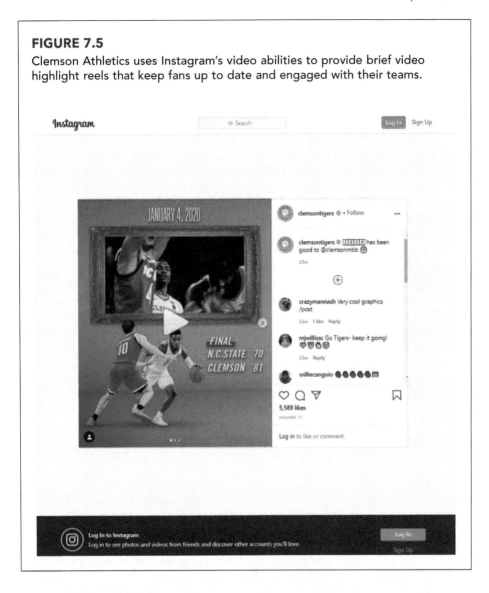

Greenfly was cofounded by former Los Angeles Dodger Shawn Green, who understood the importance of making meaningful connections with fans. By organizing media assets in an accessible online location, players could deepen those connections. The visual content is gathered by MLB Live Content Creators, including photographers, videographers, and social media managers. Creators attend each game, collecting pictures and video on and off the field, and then upload the assets to the Greenfly platform.[16] In 2019, approximately 1,200 pieces of content were available every day for use across platforms and in near real time; as Greenfly suggests, one of the greatest benefits is that the platform is "ultimately giving fans the unique perspectives of the game and its players they cherish and share."[17] Other organizations partnering with Greenfly for distribution of authentic content include Minor League Baseball (MiLB), the World Surf League, and the Asian Football Championship.[18]

In addition to all of the benefits of personal branding and direct engagement, social media has elevated some athletes to ultimate influencer status. These athletes enjoy large followings, and their opinions and thoughts on social and cultural events, along with their advocacy efforts, are shared around the world.

In 2011, Nike signed the newly minted San Francisco 49er Colin Kaepernick to an endorsement deal that was followed by Nike's partnership with the NFL in 2012.[19] In 2016, Kaepernick took a knee more than once during the US National Anthem as his expression of protest against police brutality and racial injustice (see Figure 7.6).[20] When news of this hit the Twitterverse, fans and haters alike exchanged jabs and shared thoughts across various platforms, heightening awareness and prompting conversations about police brutality and patriotism in America. While still under contract with Nike, Kaepernick ended his contract with the 49ers. During this time Kaepernick filed a lawsuit against the National Football League, alleging collusion on the part of league officials that kept him from being picked up as a free agent.[21]

Having not played in a game in the last two seasons, it may have come as a surprise that Nike not only renewed Kaepernick's endorsement contract but went a step further, announcing that the former player would be a highlighted athlete in their thirtieth anniversary "Just Do It" campaign. Following the announcement, Nike stock dropped as much as 3 percent and #BoycottNike began trending on Twitter.[22] Kaepernick's role as a Nike featured athlete was challenged by the public. Nike stood behind him, believing that their decision would be viewed positively by their audiences—strengthening their reputation and adding to revenue. They were correct. Nike stock rebounded following the release of the advertisement featuring Kaepernick.[23] And in December 2019, after Nike released the "True to 7" sneaker featuring Kaepernick's personal logo on the shoe's tongue and a portrait of Kaepernick on the heel, the shoe sold out online within minutes of being made available in North America.

FIGURE 7.6

Now-former San Francisco 49ers quarterback Colin Kaepernick takes a knee during the National Anthem to protest racially motivated police brutality in 2016.

FIGURE 7.7

Megan Rapinoe is an American professional soccer player who leverages her online presence to advocate for causes that she supports.

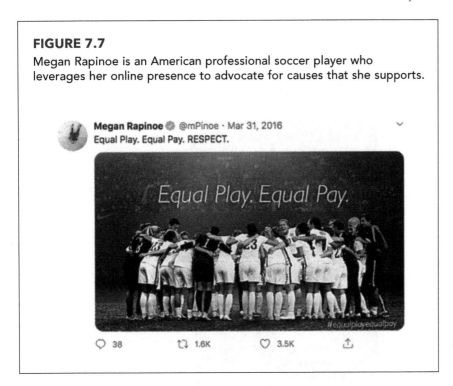

Many athletes use their notoriety and the power of social media to advance social causes and concepts. Megan Rapinoe, one of the most impressive members of the Women's Soccer League, found herself with a platform to affect change because of her career success. Her newfound celebrity allowed Rapinoe to become an advocate for equal pay, gender quality, racial equity, and various LGBTQIA initiatives that she actively promotes on her social platforms including Twitter (see Figure 7.7).[24]

In addition, Boston Celtics' center Enes Kanter has made quite a name for himself not only for his basketball prowess but as a social media activist, as well. Kanter advocates for democracy and freedom as he uses his social media accounts to educate others about political unrest in his home country of Turkey.[25] The photos in Figure 7.8 from Kanter's Instagram account in 2019 serve as strong examples of how he expresses his thoughts and activist initiatives using social platforms.

Fans

We've gone beyond watching sports from home and engaging with other fans in an arena or stadium. Social media has broadened the sporting community. The use of mobile devices allows us to make digital connections with fellow fans and the sports organizations in real time (see Figure 7.9). Fans can now share video of that great play on their own platforms, which can be viewed by the tens, hundreds, or even thousands of people in their networks. Creating dialogue among a broad range of fans is as easy as typing a Tweet or sharing an Instagram story. As they share experiences and opinions with one another, fans are cultivating digital relationships with like-minded—*and sometimes not so like-minded*—people around the globe. These interactions have opened a new space for fandom to be shared before, during, and after sporting events. The ability to connect directly has also enabled fans to communicate with their teams and favorite athletes like never before, helping strengthen those

FIGURE 7.8

Boston Celtics center Enes Kanter is an activist for human rights and freedom and uses his celebrity and social media presence to bring awareness to global challenges.

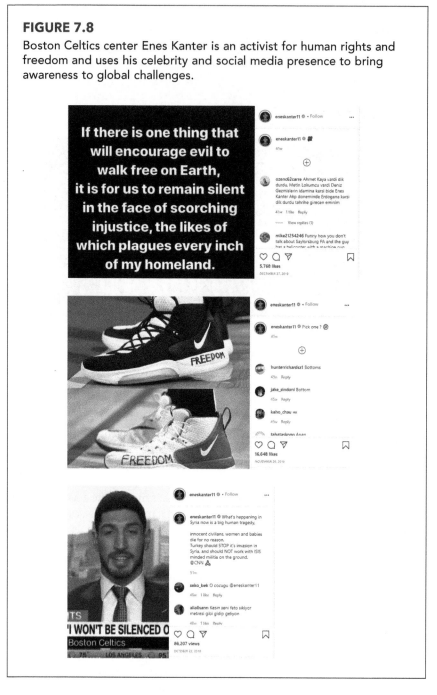

bonds of loyalty that all brands strive for. Want to congratulate your favorite soccer player on her game-clinching goal? Now you can with some quick strokes of the thumb, and they might even thank you for your kudos!

Sports Broadcasters and Journalists

As noted by NBC Sports sportscaster Mike Tirico in the opening of this chapter, his career and those of his peers at NBC and other networks like ESPN have been drastically changed by the onset of social media. These

FIGURE 7.9

FC Barcelona fans can't put down their devices during the International Champions Cup 2019 match versus SSC Napoli.

communications professionals are now expected to be in the game 24/7. Like their colleagues covering news beats, sports journalists have gained the ability to share news as it happens rather than succumb to the restrictions of antiquated television and print news cycles. In addition, the journalists' presence in the social sphere means that they are also responsible for building their own brand and relationships to cultivate a following and interest in the content they are creating. The advent of social media has caused many journalists to work strategically on behalf of their personal and professional brands to build awareness and relationships to ensure their success, much like public relations practitioners. This enhanced role brings with it the pressure of wanting to break the big stories first while maintaining accuracy and integrity.

Given the low barriers to entry of the digital space, social media has enhanced the ability of broadcasters and journalists to track industry happenings, teams, athletes, and their competition. The armchair quarterback of yesteryear can now have a blog and a Twitter account and is capable of reporting on sports just like the trained pros.

Sports Marketing and Social Media

Sports are a multibillion-dollar industry. **Sports marketing** is a niche within the marketing industry specializing in the promotion of sport- and nonsport-related events, goods, and services in conjunction with sport-focused individuals and organizations.[26] This profession has benefited from the digital space.

Olivia Stomski, director of the Newhouse Sports Media Center at Syracuse University, believes that social media is a tool to communicate a brand's culture. "Sports fans turn to social media for instant updates on scores, trades and injury reports—so it is a captive audience for brands to capitalize on authentic exposure and build awareness for their products."[27] She adds that the intimate nature of social media leads not only to exposure to products but also to creation of relationships with consumers based on their favorite sports, teams, and athletes.

As you've learned by this point in the text, as a communications channel, social media tends to be cost effective across the board for companies and organizations. This is true for the sports industry as well. Aside from the fixed costs associated with doing business (e.g., employee salaries and benefits) and the financial commitment associated with paid social media, any brand can open an account, establish their social media presence, and engage online consumers. As Stomski notes, the primary benefit to marketers and communicators is the ability of social media to reach desired audiences in a direct and targeted way while offering the opportunity for engagement with the right message or call to action.[28] She explains that a well-crafted marketing and partnership strategy has the capacity to elevate both sports brands and consumer brands.[29] A great example of this approach is the 2018 FIFA World Cup (see Box 7.1).

Box 7.1:   FIFA World Cup Russia 2018 FIFA World Cup Russia 2018

In 2018 the Fédération Internationale de Football Association (FIFA) declared the Russia World Cup to be the "the most engaged FIFA World Cup™ in history," giving credit to their savvy social media strategy and partnerships.[30] FIFA's expanded social media strategy resulted in 7.5 billion engagements across their digital platforms; this included 1.25 billion video views and more than 580 million interactions on FIFA social media platforms over the duration of the tournament.[31] To accomplish this, FIFA expanded their social reach by adding platforms including VKontakte in Russia and investing more in the Chinese audience through Weibo and WeChat.[32]

FIFA understood the importance of generating content that took into account the cultural differences of its fans. Using a visual storytelling approach, they created authentic content representing all competing teams, which they obtained through on-the-ground reporters across the globe; they then shared the content across all of their platforms and on the FIFA app.[33] Reporters were able to provide genuine, captivating images of the action as it happened; to ensure that no football fan was left out, the content was delivered in sixteen languages. FIFA's strategic brand partnerships—with companies including Coca-Cola, Hyundai, and McDonald's—provided additional opportunities for global social engagement across brand social platforms and apps.[34]

FIFA's investment in strategic social media, with its focus on targeted content and fan engagement, paid off. Their World Cup app became the

Official Emblem of the FIFA World Cup Russia 2018

number one sports app in more than 128 countries, and FIFA.com was ranked as the number one football website in the world.[35]

Think about It: With fans and reporters being able to engage, how did this campaign differ from other sports-related social media campaigns you've seen?

E-SPORTS: THE GAMERS' GAME

E-sports, or electronic sports, is the industry of competitive video gaming. Newzoo, a leader in e-sports metrics for business, defines the term as "Competitive gaming at a professional level and in an organized format (a tournament or league) with a specific goal (i.e., winning a champion title or prize money) and a clear distinction between players and teams that are competing against each other."[36]

The first organized video game competition, the Space Invaders Championship hosted by Atari in 1980 (see Figure 7.10), boasted 10,000 participants.[37] The winner, Rebecca Heineman (then credited as Bill Heineman), is known as the first video game champion; they would go on to a successful career in the video game industry.[38]

E-sports has grown exponentially since the days of Space Invaders. In 2019, the League of Legends Championship offered fans more than 1 billion hours of viewing and hit a record of 44 million concurrent viewers.[39] Some of you may be asking yourselves, "But are e-sports 'real' sports?" As you'll learn shortly, the revenue generation model and revenues produced through e-sports help strengthen the argument that e-sports are in fact sports. And then there's this: In 2013, the US government officially recognized professional League of Legends players as professional athletes; this opened doors for greater opportunity and travel in the pursuit of gaming excellence and competition,[40] solidifying the idea that e-sports are indeed "real sports."

FIGURE 7.10

Atari's 1980 Space Invaders Championship, regarded as the first organized e-sports event.

Building an E-Sports Community

In 2011, Justin.tv launched TwitchTV. Described by the company as a network "dedicated to supporting, entertaining and inspiring the e-sports community," TwitchTV "features the highest quality competitions on all games and platforms, with the top gamers, the biggest tournaments, and the best commentary."[41] Justin.tv sought to provide a platform not only to stream content, but to create a community for gamers around the world.[42] Since its launch in 2011 with 3.2 million unique visitors per month, a great deal of change and growth have taken place. Amazon acquired Twitch in 2014 and now operates the streaming service as a subsidiary.[43] Today, Twitch has more than 3.8 million monthly active streamers broadcasted on the platform. Twitch is not the only player in this game (pun intended!). The e-sports industry has grown to include companies like EA Sports, ELeague, and Blizzard Esports, among others.

E-Sports by the Numbers: Revenues and Brand Opportunities

According to the Global Esports Market Report of 2020:

- "Global esports revenues will grow to $1.1 billion in 2020, a year-on-year growth of +15.7 percent, up from $950.6 million in 2019.
- "In 2020, $822.4 million in revenues—or three-quarters of the total market—will come from media rights and sponsorship.
- "Globally, the total esports audience will grow to 495.0 million people in 2020, a year-on-year growth of +11.7 percent."[44]

In the next few years, the World Economic Forum predicts that e-sports will surpass more than $1 billion in revenue (see Figure 7.11).[45] E-sports funding

FIGURE 7.11

2020 Global Games Market Report according to Newzoo

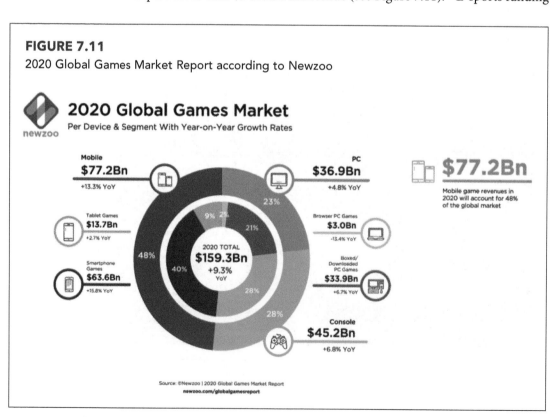

streams are similar to those of traditional sports. Monies earned are based on ticket fees, merchandise, sponsorships, advertising, and media rights, providing brands multiple opportunities to connect with their target consumers across the digital space as well as through in-person gaming competitions and events.

So how do brands leverage the e-sports market? In many ways, the brand connection to e-sports is like traditional sports marketing and advertising and includes sponsorships, promotions, and ad buys. Gillette, a brand specializing in men's grooming accoutrements, announced a campaign partnership with Twitch called the "Gillette Gaming Alliance." The partnership included the selection of eleven gamers around the world who would develop content for viewers and be Gillette brand ambassadors. This extended to the virtual space through "Bits for Blades," a program that allowed Twitch users to earn Twitch bits, a virtual currency that could be used to purchase Gillette products. In addition, the company took the partnership offline through TwitchCon Europe, offering opportunities to interact with the brand in person.[46]

E-sports celebrity partnerships are also an option. Red Bull sought to increase brand awareness within the gaming community, already known to have a penchant for energy drinks to keep them going through intense gaming sessions (see Figure 7.12). The brand partnered with one of the most well-known and popular gamers in the business, Ninja. Red Bull ran a contest in which the winner was offered the opportunity to meet Ninja. Promotional content, including videos and still images of Ninja interacting with the brand, were shared across Red Bull's social media platforms, website, and Twitch, driving traffic to Red Bull's owned sites and

FIGURE 7.12

Red Bull's commitment to building a brand relationship with the e-sports community includes multiple partnerships and dedicated digital platforms.

Relational/Societal/Self: The Rise in Global Regional Sports

As the digital space continues to permeate the sports industry, we are seeing growth not only in e-sports but in the global popularity of regional sports. Through digital technologies and global social platforms, American football is catching on around the globe. NFL teams are playing games in full stadiums in Europe, and there's been increased interest in soccer/ football in the United States. These examples, along with a multitude of others, suggest that both sports marketing and the sports communications industry will continue to expand as teams, brands, and athletes find it necessary to augment their current skill sets with a stronger focus on social strategy, digital delivery, and multicultural marketing in order to grow their audiences.

Think about It: How would you use the cultural power of sport and the communications power of social media to enhance relationships between people from different backgrounds? How can sport and consumer brands play a role in bringing people together? How can sport and consumer brands play a role in your personal life?

creating awareness among this hard-to-reach younger male demographic.[47] In addition, Red Bull offers @RedBullGaming on Twitter, where e-sports enthusiasts can experience content created with their gaming interests in mind. For more on the effects of the digital space on e-sports and regional sports, see the Relational/Societal/Self feature.

CHAPTER WRAP-UP

Social media has transformed the ways in which sports are consumed and marketed. The capacity of the digital space to connect fans with their favorite teams, brands, and athletes is at an all-time high and continues to expand, providing a plethora of opportunities for business-to-business brand partnerships. The future of sports communications is global; those looking to break into this fast-paced, constantly changing industry should be prepared to strategically expand their reach and create meaningful ways to engage cross-culturally. Careers in the field run the gamut from business to advertising, marketing, and public relations, including sports agents, broadcasting and sports journalists, sports media producers, podcasters, e-sports commentators, social media managers, publicists, corporate public relations/advertising/marketing specialists, and communications agency account managers, among others.

CRITICAL-THINKING QUESTIONS

1. How does social media impact sports brands? How does that compare to its impact on consumer brands?

2. How has social media changed the relationship between sporting events and sports fans? Support your response by thinking about your own interactions with your favorite sports teams or athletes.

3. Should athletes use their celebrity to advocate for social change? Why or why not?

4. Do the same marketing and communications principles apply to e-sports and traditional sports? Explain your answer.

ACTIVITIES

1. Think about a time when your experience with an athlete or sports team influenced your choices. Describe the situation and use the mass communications theories explored to this point in the text (gatekeeping, agenda setting, framing) to explain why your experience led you to the choice you made.

2. Imagine that you are the account executive at a public relations and marketing agency for a major brand of your choosing seeking to develop an integrated campaign in conjunction with your favorite professional sporting event. What media mix would you choose and why? Which specific platforms of social media should be included?

3. Based on what you learned about framing and agenda setting, read the following headlines and write down your quick thoughts as to what the story might be about. Then look the story up on ESPN.com and see if your assumptions about the story are in line with what the article says. Apply the principles of both framing and agenda setting to your responses.

    a. *Headline 1:* XFL's Wildcats fire DC Johnson after one game
    b. *Headline 2:* Vanessa Bryant expresses grief, anger in Instagram post
    c. *Headline 3:* Sources: Tua gets positive test results on hip

4. Select a career in sports marketing that interests you. Use social media to reach out to someone who currently holds the job you would like to have and secure an interview with them. During the interview, ask how their role and the roles of their teams leverage social media.

KEY CONCEPTS

E-sports
Sports communication
Sports marketing
Strategic Sports Communication Model (SSCM)
Two-way symmetrical communication

MEDIA SOURCES

Esports Marketing blog: https://esports-marketing-blog.com.

Esports Observer: https://esportsobserver.com.

NBCSports: https://www.nbcsports.com.

Twitch: https://www.twitch.tv.

Espn.com: search esports.

Esports Charts: https://escharts.com/blog.

Political and Civic Communication

SOCIAL MEDIA, PUBLIC DISCOURSE, AND ACTIVISM

LEARNING OBJECTIVES

8.1 Describe the relationship between social media and political communication.

8.2 Summarize the theories and social movements of social media.

8.3 Explain the characteristics of social media as a form of free press.

8.4 Identify how social media can serve as an agent of change.

The past few years have seen a rise in the impact of social media on public discourse within society. This has occurred through both communication and political participation.[1] The Women's March is a prime example of how political communication occurs today.

On January 21, 2017, the day after the inauguration of US President Donald Trump, a worldwide protest and social media movement became the largest single-day protest in US history. The Women's March on Washington,[2] along with many other local marches worldwide, was shared on nearly every social media site and streamed live on YouTube, Facebook, Twitter, and Snapchat. The march reported more than 5 million participants in the United States and well over 7 million worldwide. Across the globe, approximately 700 marches were organized by everyday citizens through websites, text to campaigns, and social media engagement. As a result of the inaugural march, the organization has grown in scope and is now an annual event, promoted and covered on virtually every social media platform available worldwide.[3] With the mission to "harness the political power of diverse women and their communities to create transformative change,"[4] the Women's March movement is "dedicated to ending violence, standing up for reproductive rights, LGBTQIA rights, disability rights, worker's rights, civil rights, immigrant rights, and environmental justice."[5]

POLITICAL COMMUNICATION IN AN ALWAYS-ON CULTURE

Social media offers opportunities for citizens throughout the world to come together and share information and ideas, providing long-term solutions and tools that can strengthen civil society and the public sphere. As more people become connected online, revolutionaries across the globe are being empowered like never before. They use social media platforms in developing, executing, and sustaining modern social movements while defining government and governance.

Use of tools in the mobile age has created opportunities for citizens not only to organize movements, but also to report as citizen journalists, launch viral content, and livestream national and state events from a first-person perspective that was largely absent from the political environment until the adoption of smartphones. An early (2010) study investigated the link between civic and political involvement and mobile phone use. Researchers found that the "use of technology for information exchange and recreation are positive predictors of participation in civic life"; however, "associations are moderated by mobile communication competence."[6] Since the late 1990s, civic engagement in society had been on the decline, that is, until the 2016 US presidential election.[7]

The rise of the Internet at the end of the twentieth century and the mass appeal of this new media gave rise to arguments much like we see today with emerging technologies like streaming channels. One view argued that the new media would displace face-to-face sociability and interaction,[8,9] and the opposing viewpoint pointed to the technology's ability to connect people in previously unknown ways.[10] This polarization still exists in research and probably in your own living room, especially when it comes to political activity online.[11,12] When this polarization is used as a social media strategy to divide generations, people, and countries,[13,14] it creates what is referred to as a **filter bubble**,[15] the algorithmic curation and personalization of systems that decrease the likelihood of finding ideologically challenging content online.[16] In other words, you get only your preferred political "side of the story," sometimes with even more radical exposure, in increasing doses over time.[17]

This idea is at the heart of many modern social media scandals and in some cases affects policy and legislation in countries concerned with the polarization of their populations. One example is the data scandal at Cambridge Analytica,[18] a data company that systematically mined user data through apps on Facebook with the intent to sell and perhaps weaponize user data for political purposes. A whistleblower report triggered concerns about data safety and privacy of many online tools used daily across the globe. This included not only social media giant Facebook but also Google, which has 3.5 billion daily searches and 1.2 trillion annual searches worldwide.[19] Google accounts for more than 90 percent of Web search volume globally;[20] their Web browser, Chrome, holds 64 percent of the market share worldwide (see Figure 8.1).[21]

FIGURE 8.1

Statcounter Global Stats, January 2019–January 2020 Browser Market Share

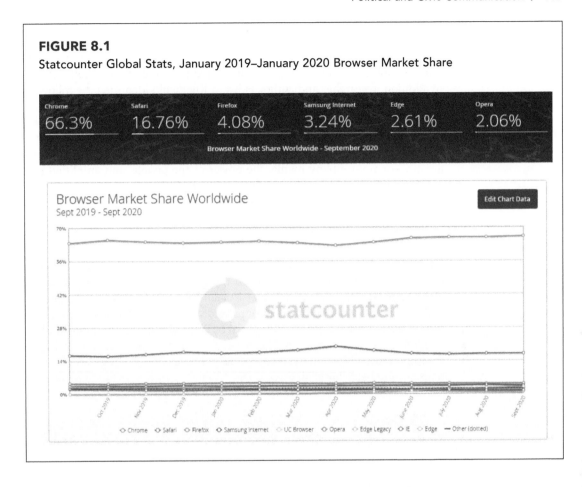

Communication within the political realm demands transparency and relationship-driven, trustworthy engagement among all audiences. Researcher, author, and professor team Patricia Farias Coelho, Pedro A. P. Correia, and Irene Garcia Medina offer the following mass communication trend analysis with regard to social media: "New applications for the various social and mobile platforms will tend to a high customization effectiveness of on-line advertising with a social and interactive nature of the on-line marketing, viral and word of mouth with a growing consumer participation in public and political communication."[22]

THEORIES, SOCIAL MOVEMENTS, AND SOCIAL MEDIA

As the social sphere continues to develop, understanding the characteristics and motivations of citizens is invaluable for communicators who deal with message strategy and media outreach. The current political environment in the United States has created an atmosphere of renewed vigor and uprisings in various populations. Mass communication theory and practice need new ways to conceptualize the relationship between civic engagement and audiences.

As you learned in Chapter 1, media scholar Henry Jenkins identified the concept of shifting sentiments as *participatory culture.*[23] Recall that a participatory culture has minimal impediments to public engagement and/or expression, development and sharing of content, and fostering of social connections. In addition, researcher and author Howard Rheingold identified the following *participatory media*: blogs, wikis, RSS, tagging and social bookmarking, music/photo/video sharing, mashups, podcasts, digital storytelling, virtual communities, social network services, virtual environments, and vlogs.[24] Also as noted in Chapter 1, these distinctly different media share three common characteristics—many-to-many media, the power of the people, and amplified networks—all of which have the power to carry strategic messages to the masses.

Together, collective action, identity, agenda setting, and frame alignment, concepts developed from the social sciences, form what political science theorists consider the *collective action (CA)*[25] *framework.* These ideas demonstrate how individuals communicate to frame or analyze collective messages and data for individual use. Sharing attributes of mass communication, framing, and agenda-setting theory developed from the greater concept of framing in the social sciences.[26] Recall from Chapter 7 that *framing* comprises a set of concepts and perspectives on how people, groups, and societies communicate about reality.[27] *Agenda setting,* a theory developed by Max McCombs and Donald Shaw in 1968 and first presented in Chapter 4, is defined as the "ability to influence the importance placed on the topics of the public agenda";[28] it impacts attitudes, opinion, and behavior at all three levels.[29] Table 8.1 compares the two theories.

TABLE 8.1 Framing versus Agenda Setting	
Framing	**Agenda Setting**
• Content creator chooses the way in which the information is brought forth and the frame in which the data is presented • Affects how the audience thinks about the information • Creates the structure for ideas	• Content creator selects the topics for consideration and consumption • Affects what the audience consumes based on the selection • Content available is consumed

Although use of these frameworks predates the Internet, it is of interest to use them to assess online assembly through social media to illustrate the impact on social movements and civic communication. The perspective from which a story is told can add to the filter bubble; algorithms operationalize the framework as a sorting mechanism to calculate the information consumed more accurately and to innovate. Here's the bottom line: People tend to process information in the way it is presented. So, filter bubbles build a virtual wall, allowing users to see only information that is directly related to the views and opinions they agree with.

The framing process allows comparison or explanation of a specific event or social movement across multiple schools of thought. So, multiple conversations in multiple fields can occur about the same social movement, providing additional insight that can prove deeply significant to history, culture, and—most important to armchair political activists—media coverage. Framing allows new media to be brought into the social movement fold with relative ease.

Information communication technologies (ICT) represent the convergence of audiovisual, telephone, computer networks, computer, and software. ICT is critical in developing and executing modern social movements, particularly at the grassroots level,[30] but it has mixed outcomes with regard to sustainability.[31] Manuel Castells, a prolific proponent of the networked society, describes the displacement of mass media by mass self-communication as altering the communication model from one-to-one to many-to-many.[32] The beauty of this is that, through nearly equal access to the Internet, social media can become a decentralized, nonmarket, peer-produced, nonproprietary, open-sourced, and commons-based resource in nature.[33] In order for a social media–driven social movement to live, or to be an event, the activism must also have a presence in the nonvirtual world, on public display in plain view. Every social movement that embraces social media is shaped by the technology available at the time of the movement was born.[34] Such **cyber activism** results in a change in the power dynamics between traditional media and social media. Activist groups advocating social change often have strained relationships with traditional mainstream media, yet social movements still rely on mainstream media for legitimacy.[35]

SOCIAL MEDIA AS AN ALTERNATIVE FREE PRESS

Social media have created collective spaces where people can discover and share information across time, space, and social and cultural boundaries to create a participatory culture. Users are more likely to actively participate in social media that can increase perceived social and public equity. Because bringing marginalized people and communities together can magnify a social movement and create opportunities for collective action, social media has become integral in grassroots communication and political participation.[36]

Everyone becomes a reporter of the news, as it occurs (see Figure 8.2). "Recognizing the need to create a culture of sharing and participation by partnering with news audiences, media organizations are now presenting multiple opportunities for users to comment, share, and create content to varying degrees."[37] Through *citizen journalism* (see Chapter 3), activists can directly reach their target audience, supporting and permitting the bypass of the traditional media channels with messages in real time. Author, professor, prolific Twitter user, researcher, and reporter Jay Rosen is the founder of Assignment Zero, the first journalism project run by the public. Rosen suggested that the blurring of the lines bordering the spheres of consensus, legitimate debate, and deviance has complicated the practice of journalism in the United States.[38] Traditionally trained journalists are taught to uphold the journalistic virtues of objectivity and balance, but the rise of citizen journalism has challenged those standards.

Bloggers and civilian journalists threaten to expose the unwillingness of some traditional journalists to delve deeper into stories that go against legitimate debate and consensus. Such exposure weakens their authority and makes readers less likely to trust their impartiality. By being able to connect with one another and share the stories and accounts, citizen journalists are learning that "the 'sphere of legitimate debate' as defined by journalists doesn't match up with their own definition."[39] In the past there was nowhere for this kind of sentiment to go. Now it is collected, solidified, and expressed online. Bloggers tap into it to gain a following and serve demand. Rosen has long believed that citizen journalism promotes social democracy.[40]

FIGURE 8.2
Smartphone Selfie Man in Yellow Shirt with #

Social media social movements such as #OccupyWallStreet (OWS) were among the first to use bloggers. These bloggers used **content management systems** or blogging platforms such as WordPress and **microblogging** platforms such as Twitter and Facebook as the primary means to communicate the protest and report in real time to the outside world what was happening in the field. They also used **livestream** channels to broadcast the protests in real time, often painting a very different picture than traditional media. Occupy activists blogged in-depth stories from the field, documenting them with photos, and podcast the voices of the protesters, which amplified their messages.[41,42] A member of another early social movement, the Tea Party Movement (TPM), also used information and communications technology (ICT) for collective action. The TPM started on February 19, 2009, when CNBC reporter Rick Santelli unleashed a rant against the Obama administration's home refinancing proposal on the floor of the Chicago Mercantile Exchange.[43] The video of his tantrum (taken by an onlooker) became a YouTube viral sensation, and a social movement was born. Facebook for TPM became such a central organizing point that an actor within the movement made a Facebook replica network called the Tea Party Community (TPC) to serve as their own social hub.

Social media offers citizens the world over opportunities to share information and ideas, potentially providing "long-term tools that can strengthen civil society and the public sphere."[44] Not surprisingly, there is growing scholarly interest in the mediation of activism and political campaigning. However, the novelty of the topic, the unique qualities of available data, and often unwieldy data set sizes have limited existing accounts to analyses of single cases.[45,46] This makes it difficult to generalize from the findings, limiting our ability to build theory about the uses of social media in moments of political activism.

As protest movements grow more diverse, so must our theoretical framework and investigations of the nature of protest movements in online spaces.[47,48] One important aspect of this potential public sphere is how it facilitates social and political activism. By allowing activists to reach a substantial portion of the public, social media enable a broader range of tactics, beyond appeals to the established media, and raise the question of whether traditional social movement theories can explain such movements adequately.[49]

In classic accounts, the problem of achieving effective coordination within movements was so great that it became central to how activism was structured.[50] The solution was to create bureaucratic organizational forms that could formalize members' participation and direct their actions.[51,52] The rise of inexpensive, networked digital media, with marginal costs of communication approaching zero, means major changes in the nature of mobilization and engagement.[53,54,55] Traditional political movements linked to candidates or issue campaigns have responded to the opportunities of the new media environment by becoming hybrid organizations, centrally managed but with a relatively entrepreneurial base.[56]

At the same time, broader social changes are also contributing to new activist forms. Residents of late modern society find themselves increasingly responsible for elements of life—such as economic security, risk management, and identity maintenance—that once were delivered by social institutions.[57] As a result, late modern citizens face a new set of tasks on their agendas: the creation and maintenance of a personally satisfying sense of self—or "personal identity project."[58] Political identities are expressed via lifestyle and consumption choices, and become highly personalized in nature.[59] Large, loosely knit social circles of networked individuals expand opportunities for learning, problem solving, decision making, and personal interaction. The new social operating system of *networked individualism* liberates us from the restrictions of regimented groups, requiring networking skills and strategies to maintain ties and balance multiple overlapping networks.[60] At the extreme, individual potential collaborators drop in and out of specific movements as they please,[61,62,63] taking their networks, and alternative and free media, with them. President Barack Obama was called "the first social media president," which is to say, he met people where they were comfortable connecting. There is no better example of that than his final State of the Union address (see Relational/Societal/Self feature).

Relational/Societal/Self: The Social Media President @POTUS Final #SOTU

The Obama administration's chief digital officer Jason Goldman published to his Medium platform and to the White House Web page the following official accounts just before Obama's final State of the Union (SOTU) address in 2016: "[The] American people will see a multi-platform streaming and social broadcast of the State of the Union that reflects the ways people experience live events in 2016. We'll be reaching people where they are—and making it possible for them to engage, respond, and share the President's speech themselves in new and different ways."[64]

So why the change in 2016? Goldman addressed this on his blog:

You'll often hear discussion about how to "break through the clutter" online—the premise being that the conversation online gets necessarily dumbed down.

Now, there's a lot of valid criticism about all the noise in online media, and the risks—but there are countless examples of people embracing the clutter and using the Internet to come together to make positive change. We believe that by "broadcasting" the State of the Union across social media and streaming video platforms we are helping American citizens con-nect to the government that serves them.[65]

In a preview video about the State of the Union, President Obama said: "I don't think I've ever been more optimistic about a year ahead." He also said, "This address will be for you. We've taken both of these messages to heart, in an effort to meet people where they are."[66]

The "first social media President" invited all Americans to take to Facebook and make plans to watch the speech via a Facebook event,[67] watch the trailer to get prepared, then "get cozy with your favorite internet-connected device. And finally, keep engaging with the White House: We're listening."[68,69]

Think about It: Examine the POTUS social media accounts now. What is the tone that these accounts are trying to set? How does it differ from that of the previous administration?

The SOTU has evolved with advancing media and with an ever more discerning American public. Article II, Section 3, of the Constitution tells us this: The President "shall from time to time give to the Congress Information of the State of the Union."

You'll notice that exactly how the president is supposed to share the State of the Union (SOTU) is left unspecified. In 1801, Thomas Jefferson decided that speeches were too "inconvenient" and redolent of the monarchy, so he started sending reports instead. It was Woodrow Wilson in 1913 who once again directly addressed Congress in person. And ten years later, Calvin Coolidge's voice reverberated through living rooms across the country as the address was broadcast on radio for the first time. Looking at other SOTU firsts, we see the evolution of media in the twentieth century:

- First TV broadcast took place when President Harry Truman was in office in 1947
- First president to deliver the speech in primetime was Lyndon Johnson in 1965
- First live webcast on the Internet happened in the President George W. Bush administration in 2002
- First high-definition television broadcast of the address also took place under George W. Bush in 2004
- First enhanced State of the Union livestream: President Obama, 2011[70]

In addition to broadcasting SOTU on the White House State of the Union Web page and the White House YouTube channel, another first in 2016 was streaming it on-demand on Amazon Video.[71] Amazon also paired with the White House to make the speech available across all devices, so that Americans could watch the State of the Union address in the same way we're used to consuming video content in 2016—on our phones or cast to our television sets on demand. Amazon Genius was also active,[72] allowing people to review past SOTUs and actively link to the items that matter in an integrated capacity with live imaging, background, hyperlinks, etc. This allowed even the most passive viewer of democracy to get up to speed in no time.

As in past years, you could also watch video excerpts released in real time on Facebook and Twitter, view live GIFs on Tumblr, and—for those with shorter attention span—watch videos on Vine and look at photos on Instagram. These efforts built on previous White House efforts to connect with users across a range of social media sites and make the experience of the speech appropriate to each platform. No small feat.

The president himself also changed the way he delivered the SOTU that year; instead of the "usual," laying out a laundry list of policy proposals for 2016, his office reported that "He'll look beyond the next election and instead talk about some of the most important issues that will shape our country for generations to come"[73] in an effort to engage young people in creating a better country.

Here's why "meeting people where they are" matters in governance for our society:

- We are generally a passive voting audience; in theory, if you meet us where we are we are more likely to participate in governance.
- In a democracy, the idea of participation, which requires accessibility, is among the most important of ideals. Taking it to the people expands this notion.
- Despite relative apathy toward government relations in general (until they are impacted personally), transparency in government and the idea of RADICAL transparency, the type above reproach, is demanded by the American people.
- To pull younger generations into and to keep older generations informed about the democratic process, we must cater to "now" tactics. Social media can serve as a generational bridge.
- If voters don't feel like they can be heard, apathy will continue. Multiple social media channels allow people to close that communication feedback loop (a la Shannon and Weaver's model; see Figure 3.2) with elected officials or those on the ballot in real time. This forces officials to actually address needs regardless of their constituents' proximity to the White House or Washington. Social media in general has facilitated the distribution of political power.
- Prior to the 2016 SOTU, the White House Facebook page and Web page displayed a countdown clock, complete with clips from the administration, rolling factoids, and video entertainment. This true multimedia experience leading up to the president's address was reminiscent of a pregame show for the Super Bowl. Part of the hype and "warm up" to the 2016 SOTU was Vice President Joe Biden on stage "warming up the Internet."
- Meeting people where they are is an extension of the Obama administration's attempts to operate a particular type of constituent outreach. From the very beginning of his campaign cycle up to the end of his presidency, social media played a key part in Obama's role as leader and figurehead. He has been dubbed the first presidential "social media ninja"[74] for his varying presences ["even on Medium!"[75]] and the amazing content machine overseen by his chief digital officer. The world had never before experienced this type of opportunity to interact with its most powerful man and administration at this level.
- Social media allowed transmission of personalized messages from POTUS to individuals in their homes on their own devices, our most intimate pieces of property. Intimacy matters. It is somewhat ironic that we are less interpersonally in touch than ever before because of technology that was developed to keep us "more connected."

SOCIAL MEDIA: A CHANGE AGENT

As a change agent, social media is less about the tools and more about the power of their application to create, maintain, or end collective action, literally creating change and also facilitating those who wish to gather for change. Social media is a tactic for supporting, not supplanting, existing strategies, as it rarely works in a vacuum.[76] Ironically, the best way to get people away from their computer is through the computer. Think about it. It's impossible to organize thousands of people to march without the Web. Without the Web, you can't organize thousands.[77]

Platforms such as Facebook and Twitter have become the foundation on which passionate change makers can build networks of individuals and take action to the streets. Whether this is the beginning of actual change is debatable because it is difficult to measure. Social media undeniably amplifies efforts to effect change all over the world. However, these efforts don't work solely because of social media. Although enthusiasm for ICT is common, utilization of mainstream media through primary activist accounts is still important. Activists can use both mainstream and social media in their messaging to involve those other than protestors and sustain the social movement.

Some countries attempt to control, censor, and monitor social media. These efforts are unlikely to be successful in the long run, as these are durable tools that can strengthen civil society and the public sphere.[78] Remember that the Occupy Wall Street (OWS) movement, one of the first digital social movements, was "born on the Internet, diffused by the Internet, and maintained its presence on the Internet."[79] The digital origins of the OWS movement created street protests. That is not to say that the Internet or ICT created the movement. Instead, the digital disbursement of the movement's message spurred collective action by boots on the ground. Fast-forward to today's social movements—has much changed?

Authors Clay Shirky and Malcolm Gladwell, two prominent early social media theorists who specialize in the topic of social media, take opposing sides on this issue. In 2008, Shirky argued that the political use of social media ultimately enhances freedom:

> Social tools create what economists would call a positive supply-side shock to the amount of freedom in the world. [...] To speak online is to publish, and to publish online is to connect with others. With the arrival of globally accessible publishing, freedom of speech is now freedom of the press and freedom of the press is freedom of assembly.[80]

In contrast, Malcolm Gladwell[81] argued that activists in revolutions and rebellions risk their lives, which requires a courage derived from strong social ties and friendships with others in the movement. "The kind of activism associated with social media isn't like this at all. The platforms of social media are built around weak ties."[82] In his view, Facebook and Twitter activism would only succeed in situations that do not require individual people "to make a real sacrifice,"[83] such as registering in a bone-marrow database or retrieving a stolen phone. According to Gladwell, "[t]he evangelists of social media [such as Clay Shirky] seem to believe that a Facebook friend is the same as a real friend and that signing up for a donor registry in Silicon Valley today is activism in the same sense as sitting at a segregated lunch counter in Greensboro in 1960."[84] He feels that social media would "make it easier for activists to express themselves, and harder for that expression to have any impact,"[85] and that social media "are not a natural enemy of the status quo" and "are well suited to making the existing social order more efficient."[86]

This brings us to author Evgeny Morozov's[87] characterization of social media activism as **slacktivism**:

> feel-good online activism that has zero political or social impact. It gives those who participate in 'slacktivist' campaigns an illusion of having a meaningful impact on the world without demanding anything more than joining a Facebook group. [...] "Slacktivism" is the ideal type of activism for a lazy generation: why bother with sit-ins and the risk of arrest, police brutality, or torture if one can be as loud campaigning in the virtual space?[88]

In response to the work of Gladwell and Morozov, Clay Shirky[89] acknowledges that social media "does not have a single preordained outcome."[90] Instead, social media would serve as "coordinating tools for nearly all of the world's political movements, just as most of the world's authoritarian governments (and, alarmingly, an increasing number of democratic ones) are trying to limit access to it."[91,92] Shirky admits that there are attempts to control, censor, and monitor social media all of the time, but maintains that the chance of failure is unlikely; as previously stated, social media is comprised of "long-term tools that can strengthen civil society and the public sphere."[93]

Shirky feels that the positives of social media outweigh the negatives with regard to its impact on democracy. He maintains that: Social media = more democracy = more freedom. While acknowledging that contradictions make his argument more complex, he argues that the slacktivism argument is irrelevant because "the fact that barely committed actors cannot click their way to a better world does not mean that committed actors cannot use social media effectively."[94]

Today, "slacktivism" has been replaced by the term hashtag activism. **Hashtag activism** happens when large numbers of postings with a social or political claim appear on social media under a common hashtagged word, phrase, or sentence.[95] The hashtags connect the posts, lending a sense of narrative to them. It is the same idea as slacktivism. However, different media create different responses, making it essentially *faux activism*, or sharing issues with followers, family, and friends in an effort to create widespread discussion and action. Everyone can express their opinions via this expansion of mass communication in a democratic way,[96] but the jury is still out on whether this is true activism that creates change or simply an expression of online outrage or support.[97]

CHAPTER WRAP-UP

It's evident that, just over the last decade, social media has become a powerful tool for political communications. The shift from passive to active participant is unmistakable. People's continuing efforts to turn to digital sources to learn about and become part of the story is one of the most monumental changes. Social media platforms such as Facebook, YouTube, and Twitter have become powerful political tools for everyday citizens and political candidates alike. The ability to build networks and collaborate is one of the inherent benefits of engaging in political communications via social media.

CRITICAL-THINKING QUESTIONS

1. How have social media–based social movements changed over time, and why?

2. What communication models other than those mentioned in this chapter can help shape or explain social movements? Explain your answer.

3. Social media have become powerful political tools in campaigns and governing over the last ten years. What major trends can you identify?

4. Have you ever participated in a political demonstration or taken part in online activism? Why or why not?

5. What skills do political communications practitioners need to have in their toolboxes today, and why?

ACTIVITIES

1. Select a prominent current social movement. Using a communication model from this chapter or another one, analyze the communication tactics and techniques used to propel the movement. What improvements would you suggest to movement organizers to improve its outcome? Do you think the model you chose could/would help them with their communication strategy? Why or why not?

2. Video news releases (VNRs) are a standard tactic used for political communications. With the increase in altered videos, distrust in media, and the proliferation of fake news, come up with ways to share news authentically via traditional and online channels.

3. Imagine that you've been hired as an entry-level communications specialist to run the political campaign for the next senator in your hometown. Outline a social media plan to help this person connect with Generation Z.

4. Research and discuss the change of the norms for presidential communications from the 1980s to the present. Have presidents become more connected to us? Does it matter?

KEY CONCEPTS

Content management systems
Cyber activism
Filter bubble
Hashtag activism
Information communication technologies (ICT)
Livestream
Microblogging
Slactivism

MEDIA SOURCES

Social Media and Political Communication: https://www.researchgate.net/publication/332232794_Use_of_Social_Media_as_a_Tool_for_Political_Communication_in_the_Field_of_Politics.

Political Advertising: https://www.ethics.state.tx.us/data/resources/advertising/Gpol_adv.pdf.

Social Media and the Election: https://www.politico.com/2020-election/candidates-views-on-the-issues/technology/social-media.

Candidates Take to Social Media: https://www.wsj.com/articles/presidential-candidates-take-to-social-media-11574942401.

Generation Z and Politics: https://www.businessinsider.com/gen-z-changes-political-divides-2019-7.

Health Communication

#CARAVANTOCANADA

LEARNING OBJECTIVES

9.1 Identify the trends within the field of health communication related to social media.

9.2 Understand the impact of data on the role of social media in health care.

9.3 Assess the impact of social media on community building, marketing, and the future of health communication.

Frustrated by what she described as the "life-threatening" cost of insulin in the United States, diabetes advocate, author, and speaker Quinn Nystrom organized a trip from Minneapolis to London, Ontario, Canada. Its purpose was to increase awareness of the rising cost of pharmaceuticals in the United States. Using multiple communications channels—including email, mass media, and social media—to recruit fellow diabetics and caregivers to join her on the trip, Nystrom documented the trip in real time via social media platforms using the hashtags #CaravanToCanada and #insulin4all to keep supporters in the loop. Fifteen people purchased insulin at a Canadian pharmacy at a total cost of $1,924.10; the same amount of the drug would have cost $23,789.24 in the United States.[1]

Nystrom's strategic use of social media generated global media attention, catching the eyes of political figures throughout the United States and Canada. This included then-US senator, presidential candidate, and

Type 1 diabetes parent Bernie Sanders, who joined the group for their third caravan, which visited the birthplace of insulin, the Banting House.[2]

Before social media, organizing an effort with this impact would have been close to impossible or, at best, terribly difficult. Social media–savvy organizers can put together these types of trips within days' notice and can create change immediately with a trending hashtag on Twitter. Due to the popularity of her fight and the support she gained from #CaravanToCanada, in 2020 Nystrom entered the congressional race in Minnesota on a platform to fix the "broken healthcare system" (see Figure 9.1). Social media in the form of an organized hashtag has inspired Nystrom to run for Congress to enact change in healthcare policy.

FIGURE 9.1

Quinn Nystrom, a diabetes-education advocate, opted to run for Congress in her home state of Minnesota following the #CaravanToCanada in order to impact policy at a higher level.

Quinn Nystrom ✓
@QuinnNystrom

Diabetes advocate, speaker, author | Running 4 Congress in #MN08 to fix our broken healthcare system | not taking Pharma or Health insurance pac $$ so donate 🔻

◎ Minnesota   🔗 secure.actblue.com/donate/quinn-n...   🎂 Joined April 2009

660 Following   **3,052** Followers

Followed by Annie Grayer, Cara Korte, and 8 others you follow

| Tweets | Tweets & replies | Media | Likes |

🔖 Pinned Tweet

Quinn Nystrom ✓ @QuinnNystrom · Jan 15

Yesterday my insulin pump broke. I need this to live. Today:

🔻 $1500 in medical bills
🔻 4 medical calls, 5 forms to sign, 2 hours on hold
🔻 min 2 weeks wait for a new one

This is healthcare in the US. This is wrong. I'm running 4 Congress to fix it. Follow me & RT to help.

◯ 13   ⟲ 116   ♡ 245   ⬆

TOP SOCIAL TRENDS IN HEALTH COMMUNICATION

Today's health-care media landscape relies heavily on online resources for sharing, knowledge building, social support, community building, and interventions for patients and practitioners alike. The National Communication Association defines **health communication** as the process by which people communicate in different health-care contexts.[3] Nestled within communication studies, health communication is a broad discipline that has come to mean a variety of things, depending on the audience and the situation. Researchers studying health communication aim to develop and refine strategies to enhance health communication in order to avoid risks related to or pertaining to health. These risks could be to personal health, public health, specific disease-related contexts, or management of health-care data; the list goes on and on.

The term *health communication* first appeared in 1961 when the National Health Council (United States) created and administered the National Health

FIGURE 9.2

"TikTok Famous" Dr. Nicole Baldwin with the list of diseases that vaccines prevent. Her tweet regarding her video on TikTok racked up more than 26,000 retweets and almost 60,000 likes.

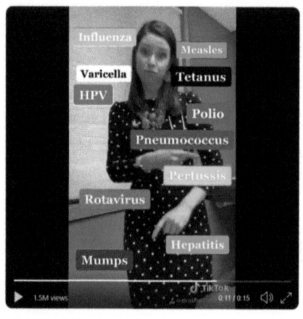

Forum. Its purpose was to discuss challenges facing all types of practitioners in communicating complex information related to health.[4] The term was adopted by the International Communication Association, as a field of specialization or study, in 1975.[5] Health communication practices draw on work from practitioners and scholars across a wide variety of disciplines and sciences. Enhanced practices help to better address public health challenges, like the coronavirus, for example, which do not often fit neatly into one box, but instead affect broad swaths of industries, people, and areas of the world.

Addressing public health challenges is no small feat. It takes the application of a number of theories and models to process behavior. To create lasting change, additional models may need to be brought in from other disciplines in order to influence target audience attitudes, beliefs, and behaviors.[6] Sound complicated? Well, it is. Health communication practitioners must navigate a world full of challenges in a rapidly evolving environment. As they encourage the general public to examine, adopt, and sustain healthier behavior in real time, policy makers, professionals, and administrators continually introduce

FIGURE 9.3

Screenshot of the end of Dr. Nicole Baldwin's video. In the words of the CDC, "vaccines don't cause autism."

Dr. Nicole Baldwin
@NicoleB_MD

Tried my hand at #Tiktok - this one struck a nerve.
#VaccinateYourKids #VaccinesWork #somedocs

1.5M views   0:14 / 0:15

5:28 PM · Jan 11, 2020 · Twitter for iPhone

26.8K Retweets   **59.9K** Likes

new terms of engagement, which can sometimes change in hours or even minutes.

Dr. Nicole Baldwin, an Ohio pediatrician who works in emergency medicine, posted a 15-second video focused on the controversial issue of vaccination on TikTok, the popular social media platform. "Real People. Real Videos," owned by ByteDance, Baldwin's video, went viral, amassing more than 1.5 million views in just a few days. Reposts on Twitter and Facebook garnered hundreds of thousands of views, likes, comments, retweets, and shares (see Figure 9.2). Her overwhelming popularity allowed Baldwin to engage in her own public health initiative, showing the types of diseases that vaccines prevent, including influenza, HPV, hepatitis, measles, polio, and others.

Baldwin ended her video with what vaccines do NOT do, quoting directly from the Centers for Disease Control website (see Figure 9.3).[7]

FIGURE 9.4

Dr. Nicole Baldwin's Facebook post, in which she verifies the fallout of her TikTok viral video regarding vaccines. Antivaxxers launched a campaign against Dr. Baldwin on all facets of social media, including Yelp! reviews and local Google platforms.

Dr. Nicole Baldwin
January 17 · 🌐   •••

ICYMI...Over the past 5 days I have been the subject of a large, coordinated global attack from the antivaxx community both online and offline due to a provaccine video that I created on Tik Tok and shared across my social media platforms.

It has taken a team working around the clock to ban over 5000 attackers from my Facebook page alone. Fraudulent reviews have been posted on multiple rating sites, most notably Google and Yelp. All reviews have been reported and are under investigation.

Photos of mine have been altered with antivaxx propaganda and shared across all social platforms. These too have been reported.

Attackers have been calling my office and harassing my staff as well as threatening my practice. These calls are under investigation by the police.

What can YOU do to help:

👏 Continue to spread the word - VACCINES ARE SAFE. VACCINES ARE EFFECTIVE. VACCINES DO NOT CAUSE AUTISM.

👏 If you see harassing comments on any of my social media platforms, please report those and send me screen shots of any threats.

👏 If you see fraudulent reviews online, please report those as well.

👏 If you see photos of me that have been altered, please screenshot, send it to me and report the user.

👏 If you would like to join the fight against antivaxx attacks such as this, check out www.ShotsHeard.com to join a team that combats these attacks.

Thank you to my office staff, my online team, and my amazing online community for your support in this fight!

#vaccines #vaccinateyourkids #somedocs @ohioaap @ameracadpeds

What began for Dr. Baldwin was an entirely different kind of virality than what she experienced on the job: a widespread global attack from the antivaccination (antivaxx) community both on- and offline, including fake reviews, death threats, and in-person visits to her home and clinic from opposition fanatics, which she recounted in a Facebook post (see Figure 9.4).

This is not the first time virality has impacted a physician or their practice. Another victim of antivaxxer harassment is Dr. Todd Wolynn. A coordinated attack occurred after his physician-owned practice, Kids Plus Pediatrics, produced a public service announcement of the power of the human papillomavirus (HPV) vaccine as a cancer prevention tool.[8] In response to these attacks, Wolynn created a nonprofit to help protect members of the medical community from rapid-fire social media attacks. Called Shots Heard Round the World, the nonprofit group is described as "a rapid-response digital cavalry dedicated to protecting the social media pages of health care providers and practices."[9] This organization created the "kids + anti-anti-vaxx toolkit: a strategy guide to prepare for, defend against, and clean up after a Facebook anti-vaxx attack."

The most recent outcry from the scientific field came from a team of eighteen scientists who, in an open letter published by *The Lancet*, disputed a conspiracy theory that the COVID-19 virus (coronavirus) is a bioweapon that was created in China near the center of the first outbreak in Wuhan. This effort coincided with a social media and digital campaign launched by the World Health Organization to provide a "vaccine against misinformation."[10]

HEALTH CARE, BIG DATA, AND SOCIAL MEDIA

Speaking of information, the health-care industry collects a lot of it, 170 **exabytes (EB)** of data annually. What exactly is an exabyte? Well, it's a unit of computer data storage: two to the sixtieth power. In general terms, an exabyte is one quintillion bytes or a billion gigabytes.[11] Still a little fuzzy? Think about this: An exabyte of storage could store 50,000 years of DVD video footage.

Health care has gotten off to a slower and shakier start than other industries with regard to taking full control and advantage of big data. That said, today's sophisticated data collection, with the help of sensors and wearables like glasses, watches, and smart clothing, have given us the ability to engage the **Internet of Things (IoT)** and provide data better than "self-reported" outcomes. Health-care providers and companies are using this data to improve patient care, eliminate barriers to health and wellness, reduce the spread of disease, predict disease outbreaks, eliminate waste, and reduce consumption. It is also being used to cure conditions, monitor fraud, and digitize and quantify nearly every aspect of the human condition with the goal of improving it. According to Eric Topol, MD, executive vice president of the Scripps Research Institute, human beings can be digitized at different levels, much like Google maps satellite view, traffic view, and street view: "Providers can create a "Google medical map" of a human being from external features anatomy (by scans) to physiology (by sensors), to DNA, RNA and chemical composition. We can quantify the environment, which we could never do before—now it's obtainable information."[12] Information has been readily available for decades but only recently has it been put to use to create focused outcomes in health (see the Relational/Societal/Self feature).

Relational/Societal/Self: Using Health Information to Innovate

Since 1976, experts from SAS, an international leader in innovative analytics, have been using information and data to improve consumer outcomes in the health-care industry. SAS has used this data to identify the top emerging areas of data-related topics in health care. Here we categorize these trends into the three major themes of this text—relational, societal, and self—to refocus it into actionable areas for the best impact:[13]

Relational:

- Helping providers and patients communicate/ understand/keep an open mind about data analytics and collection methods that transpire between provider and patient or vendor and patient;

- Unraveling complex fraud schemes through a hybrid approach of personal education and machine learning/ artificial intelligence, protecting all types of resources in all populations and providing continuity of care.

Societal:

- Data sharing in research to amplify/expedite progress. As cancer, for example, affects people from various backgrounds, sharing of cancer research could have a large impact in expediting cancer treatment or finding a cure;
- Blockchain technology and payment integrity in health care creates data security through com-

plex encryption from end to end throughout a transaction.

Self:

- Using data, machine learning, and artificial intelligence can stop an illness/prevent an injury or lessen their impact on the individual;
- Analytic simulations/ simulators can improve outcomes and lessen patient downtime;
- Analytics can be used to free up surgeon time in the operating room, allowing them more time at the patient's bedside.

Think about It: What are the ethical implications for companies like SAS of the concerns surrounding privacy and data mining?

Walmart—the nation's largest private employer, one of the largest e-commerce platforms on the Web powered by social media, and market disruptor—provides insurance to more than one million workers and their families in the United States. In the fall of 2019, it announced its entry into the health-care market with Embold Health, a provider that synthesizes large amounts of data from public and private insurance programs to create reports and track individual physicians and outcomes. Their goal is to "use this data to curate a group of physicians with a track record of providing consistent quality care and then provide that to associates so they can make more informed decisions regarding their care."[14]

Starting out as an experiment to give access to the best providers and provide the safest, most economical outcomes for their workers, Embold Health morphed first into telehealth in more rural areas and then opened its first stand-alone health clinics in Georgia, South Carolina, and Texas. These clinics offer primary and dental care at reduced rates.[15] Walmart saw an opportunity to bring together three incumbent partners—Doctor on Demand, Grand Rounds, and HealthSCOPE Benefits—to create a new, nimble, and creative service with two goals: (1) to aid their own employees, and (2) to improve the greater health-care environment in the United States. According to Linda Woods, Walmart's senior director of US benefits, "if we get this right, we can raise the tide for all health care."[16]

THE INFLUENCE OF SOCIAL MEDIA ON COMMUNITIES, MARKETING, AND THE FUTURE OF HEALTH COMMUNICATION

As the health-care industry grows, more opportunity to apply social media data to health care presents itself. The ways in which the health-care industry can use social listening and intelligence collecting are many. Here are a few that grow increasingly important to consider for those interested in health communications.

Social Media and Community Building

One of the modern marvels of social media is how quickly messaging can travel. Unsurprisingly, community building, or the gathering of like-minded individuals, is rather quick to occur via social channels as well.[17] In health communications this idea of community includes the traditional social media delivery outcome of "messages of enlightenment" (or education).[18,19] More recently, it has also been used for two other purposes:

- **Listening.** Listening[20] to existing cultures and communities can help deliver more patient-centered dialogue in those communities online[21] (through hashtags, chats, groups, etc.).
- **Social justice.** It is important to acknowledge the marginalization of certain communities (on- or offline) based on social status.[22]

For example, in communities where those with disabilities have gathered, both formal knowledge sharing (enlightenment) and informal community education can occur.[23] With just a small amount of research, major themes can be observed and analyzed in order to better address the health-care needs of this community. A simple Google Scholar search reveals that a review of literature has already occurred in this area. Six major themes were identified: community, cyberbullying, self-esteem, self-determination, access to technology, and accessibility.[24] Say that you were building a campaign with a disabled population as your target demographic. Using this information, you could (1) find online areas of gathering, (2) create appropriate messaging, (3) discover meaningful ways of implementing outreach, (4) construct value-added campaigns based on identified needs, and (5) enhance your understanding of a perspective that may be different from your own to increase empathy. Without analysis of this research, would you be able to create a campaign as relevant or appropriate to the target population? Probably not.

Social Media in Interactive Marketing

Many health-care organizations use digital media of all types for marketing, communications, and public relations. Such alternatives to advertising are presented to an information-hungry public that tends to Google symptoms in an effort to self-diagnose before calling a primary care physician or visiting the emergency room.[25,26,27] The following practices by health communicators in the area of interactive health-related marketing have emerged:[28]

- Promote mission statements on social media that resonate with potential health-care recipients. Mission alignment can be powerful in guiding a patient in selecting a health-care provider.

- Recognize both the opportunities and the pitfalls of the use of social media for public health education by health communicators. The relatively new use of social media in medical settings means that there is no precedent for dealing with a rich assortment of health regulations (such as OSHA, HIPPA). Sensitive topics hosted on social media channels in groups or chats could open the host to liability or litigation surrounding privacy and ethics. This shouldn't deter the use of social channels for this purpose, but activity related to health concerns warrants an additional level of care and consideration (perhaps even consultation with legal).
- Create supportive social networks. When patients leave a health-care practitioner feeling alone or discouraged, finding common ground through social media may be the best way to alleviate a confusing or upsetting diagnosis. Condition-specific social networks that bring together those with similar diagnoses can provide tremendous support. For example, Panoply, a condition-based social network, takes a proactive approach to assisting those suffering from mental illness by bringing together users suffering from specific conditions such as depression to lessen the stigma normally surrounding those conditions.
- Know that the ability to understand, create, and distribute impactful health-care content on social media doesn't come automatically. Managing information to create actionable guidance and build awareness, and publishing credible data are critical in promoting health services in a social media health-care environment.
- Understand that interactive audience communication facilitates two-way communication between provider organizations and consumers and enhances engagement quality. Consumers can be guided or funneled toward desired actions and support, and important feedback on wellness initiatives can be elicited. Interactive social media has been used by health communicators to "reduce suicide occurrences and improve outlooks among patients diagnosed with cancer."[29] Although not considered a replacement for in-person care, it can be considered a supplement or an early warning system for providers with patients in high-risk categories.

A number of health-care-related groups have published guidelines regarding social media professionalism. To learn more about health-care communication ethics and the professional conduct expected of health communication professionals, consider reading the guidelines that have already been established for social media communications for the following groups: the American College of Physicians (ACP), the Federation of State Medical Boards (FSMB), and the American Medical Association (AMA).[30]

Future Fuel for Health Communication

At the 2019 Healthcare Information and Management Systems Society (HIMSS) conference, more than 43,000 health executives, academics, policy makers, nonprofit board members, and government officials gathered to discuss technology advancements, policy issues, and all things related to health care. Pan Communications, a global leader in integrated strategy for health care and technology, summarized their findings. The top three trends identified during this conference included the following:[31]

- *Consumer-Centricity:*[32] *Consumer-centricity* is the idea that empowering and engaging patients is critical to patients' sound decision making regarding their own health care and health-care decisions. Predictability ranking was among the top desires for innovation expressed by conference participants, particularly in the area of artificial intelligence (AI). Providers and companies must continue to provide tools and resources such as AI to better engage and interact with patients in an effort to provide a better overall user experience (UX). A continuum model of care can connect patients to all resources in medicine and within the community at large.
- *Interoperability:*[33] If consumer-centricity is going to be effective, it will be as a result of *interoperability,* the idea that all parties—regardless of network—seamlessly provide care; this includes the ability to track, monitor, and report progress to any other provider, plan, and caregiver. To make this happen, organizational systems must coordinate across organizational boundaries, ideally raising the quality of care and reducing costs in the process. The Office of the National Coordinator (ONC) for Health Information Technology, a staff division of the Office of the Secretary within the US Department of Health and Human Services, has proposed new rules for implementation in 2020. These involve reconsidering the identity of a patient; instead of being a person acted on, each patient would be in control of their own medical record, eliminating current barriers to sourcing medical records from one provider to another, for example.[34] The ONC ruling calls on health-care providers to open application programming interfaces (APIs). This would allow standardization and interoperability and enhance the user experience.[35]
- *Cybersecurity:*[36] Consumer-centricity and interoperability are both super important, but could either one work without enhanced cybersecurity? Probably not. The idea of having medical records available at the touch of an app to anyone at a moment's notice sounds great, if they are secure. However, we can't "free the data" without a plan for securing it. If data sharing arrives through separate infrastructures (health systems, insurance companies, providers, vendors, etc.), how will it be secured? Cybersecurity is and will continue to be a top trend in years to come as discussion of best practices, creation of enhanced collaboration opportunities, and execution of mutual agreements will be a complicated and nuanced practice.[37]

Like any type of data collection, none of these trends can be operationalized without collecting, securing, sorting, and classifying information, and then extracting it for use. Data without the capacity to become actionable is simply information that cannot be used to allocate resources or maintain health. For more on ways to make this data actionable, see the In Theory feature.

IN THEORY | Adopting Mass Communication Models for Health Communication in the Age of Social Media[38]

Two public health-care administrators and researchers, Yosef Albalawi and Jane Sixsmith, created a pilot study that adapted the agenda-setting model of mass communication (see Figure A). This model, first expressed by Lippman[39] and later developed by Lasswell and Cohen,[40] was subsequently refined by McCombs and Shaw (see Chapter 4).[41] Researchers Rogers and Dearing proposed yet another version of the model with three components: media agenda, public agenda, and policy agenda (see the left panel of Figure A).[42] The application to health communication began through Kozel et.al. in an effort to link agenda setting to the process for establishing effective health legislation, policy, and programs.

When they discovered that health practitioners did not understand the agenda-setting model or how to apply it to health education, they offered tools and training for those in leadership to improve the state of practitioner education. Their goal was to increase the ability of health-care practitioners to set policy, something that had usually been limited to lobbyists and legislators.[43]

The idea of agenda setting in health promotion is intended to improve communication in the health-care community, specifically through the public health promotion lens. This lens informs public health design, implementation, and evaluation of interventions. Albalawi and Sixsmith's study analyzed agenda setting within social media in general and, more specifically, investigated Twitter as a means of sharing information.[44] Based on the outcome of their study, the researchers introduced an alternative to the agenda-setting model that considered the use of social media tools in a digital age (see middle and right panels of Figure A).

Think about It: Are there any other models in mass communications that can build upon the use of social media tools in the digital age, in respect to health communications? Defend your answer. Do you see more opportunity for models to be applied to practice in a health-care setting? Choose an area of practice and attempt to align one or two models to create your own drawn model.

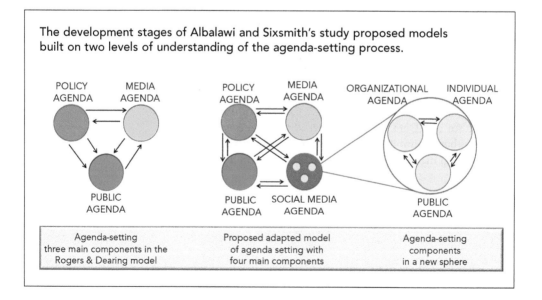

The development stages of Albalawi and Sixsmith's study proposed models built on two levels of understanding of the agenda-setting process.

POLICY AGENDA   MEDIA AGENDA

PUBLIC AGENDA

POLICY AGENDA   MEDIA AGENDA

PUBLIC AGENDA   SOCIAL MEDIA AGENDA

ORGANIZATIONAL AGENDA   INDIVIDUAL AGENDA

PUBLIC AGENDA

| Agenda-setting three main components in the Rogers & Dearing model | Proposed adapted model of agenda setting with four main components | Agenda-setting components in a new sphere |

CHAPTER WRAP-UP

The need for effective health communication is growing and will continue to grow as the world's population ages and chronic disease and illness become more widespread. The integration of communication channels has literally put the delivery of health information at our fingertips. On the plus side, this is empowering. On the minus side, it can be confusing, sometimes spreading bad information faster than it can be remedied. For people with limited reading or technical skills, or those intent on self-diagnosis ("paging Dr. WebMD"), the proliferation of information can pose a challenge. This is why it's important for public health professionals and communicators to become adept at the creation, delivery, and monitoring of consumer health information.

CRITICAL-THINKING QUESTIONS

1. What are some characteristics of the most successful social media health communication social movements, such as #CaravanToCanada?

2. Can generating global attention on an issue like insulin pricing make permanent change? Why or why not? Identify a social media-turned-policy situation that made the jump from social movement to legislation.

3. Do the benefits of social media outweigh the detriments for a field like health communications? Explain your answer.

4. Has anyone you know benefited from the use of social media and community building following a tough diagnosis? How did it help? How did it hurt?

5. Is the use of social media as a marketing tool to improve their patient intake funnel an ethical practice for hospitals and caregivers to use? Explain your answer.

6. What effect does professionalism have on the use of social media in health care? Explain how codes of behavior help (or hurt) the industry.

7. Has there been enough focus on security in the social media age with regard to health-related topics? Have you seen the protection of health information work against someone? Where could it help them?

ACTIVITIES

1. Research three to five health-related social movements (other than #CaravanToCanada) online. Have any of them been successful at creating policy change? Why or why not? Create a list of characteristics that the most promising or most successful movements have in common. Could you rewrite this as a strategy for a new health-care social movement?

2. Do a quick online analysis of codes of ethics or professionalism pertaining to social media for groups like the American College of Physicians (ACP), the Federation of State Medical Boards (FSMB), and the American Medical Association (AMA), all of which have published guidelines regarding social media professionalism. Write your own code of professionalism from items that are common to these three. Track down others that you could incorporate to enhance your personal code of professionalism for practicing online as a health communicator. Share via blog, with your professor, or discuss in class.

3. As described in the chapter, Walmart has gone "all in" on the idea of health care for the masses. If their pilot program works, how will this move impact the local medical communities where Walmarts are located? What will happen if the Walmart model is successful, but a store shuts down or moves to a different community? Is it possible for a community to be too dependent on a brand? Research Walmart as a brand first and then create your hypothesis by answering these "big picture" questions. Discuss the ramifications of for-profit businesses running health care for the masses and offer alternatives.

KEY CONCEPTS

Exabytes (EB)
Health communication
Internet of Things (IoT)

MEDIA SOURCES

Health Communication Toolkit: https://www.cdc.gov/healthcommunication/toolstemplates/socialmediatoolkit_bm.pdf.

CDC Social Media Guidelines: https://www.cdc.gov/socialmedia/tools/guidelines/guideforwriting.html.

The Society for Health Communication: https://www.societyforhealthcommunication.org.

Interactive social media interventions to promote health equity: https://www.ncbi.nlm.nih.gov/pmc/articles/PMC4964231.

ACH Online: https://www.achonline.org.

Entertainment Media

LOOK WHAT YOU MADE HER DO

LEARNING OBJECTIVES

10.1 Explain the impact of social media on the television, music, and film industries and how they market and advertise their products.

10.2 Demonstrate the various ways in which social media is used by celebrities.

On August 18, 2017, Taylor Swift's social media accounts went dark, including her Instagram, which had 102 million followers at the time. No images remained on her Twitter or Facebook profiles, and even her website went black.[1] The social sphere reacted quickly and strongly to what was literally a "Blank Space"; the absence of Swift's social media presence left fans wondering about the artist: "I WOKE UP LITERALLY 7 MINUTES AGO WHAT IN THE WORLD IS GOING ON WITH TAYLOR SWIFT."[2]

You might ask yourself why a superstar like Taylor Swift would eliminate a brand presence that she spent nearly a decade building.

After her accounts were cleaned, Swift began posting perplexing short videos of what appeared to be a reptile across her social platforms over a three-day period, leading fans to use social media to make their own predictions about what the star was trying to tell them.[3] Finally, on August 23, Swift used Twitter and Instagram to reveal the cover art for her new album

Reputation, set to drop on November 10, 2017, and announced that the first single would be released on August 24th.

In a sea of artists clamoring for album sales, concert sales, and attention, Swift and her team used the power of her social community to build suspense, engagement, and excitement among her droves of followers. Her strategic approach to keeping her audience engaged helped ready the market for her new release, and the fresh approach allowed Swift to break through the noise. What's more, *Reputation,* which featured a more mature sound, would mark a new chapter in Swift's music career; removing the star's digital presence presented a "clean slate for a new era."[4] The strategy appears to have worked; by the end of the first week postrelease, *Reputation* was number one on the Billboard Top 200 chart, and first-week sales numbers passed the $1 million mark, making it her fourth album to reach that milestone.[5] Swift is known for her social media prowess, often surprising her fans and exceeding music chart expectations.

The global reach of social media has allowed both professionals and amateurs to cultivate followings and share their craft with audiences around the world. The connective nature of the arts has found new channels through which they can entertain, educate, and communicate. Conversations happen globally surrounding the experiences that people share, based on the media that they are consuming. This chapter explores how audience behavior influences social conversations happening on the Internet and how the television, music, and film industries are maximizing the social sphere to enhance the entertainment experience for consumers while expanding opportunities for brand engagement.

SOCIAL MEDIA'S IMPACT ON THE ENTERTAINMENT INDUSTRY

Social media has become an integral component of television, music, and film. If you think about it for a moment, that makes perfect sense. All of these forms of media entertainment—whether a television show, a song, or the next hit release movie—involve some type of shared experience; intended for more than one person to experience, their impact is amplified through our group psychology, connecting people regardless of location.[6] We log onto our chosen social platform to view messages and multimedia, interpreting them through our own lenses and filters, yet we are not alone. In fact, billions of people out there have had the opportunity to engage in the same way, and some of them may even choose to connect with us. We find ourselves sharing with others what we've taken away from an experience through [an electronic] word of mouth.[7,8,9]

Why does any of this matter? And, how exactly has social media impacted our engagement with entertainment media? Uses and gratifications theory (UGT) suggests that audiences are active, motivated consumers of media with media choices rooted in the desire to fulfill a psychological or social need.[10] Entertainment media is where people go to gain information (by watching the news or educational programs), to feel part of something (like when we see ourselves reflected in a celebrity), to be entertained, to socially engage, and sometimes to escape the stresses of our lives. In other words, entertainment media plays a big role in who we are and the messages we are exposed to. Understanding the ways in which social media impacts the entertainment industry is important to us as consumers of media, and to the brands that seek to reach us. For more on uses and gratifications theory, see the In Theory feature.

Social Media's Impact on Television

Social media has certainly changed the way people watch television and the ways in which its producers reach their viewers.[18] Television has come a long way. At its start, there were only three stations to choose from: NBC, CBS, and ABC. Technological advancements first brought us cable and now digital offerings. Television is no longer just a box sitting in the family room, but a type of media that can be consumed through your laptop, smartphone, or tablet by downloading an app or by checking out streaming content on any number of social platforms.[19,20] Television viewing has become a social experience that connects people through shared interests and social platforms.[21]

IN THEORY | How Uses and Gratifications Theory Explains Why People Use Social Media

When researchers need to understand what people do with media, they utilize **uses and gratifications theory (UGT)**. Developed by Elihu Katz and Jay Blumler, UGT falls within media effects literature in the study of mass communications; it attempts to illustrate the relationship between an audience and the media and identify how that audience uses the media.[11] The basic premise of this theory is that individuals seek out media that fulfills their needs and leads to ultimate gratifications.[12] Anita Whiting and David Williams identified ten uses and gratifications that directly correlate to social media. These include "social interaction, information seeking, passing time, entertainment, relaxation, communicatory utility, convenience utility, expression of opinion, information sharing, and surveillance/knowledge about others."[13,14]

When consuming media, audiences seek to meet five categories of psychological and/or physical needs: (1) entertainment; (2) information and education; (3) identification with characters of the situation in the media environment; (4) social interaction; and (5) escape.[15] Translated for social media, UGT directly translates; practitioners can effectively target an audience based on cognitive, affective, personal integrative, social integrative, and tension-free needs.[16] Media serve to aid in the fulfillment of these needs in a number of ways; entertainment is perhaps the most obvious. News broadcasts and educational programming meet our need to be informed and educated. Media can also be used "to connect with, or escape from real-life relationships, and can also be used to form parasocial relationships with media characters and celebrities." All of this helps meet our psychological needs as well as the sometimes physical craving for social interaction.[17]

Think about It: Using the areas developed by Whiting and Williams, classify and describe your interactions on social media at a personal level with family and friends, with external connections on social platforms, and as a future social media practitioner. How does your approach differ from audience to audience? How do the social media platforms that you seek out fulfill your needs? How can practitioners use UGT to understand better the needs and actions of their target audiences?

These changes have presented a number of opportunities and challenges. Opportunities include the ability to reach and interact with a more targeted and more highly engaged audience. A major challenge for networks and advertisers alike who strive to engage viewers within the new models of viewing is identifying the ideal tone of their messaging.[22,23]

Social TV

The world's first televisions first started emerging in American homes in 1938.[24] When they first appeared in households, they were a new technology. Owning a television set was a status symbol, and gathering around it was an event. Friends and family were often invited over to experience the latest and greatest entertainment advancement of the time. People were glued to their favorite shows, sometimes even "shushing" their family members for talking while they aired. Times certainly have changed.

We now live in a world where 80 percent of viewers are using something other than an actual television to watch their favorite shows. Tablet, smartphones, or laptops are opened, with viewers ready not just to watch the show, but also to discuss it on the social sphere as it airs.[25] The simultaneous use of social media while watching television is often referred to as **social TV**.[26] One of the most common ways social media has been integrated into television is via the use of hashtags on Twitter,[27] allowing viewers to engage in real-time conversations about the show. In UGT terms, those engaging in such conversations are fulfilling their need for social interaction.[28] Watchers of competition shows like "The Voice," "World of Dance," or the long-running "American Idol" are sure to have noticed that each contestant's Twitter handle is shared on the screen so that viewers can follow and talk about the performances with other viewers, fans, contestants, and the judges before, during, and after the broadcast. The live components of these types of shows culminate in online discussions, and the use of downloadable apps makes voting and engaging with the show and other users even easier.

Talent drives 60 percent of television show social engagement. In response, television ratings authority Nielsen debuted "Nielsen Social Content Ratings," a celebrity-tracking feature that "measures talent promotion of television programs across Twitter, Facebook and Instagram."[29] Knowing the social media value of the talent on their shows allows producers and marketing teams to craft more strategic social campaigns that leverage the power of their own stars.

Streaming Television

Streaming media, on-demand online entertainment sources for TV shows, movies, and other streaming media, have made it possible for viewers to watch television shows from the past and present on their own time, using an array of devices. A few examples of streaming services include Netflix, Hulu, Prime Video, Epix, and Disney Plus. They have also changed media consumption habits and pushed brands to rethink their public relations, marketing, and advertising strategies. People are transitioning to streaming platforms in droves and often substitute streaming for traditional television viewing. This substitution of media channels occurs when technology advances and varies depending on "the degree to which an innovation is perceived as better than the idea it supersedes."[30] According to Denny Vida, contributor to the Nasdaq blog MarketInsite, "Streaming video is big business, and getting bigger all the time. Revenue in the industry is expected to amount to $25.9 billion this year, growing at a compound annual growth rate (CAGR) of 4.1 percent and topping $30.4 billion by 2024, according to market and consumer data provider Statista."[31] And at the top of the streaming industry is Netflix, which remains a global powerhouse in the industry with 167 million subscribers worldwide.[32] Amazon Prime Video, also available worldwide, boasts 150 million subscribers.[33] Traditional networks have begun to join the streaming phenomenon. Disney Plus recently entered the streaming game along with NBCUniversal's Peacock, sure signs that traditional networks have realized the value of expanding their platforms and recognize the power of and relevance to their audiences of on-demand video.[34]

Streaming continues to advance in order to meet the presumed desires of consumers. Quibi (short for "Quick Bites"), founded by Meg Whitman and Jeffrey Katzenberg, is a subscription streaming service designed to be consumed primarily via smartphone.[35] Quibi does not offer the traditional thirty- to sixty-minute show; it is a video streaming app focused on offering shows that appear in segments of ten minutes or even shorter. This approach is intended to reach viewers during their "in-between moments," which, according to Whitman, are those times when you might be in a checkout line or waiting for a friend.[36] Another feature that makes Quibi unique is the high-end Hollywood studio production that its founders are bringing to short-form video. Some estimates suggest that this new format for streaming could cost as much as $125,000 per minute to produce.[37] Prelaunch, there were already a number of well-known celebrities involved, including Chrissy Teigen, Kristen Bell, Idris Elba, and Chance the Rapper (who will reboot a version of MTV's "Punk'd" on the platform).[38,39] This platform will be one to watch as the streaming wars continue to drive innovation in meeting the needs of viewers and advertisers.

Socially Propelled Music

Music enthusiasts are on social media in droves. Whether checking out their favorite artist's career, watching music videos on platforms like YouTube, or discovering new sounds on the TikTok app, nine out of ten social media users are connecting with accounts and content relevant to the music industry.[40] As you can see from Figure 10.1, music is a strong driver for social media users.

Like television, the way we consume music has changed dramatically. In the twentieth century, broadcast radio played the top hits of the times. This led to the invention of records, cassette tapes, and CDs, which allowed consumers to purchase and own the music of their favorite artists. As technology has continued to advance, so has the way we consume and purchase music, challenging traditional industry models of revenue generation.[41] In addition, music subscription streaming services like Apple Music, Spotify, Pandora, and Tidal have made finding, listening to, and purchasing music more efficient and have lent themselves to sharing tunes on social media. Figure 10.2 illustrates how much the technology of music has changed over the past thirty years and identifies the platforms driving the highest revenues. The Recording Industry Association of America (RIAA) reported that streaming music services account for 80 percent of music industry revenue.[42]

Launching Pad for New Music and Talent

The ability to find, listen to, and share music on social media creates a discovery zone for new music and talent. In fact, 63 percent of users are doing just that.[43] Users can easily repost, retweet, or share a link or streaming service

FIGURE 10.1

Music Watch Infographic: Music Drives Social Media

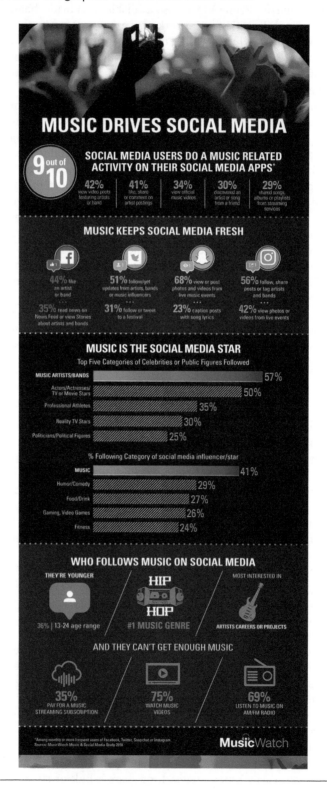

FIGURE 10.2

From Tape Deck to Tidal: Thirty Years of US Music Sales

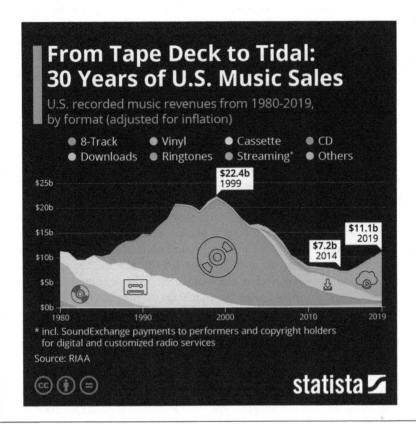

playlist of their finds to friends and followers. This helps unknown artists build a fan base, get noticed, establish trends, and possibly launch the industry's next star or influencer.[44] It is essential for artists and their labels to craft sophisticated social media strategies to maintain and grow fan bases and manage careers.[45]

Social media has broken down barriers to communication, providing direct lines between individuals and music entertainers. You might have heard stories of stars who pounded the pavement throughout the likes of New York City, Los Angeles, and Nashville to have their music heard. That might have meant dropping recordings at record labels, gigging at open-mic nights, or picking up food service jobs while trying to score auditions. But so much of that has changed. The social sphere has made it possible for new artists to make their music directly available to their target consumers. New artists highlight their work on channels like YouTube, TikTok, SoundCloud, and the (now defunct) MySpace. Take for example, Lil Xan, an American rapper, singer, and songwriter who gained recognition through the platforms Sound-Cloud and YouTube when first launching his career.[46] For many new music artists, SoundCloud serves as both a streaming service and a distribution platform.[47] Adele (see Figure 10.3) and Justin Bieber are two more examples of music artists who have social media to thank for their journey to global stardom.[48]

In 2006 Adele was a student at The BRIT School in the United Kingdom, where she was honing her vocal excellence in hopes of a singing career. Adele recorded three demo tracks and uploaded them to her MySpace page. Executives from London record label XL heard them and signed the eighteen-year-old to her first record contract, launching her career just months after graduation.[49] Although the specific platform that helped launch Adele's career is now defunct, she transitioned her online persona to her website Adele.com and has a social media presence on Facebook, Twitter, YouTube, and Instagram. Her fan base on these platforms, composed of fierce and loyal fans, boasts numbers well over 30 million followers.

Justin Bieber had been posting home videos of himself singing on a YouTube channel for a couple of years (see Figure 10.4) when his mother began receiving inquiries from multiple talent managers who had seen the teen's videos. She declined them all until 2008, when she was contacted by Atlanta-based talent manager Scooter Braun.[50] Braun discovered Bieber in a YouTube video in which he was busking in his hometown in Canada.[51] Bieber was just thirteen years old when Braun flew him and his mother to Atlanta. He connected them with music artist and producer Usher, which resulted in a signed recording deal.[52] By the time Braun had made contact with the family, Justin's fan following on YouTube was already intense; the videos on his channel had already received millions of views.[53] This was good news for the record label, as it translated to a built-in market for the release of a new album. In addition, Braun had Bieber start a Twitter account where he could interact with fans and continue to build his fan base and the Bieber brand.

By 2010 Bieber's social presence was notable. On November 9, 2010, he reached 6 million followers on Twitter and #6millionbeliebers began trending on the site (for those of you who might not be in the know, "Beliebers" is the moniker for Bieber's millions of fans).[54] Bieber boasts more than 110 million Twitter followers, second only to former US President Barack Obama.[55] Bieber

FIGURE 10.3

A 2016 Instagram post from international superstar Adele. Early in her career, Adele got a boost from social media.

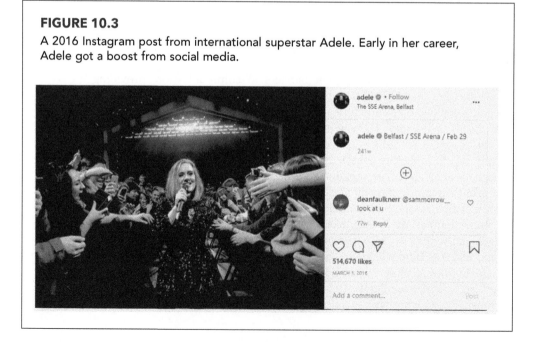

FIGURE 10.4

Justin Bieber singing a cover of Chris Brown's "With You." These home-recorded YouTube videos led to Bieber being discovered by music agents, resulting in the launch of his award-winning career.

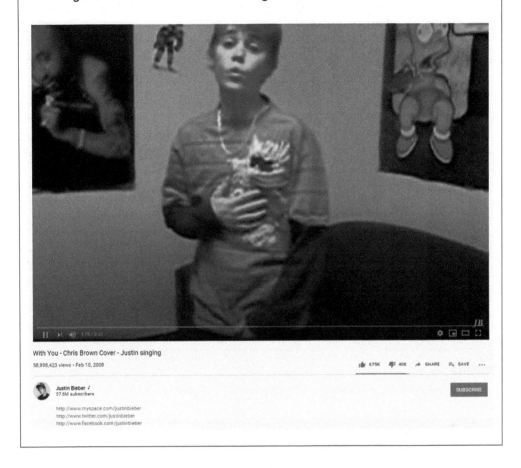

With You - Chris Brown Cover - Justin singing

58,996,423 views · Feb 10, 2008   675K   40K   SHARE   SAVE   ...

Justin Bieber ✓
57.6M subscribers   SUBSCRIBE

http://www.myspace.com/justinbieber
http://www.twitter.com/justinbieber
http://www.facebook.com/justinbieber

continues to utilize the platforms that launched his career (see Figure 10.5), tweeting his latest videos and content, and including the 2020 docu-series *Seasons,* which gives fans a more intimate look at the star, on YouTube.[56] The channel, which launched in 2007, has had more than 20 billion views to date.[57]

In the years since the Internet discoveries of Lil Xan, Adele, and Justin Bieber, platforms including Instagram and—most recently—TikTok have had a significant impact, bringing artists and sounds out of the shadows. In the article "How TikTok became the music discovery platform for the smartphone generation," author Kalhan Rosenblatt suggested that, while radio is the old standby for discovering new music, those in younger demographics are not listening to radio at the same rate as members of the older generations.[58] Millennials and Gen-Zers are on the platform, but not for the purpose of music consumption; instead, they are "using popular tracks as a way for people to have a common thread through their posts."[59] TikTok allows users to find new sounds and apply them to their posts; in effect, TikTok is crowdsourcing new music.[60]

TikTok can be an amazing platform for discovering new music and launching artists. It allows users to create communities built around music preferences that transcend the app, extending to streaming services such as Spotify, Apple Music, and YouTube as (TikTok). Users can then look for more of an artist's work, with the potential to drive artists and songs up the music charts.[61]

One of Lil Nas X's songs is an ideal example of how TikTok can influence mainstream music trends. Rap artist Lil Nas X (see Figure 10.6) was a college student majoring in computer science; he was also an avid social media user, with profiles on Instagram, YouTube, Facebook, and eventually Twitter. He dropped out of college in 2018 to pursue a music career.[62] His success on the platform TikTok would boost him to stardom and earn him a recording deal with Columbia Records in March 2019.[63]

Lil Nas X had released songs on SoundCloud, which gained some interest, but his big break came following his uploading of memes on TikTok to promote "Old Town Road."[64] The song went viral on TikTok, with users around the world producing their own short-form videos. They combined the song with a popular meme in which people would turn into cowboys from drinking '#yeeyeejuice'; that hashtag trended across platforms, connecting fans of the song.[65] Hundreds of thousands of users searched for "Old Town Road" on their streaming services, causing the song to rise to the top of multiple music listings.[66] "Old Town Road" would reach the top of the Spotify US Top 50 and global Apple Music charts. By April 2019, the song would hit number one on the Billboard charts.[67,68] And, it wasn't just everyday users of TikTok who noticed "Old Town Road." Country music artist Billy Ray Cyrus became a fan and collaborated with Lil Nas X on an uber-popular song remix in April 2019, which also topped the charts.

Lil Nas X's rise to fame provided a platform for discussions about music genres and racial implications. Billboard sparked controversy when it removed

FIGURE 10.5

Justin Bieber celebrates being the #1 streamed artist in the world.

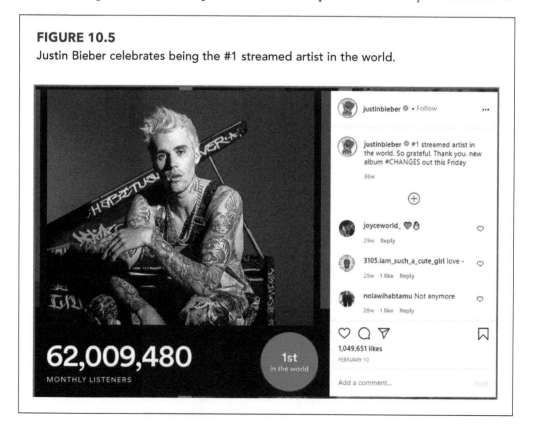

FIGURE 10.6

Lil Nas X at the LA offices of TikTok in 2019

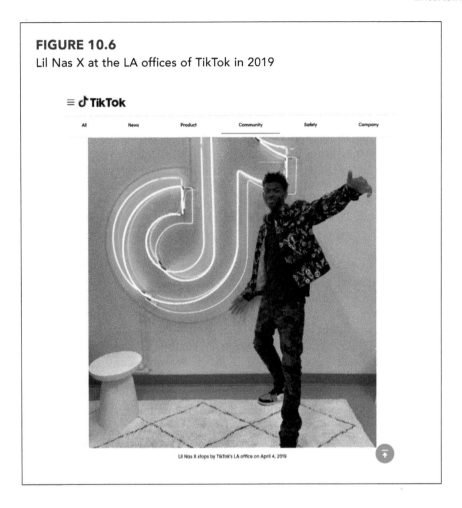

Lil Nas X stops by TikTok's LA office on April 4, 2019

the song from the country charts, stating that "It does not embrace enough elements of today's country music to chart in its current version."[69] Billboard's removal of the song prompted mainstream discussions about the role of African Americans in country music and concepts of genre-merging. "Old Town Road" combined country and rap in a new genre that Lil Nas X and others call "trap-country."

Avenues for Music Promotion on Streaming Platforms

Streaming services have opened new avenues for brands to advertise and tell their stories.[70] Spotify, for example, offers additional opportunities for the by-now familiar online display ads and videos through inclusion in sponsored playlists, in home-page ads, and on their leaderboard.[71] When Unilever, the parent company for AXE Gold products, wanted to drive awareness of their latest spray deodorant and shower gel in Germany, they partnered with Spotify on a unique campaign. By leveraging Spotify's popularity, Unilever used the app's "desktop and mobile Video Takeover ad experiences." In addition, "Sponsored Sessions … let music fans unlock 30 minutes of ad-free listening by watching a brand's video. Their accompanying display ad read '#GOLDBLEIBEN,' or 'stay gold,' and the clips played off that theme, capturing young men reaching for AXE Gold products before or after moments of high stress, sweat, or dirtiness."[72] This campaign obviously resonated with the target market. Results indicated that 75 percent of their audience felt that the Spotify ads were relevant to them; AXE Gold increased their ad recall by 168 percent and showed a 14 percent increase in brand awareness.[73]

Film, Movies, Marketing, and Social Media

The film industry is no stranger to the social sphere, having leveraged social media to build relationships with audiences in a targeted way. The digital space is able to connect the visual aspects of film and film promotion with people around shared experiences—the movies. Social media not only allows fans to come together, keep the conversation going, and engage with the films themselves, but it presents them with the opportunity to connect with their favorite industry players: the actors (and sometimes the characters they portray), producers, directors, and studios. What better way to brand your film than to give it a voice that engages with fans? So just like other industries, film maximizes the power of the two-way communication of social media to grow fan bases, build trust, and cultivate relationships.

According to Neustar, movie studios spent approximately $27.4 million on the marketing of new releases in 2018–2019; of these millions, 80 percent of the total media spend is allotted to television.[74] The remaining 20 percent is made up of multiple channels, as shown in Figure 10.7.

Why do movie studios spend so much on marketing? To sell tickets, of course! When it comes to paid media, some results may surprise you. Although digital accounts for a mere 14 percent of studios' total media spend, it represents 46 percent of paid-media-driven box office revenue. This is 4 percent more than television, which drives 42 percent of box office sales.[75] Paid Facebook media is the most efficient digital channel.[76] **Return on ad**

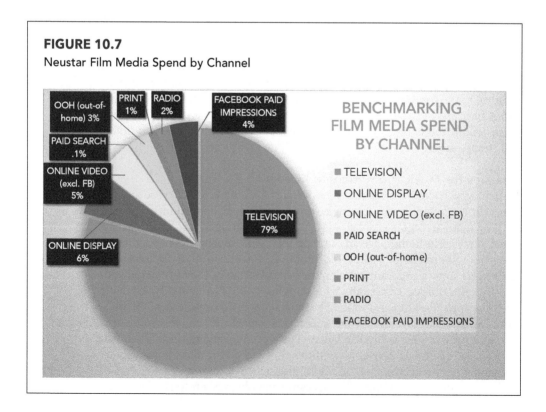

FIGURE 10.7
Neustar Film Media Spend by Channel

spend (ROAS)[77], a commonly tracked figure in advertising and marketing, represents the amount of revenue the buyer gains for each dollar spent. For example, for every movie dollar that studios spent on Facebook marketing, they earned an average of nearly eight dollars, ten times more than the ROAS for television advertising.[78] So what does all of this mean? Movie studios are realizing the value of social media marketing and advertising and are reaping the benefits in terms of revenues. In a culture requiring quantitative evidence that advertising is "working," ROAS offers a method of evaluating advertising spend that can then be used to validate a campaign's effectiveness and contribution to the "bottom line." ROAS also helps industry decision makers with future spending and strategy. It also assists them in maintaining an overall grasp on the marketplace.[79]

Earlier in the text when we discussed the differences between mass media and niche media (see Chapter 4), we noted that television demonstrates both types. Television allows advertisers to reach a mass audience through network channels, and its niche channels enhance targeting efforts, so it is a natural choice for studios looking to share movie trailers with hordes of potential moviegoers. As discussed throughout the text, social media marketing and advertising are available at a much lower cost. They also have the advantage of additional targeting capabilities; this results in more of the "right" audience receiving the message and creates opportunities for more efficient development and distribution of unique messages to each audience. Star Wars is one of the most financially successful movie franchises of all time, and Disney did not let fans down when it came to their integrated marketing strategy for "Star Wars: The Force Awakens," which would earn $238 million on its opening weekend in North America and $517 million globally.[80]

"Star Wars: The Force Awakens," which was much anticipated by fans of the franchise, was scheduled to premiere in movie theaters in the middle of December in the middle of the peak holiday shopping season. Disney made a significant investment in their marketing and advertising strategies. In addition to including a stellar mix of traditional tactics, their integrated strategy leveraged everything available in the social sphere. From using television (in cooperation with YouTube and the movie's website) to tease audiences beginning a year before the premiere, to the quintessential movie posters, earned media opportunities, corporate partnerships for merchandise and messaging, and of course social, the company covered all of the proverbial bases. Even those not interested in the film could not help but be aware that it was coming. Between January and November, Star Wars achieved 234 million social media interactions (see Figure 10.8).[81]

Disney hit their target audience by airing the official trailer for "Star Wars: The Force Awakens" during Monday Night Football on Disney-owned ESPN. The trailer simultaneously went live on YouTube, where it received an estimated 661,000 views per day for a total of 72.3 million views by the close of opening weekend.[82,83] The film's teaser trailer still holds the Guinness World Record for "the most viewed movie trailer on YouTube in 24 hours," with 30.65 million views.[84]

Opening weekend data from Facebook showed that Star Wars–related content was viewed by more than 64 million people around the globe, and these people engaged more than 140 million times.[85] On Twitter, the film's opening weekend boasted a record 4.9 million tweets; it would become the most-tweeted movie of the year.[86] Understanding how quickly conversations happen in the social sphere, it seems unimaginable that a single movie could be

FIGURE 10.8
Social Media Interactions: The Force Awakens

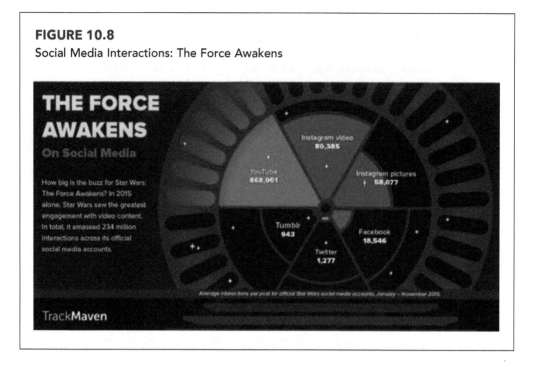

TrackMaven

discussed by millions of people for more than a year. Disney's strategy of staggering trailers that progressively provided more clues about the film's premise and investing in a mix of traditional and social media kept the conversation going, both online and in real life. By the time the official trailer aired, moviegoers were chomping at the bit to go to the theater, so much so that when tickets became available online, the number of people logging on to buy them slowed ticket platforms like Fandango and crashed MovieTickets.com.[87]

Disney's social media strategy didn't just benefit the Disney brand and the Star Wars film franchise. Their brand partners were also in the game. Disney partnered with seven brands to develop comprehensive marketing strategies that integrated with the official strategy for the movie launch: CoverGirl, Duracell, FCA-US, General Mills, HP, Subway, and Verizon.[88] CoverGirl release a line of limited-edition Star Wars cosmetics featuring the Star Wars logo. Although this pairing may not be the first partnership you'd think of, it was an excellent opportunity for CoverGirl to expand their audience reach and demographics and attach the brand to the momentum created by Star Wars. The company executed social media promotion for the products across their own social platforms using messaging that aligned with the official Star Wars branding guidelines. By mentioning @StarWars and #StarWars in their posts, CoverGirl was able to connect their content directly to buzz generated by the film expanding their brand exposure (see Figure 10.9).

As you can see, social media has expanded conversations about films, driven ticket purchases, and provided a platform for expanded brand partnerships. But how does it impact the celebrities whose job it is to entertain us?

CELEBRITIES ARE JUST LIKE US … SOMETIMES

Celebrities around the world use their social media to communicate with fans, share their opinions on global issues, and—of course—to build their brands.

FIGURE 10.9A

Cover Girl's Star Wars social media campaigns. (A) CoverGirl promotes their limited-edition Star Wars cosmetics on Twitter. (B) CoverGirl announces Star Wars special edition cosmetics line on Instagram.

← Tweet

COVERGIRL ✓
@COVERGIRL

The perfect gift for my #Padawan BFFs? Limited edition #StarWars collectors sets. 😎

3:30 PM · Dec 21, 2015 · TweetDeck

42 Retweets **91** Likes

FIGURE 10.9B

covergirl ✓ · Follow

covergirl ✓ In a galaxy far, far away @COVERGIRL+@StarWars have partnered on beauty looks created by @patmcgrathreal and limited-edition makeup inspired by #StarWars #TheForceAwakens. It's a #beautyforce like never before, channeling the duality that is within us all. #LightSide, #DarkSide—which will you unleash today? #droid #stormtrooper

269w

ldlondonstation @COVERGIRL where can you buy these in Canada?

10,646 likes
AUGUST 13, 2015

Add a comment...   Post

As a model and host of the television show "Lip Sync Battle," Chrissy Teigen's social media strategy has given her the opportunity to build a strong base of committed fans as she has developed her brand. An avid user of social media, Teigen continues grow her digital presence through proactive engagement with new platforms like Quibi (described earlier in the chapter) on which her streaming show "Chrissy's Court" premiered in 2020.

Teigen has cultivated an online persona geared toward authenticity and realness.[89] She's built an online audience by sharing intimate family moments like holidays and nights in watching television with her children and her husband, award-winning musician John Legend. Her "real talk" approach to content discusses life, motherhood, and dealing with online trolls, which keeps us regular folk coming back for more. As noted by writer Amanda Legault, "she has seamlessly made her audience believe that she, a multimillionaire celebrity, is just the same as you and me."[90]

Teigen actively engages with fans and has been known to go above and beyond for them, just as you would a friend. Would you ever think to ask a celebrity for a piece of clothing they are wearing? Rebecca Howe did just that. Howe, an avid Twitter user and Teigen fan, admired the dress Teigen wore on the show "Lip Sync Battle," so she tweeted Teigen and asked her for the dress: "@chrissyteigen but seriously when you're done with that red dress from this week's @SpikeLSB can I have it please ☺"[91] Within two minutes Teigen replied "I am done. DM me your address" (see Figure 10.10).[92]

Howe received the dress a few days later and wore it to celebrate New Year's Eve, ringing in the new year in true Hollywood style (see Figure 10.11).

Teigen's out-of-the-ordinary fan interaction with Howe led to a barrage of tweets to Teigen, including some asking her if they could have her husband when she was "done" with him.[93] The story, covered by multiple media outlets and publications including *Cosmopolitan*, *People Magazine*, and *The Daily Mail UK*, reinforced Teigen's commitment to her fans. Teigen's approach to social media earned her a place on *TIME*'s list of The 25 Most Influential People on the Internet in 2017.[94] A number of other celebrities are also using their social media to build their personal brands and influence the masses.

Kim Kardashian West built her career on sharing photos of herself doing a mixture of things, including envy-inducing Hollywood activities and intimate

FIGURE 10.10

In 2016 Rebecca Howe tweeted Chrissy Teigen, asking the celebrity for a dress she wore on television. Teigen replied to the tweet and sent the dress to her fan.

FIGURE 10.11

Rebecca Howe tweets Happy New Year wearing the dress that she received from Chrissy Teigen.

moments of her personal life. This constant self-promotion helped make the family's television show "Keeping Up with the Kardashians" a ratings hit and a top show of the E! network for years. In a 2016 interview, Kardashian West credited social media with her career: "I totally attribute my career to social media"; she went on to say that her personal brand was built from her ability to attract fans through her authentic online persona.[95] In 2019, Kardashian West's estimated rate for a sponsored post was up to half a million dollars.[96] Although Kardashian West may have been the first of the Kardashian clan to make her mark in the digital space, it was her younger half-sister Kylie Jenner who was Instagram's highest paid influencer in 2019, taking in an estimated $1.27 million per post.[97]

Dwayne "The Rock" Johnson uses Instagram to inspire fans; his posts often feature heartwarming videos of real-life fan meetings, workout videos, and inspirational content. His approach to building online relationships with his fans seems to be working, as he became the third-most-followed Instagram user in 2020.[98] Beyond connecting with and inspiring fans, pro-wrestler-turned actor The Rock uses Instagram for strategic brand promotions, including his continuing partnership with Voss water and, most recently, as a

FIGURE 10.12

Dwayne "The Rock" Johnson uses Instagram to announce his latest endeavor, Teremana Tequila, the actor's own brand of the alcohol.

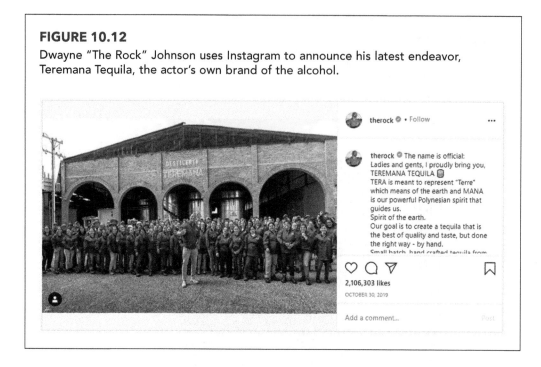

tool for the launch and promotion of his own brand of tequila, Teremana (see Figure 10.12).[99]

Celebrities who invest in building a strong and authentic social media presence can reach millions of users, which provides a significant opportunity to promote content that is important to them. Teigen, West, and Johnson have all reaped the commercial benefits of social media. They have all managed to establish themselves as influencers in the social space and have leveraged their status as revenue drivers through establishing brand partnerships and serving as launchpads for new products and projects. Consider further how artists and individual engage on social media in the Relational/Societal/Self box.

Relational/Societal/Self: Transcending Boundaries

Entertainment media has the capacity to transcend societal boundaries through global film and song releases and, in our contemporary experience, through the social sphere. This has been made possible by advancements in digital technologies that have made the world become smaller and smaller. As artists and individuals engage in relationships across borders using social sharing to make people aware of what matters to them personally, they begin to define the cultural content that is relevant to society today.

Think about It: How would you describe the impact of social media in the entertainment industry on defining culture where you live and beyond? What personal impact does the entertainment industry and the way in which you can interact with shows, actors, and artists have on you?

CHAPTER WRAP-UP

Social media and entertainment go hand in hand in many ways. Some even argue that social media itself is a form of entertainment! Film, television, and music have realized that their ability to engage with audiences in two-way symmetrical communication is an excellent way to cultivate relationships and develop brands. Social media has allowed the entertainment industry to market directly to their audiences in hyper-targeted ways, both to help ready audiences for the release of new media and new talent, and to keep fans invested in the brand. Consumer brands that partner with entertainment organizations also benefit from these established relationships, which allow them to maximize their advertising and marketing dollars through traditional sponsorships and influencer deals with their ideal target consumers.

The social space has also made it possible for regular folk to join the ranks of celebrity. Anyone willing and able to combine great talent with a strategic use of social media platforms could become the next Adele or Lil Nas X.

CRITICAL-THINKING QUESTIONS

1. How has social media enhanced your experiences with television, music, and film? Provide examples of your own social media interactions within each of these entertainment arenas.

2. Given the transition to streaming video and audio platforms, where is the future for consumption of entertainment media headed, and why?

3. Why do celebrities invest such significant efforts into building their online brands? Is it possible for a celebrity with only a minimal or no social media presence to remain relevant? Why or why not?

4. Revisit the chapter content on Lil Nas X. Have you ever discovered an artist with a new sound and shared it? Which platform were you using, and how did you let your friends know about this new sound?

ACTIVITIES

1. Imagine that you are launching your career in television, radio, or film. Design your ideal social media mix to establish your brand, relevance, and expertise.

2. Choose a hashtag related to television, music, or film on TikTok, Twitter, or Instagram and conduct a search on the platform you have chosen. Describe the life of the hashtag, beginning with its origin and describing how it is used. Which users and brands are using the hashtag and what are they talking about?

3. Write down the titles of the most recent television show or film you viewed and the most recent song you listened to. Under each title, write down answers to the following questions: How did you feel in the moment you chose the media? What did you hope to gain by the end of your watching/listening? Why did you choose to view/listen to the media on the platform you did?

4. Take a recent show that you have binged and apply uses and gratifications theory to it. How does the show fulfill your four simple needs of diversion, personal relationships, personality identity, and surveillance? Does understanding how the theory applies to your understanding and choice of viewing make you more or less aware of what drives or compels you to watch that show? Discuss this with a classmate.

KEY CONCEPTS

Return on ad spend (ROAS)
Social TV
Streaming media
Uses and gratifications theory (UGT)

MEDIA SOURCES

Digital movie releases due to the coronavirus: https://www.vox.com/culture/2020/3/20/21188408/coronavirus-streaming-movies-digital-emma-onward-invisible-man-birds-prey-way-back.

Ten rappers discovered on SoundCloud: https://www.dailydropout.com/articles/2019/3/18/rappers-discovered-on-soundcloud.

Five TV shows using the power of the second screen for social engagement: https://www.convinceandconvert.com/social-media-strategy/5-tv-shows-using-the-power-of-the-2nd-screen-for-social-engagement.

Recording Industry Association of America: https://www.riaa.com.

Quibi: https://quibi.com.

SUGGESTIONS AND ADVICE FOR USING SOCIAL MEDIA

PART —— 3

Measuring Social Media

ANALYTICS DRIVING DATA DURING A PANDEMIC

During the COVID-19 pandemic, news media outlets turned to social media to track the spread of the virus and cases of infected users. *The Economist*[1] used the photo-sharing service Instagram to trace the path of the virus and track the spread of the pandemic in real time, analyzing more than 20,000 public Instagram users to aid public health officials in containment measures.[2] This unconventional method of studying the pandemic created a database that soon contained more than 64,000 Instagram posts published in more than 2,000 cities in 125 countries, identified by **geolocation** services, which is the process of detecting geographical locations of a person or device by means of digital information through the Internet. The publication's reporters were able to show potential carriers of the virus based on symptoms and could track their accounts from location to location, often revealing the next hotspot based on contagion data and the presence of other, previously symptom-free Instagrammers in the same location.[3] Although this did not help in finding a cure, having real-time data could prove to be an unexpected—and life-saving—source of information by potentially limiting transmission and improving public knowledge of the severity of proliferation in a population that was otherwise thought to lack vulnerability to the virus.

Instagram and WhatsApp (both owned by industry giant Facebook) were already at the forefront of efforts to protect their users from false or misleading information ("fake news"), creating special algorithms to identify and track users, accounts, links, and commonly used hashtags to cut down the number of people sharing unverified information on their platforms.[4] The companies did the same in an effort to combat COVID-19 misinformation across all apps, issuing a public statement and launching their own resources through their Global Affairs division.[5]

Today's businesses routinely use analytics to connect key business metrics. However, the use of social media during the COVID-19 pandemic shows that social media analytics may be able to do more good than simply creating profits for a company. It turns out that all of those selfies and oversharing may actually be for the good of the masses! It seems unimaginable that an event as severe as a global pandemic can be tracked through Instagram posts, but this chapter will reveal the power of analytics applied to the social sphere for this and other uses.

SOCIAL MEDIA AND COMMUNICATION FEEDBACK

In assessing any form of communication activity, it is important to create deliberate mechanisms for feedback and measurement. In this way, you can come to understand both the delivery and reception of your messaging.

Each time we log onto the Internet and conduct a search, we leave behind little bits of **metadata**, a set of data that describes and gives information about other data. Think of these like crumbs from a cookie. At each site we leave bits of information: how long we stayed, where we went, how often we came back, if we clicked on a specific image, whether we made a purchase, or whether we shared a link. The list goes on and on. That trail of "cookies" can be tracked, sorted, and measured, creating personalized data that can be used by public relations and marketing practitioners to build their social media strategy. Through either **organic media**, which is activity that occurs on social media without being a paid promotion or advertisement, or **paid media**, the channels in which money is paid to place the message and control its distribution, brands use and analyze our data to drive their campaigns. Tracking social media metrics allows professionals to demonstrate the value of the work they have created and predict its impact on future campaigns. The In Theory feature illustrates how networks are connected to social media.

CHALLENGES TO MEASUREMENT

It's easy to get swayed and distracted by likes, shares, or high numbers of followers. After all, that's what most of us can see on an account, unless we have access to its analytics area. Some practitioners resort to using vanity metrics

IN THEORY | Network Effects

Social media have been associated with the transition from a one-to-many method of mass communication (think advertising in a magazine) to a many-to-many method of mass communication (social media) in which users become part of a networked communication model (see Figure A).[6] Researchers have discovered that social media returns are derived not only from individual actions taken by the user (likes, shares, etc.) but also from social interdependencies and additional message exposure as a result of *network effects*, which is when a product or service gains additional value as more people use it.[7]

Think about It: It is said that social media was developed for the masses. What does that mean? What value do you think the many-to-many model adds?

The differences between traditional media and social media and how this change occurred. Traditional media offer an outbound one-to-many approach; in contrast, social media is a network in which one-to-many becomes many-to-many, offering greater—but sometimes unruly—impact.

TRADITIONAL MEDIA

SOCIAL MEDIA

ONE TO MANY

MANY TO MANY

when they don't have access to actual data.[8] **Vanity metrics** are metrics that do not help brands understand their performance or help inform future strategies. For example, calculating the number of likes is great, but using a like as a metric does very little beyond letting the brand know how many people simply clicked the "thumbs up." To the uninformed and untrained, vanity metrics are those that are easy to "see"; however, they provide little strategic value to a person or an organization. Remember the Instagram influencer Arii who couldn't sell 36 T-shirts to 2.6 million followers?[9] Well, the failure occurred because their conversion rate was just over .009 percent—that's less effective than an online display ad.[10] This served as a wake-up call to industry leaders, alerting them that they needed to rely less on followers and more on actual influence when making decisions regarding influencer media strategy for campaign initiatives. This Insta-tragedy challenged many communications professionals to begin seeking references and success metrics from influencers before engaging in contracts for client work. It ushered in a requirement by brands to "prove you have influence" before signing influencers.

This simple example is just a start to the challenges of measuring social media, which are exacerbated by many other factors. Some of these factors, such as timing, price, and relevance, are easy to track back to poor campaign management. Virality, on the other hand, is difficult to predict. Why did that video garner 10 million views when it had a zero-dollar budget and came from a grandma in Mexico? Sometimes the answer is "Who knows?" Although many have tried, few have predicted with certainty or strategized accurately how to create overnight sensations by "going viral." Still, communications professionals often get requests from clients to "make me a viral video, please."

In 2008, Kevin Kelly, senior maverick of *Wired* magazine, published a short, shocking, and apparently future-telling article called "1,000 True Fans." Later becoming a TED Talk, the article came to represent the conceptualization of quality of buyers over quality of fans/followers/friends in a social media world. Here is one of its key takeaways:

> To be a successful creator you don't need millions. You don't need millions of dollars or millions of customers, millions of clients or millions of fans. To make a living as a craftsperson, photographer, musician, designer, author, animator, app maker, entrepreneur, or inventor you need only thousands of true fans.[11]
>
> 1,000 true fans are an alternative path to success other than stardom. Instead of trying to reach the narrow and unlikely peaks of platinum bestseller hits, blockbusters, and celebrity status, you can aim for direct connection with a thousand true fans. On your way, no matter how many fans you actually succeed in gaining, you'll be surrounded not by faddish infatuation, but by genuine and true appreciation. It's a much saner destiny to hope for. And you are much more likely to actually arrive there.[12]

Measurement, analysis, and reporting require complete context and singular metrics reported in isolation as one data point can miss the intent or true value of the whole social media story.[13] When measuring and reporting business metrics, it's easiest to consider other communication channels and their overall business goals, because social media supports the efforts of other channels in an integrated way. Focusing on the goals that an organization is already striving for can help you make the case for social media and show the benefit of your social media efforts. For example, if your organization is looking to build an email list for future communications or lead generation, you need to show how social media generated the acquisition of each email that was added to that particular list. If you are trying to sell widgets, you need to track each transaction that occurs as a result of a social media click-through to the widget purchase.

Another challenge that has been accepted in the social media world but has not yet been embraced fully is the idea that not all social media actions can be measured. Megan Marrs, a content marketer from online advertising software company WordStream, emphasizes this issue:

As with many online actions, it's often difficult to measure the offline benefits. Maybe your Facebook posts don't drive any conversions today, but a user may see those posts and become more familiar with your brand by doing so. That familiarity later on might mean choosing you over an unknown competitor or clicking your Google AdWords ad since your brand rings a bell. Social media also aids newer businesses in developing their brand's personality and building a voice. For companies that deal with dry topics relating to finance, insurance, and other yawn-worthy fields, social media can serve as a spot for introducing a more relaxed and casual demeanor of the company.[14]

In other words, brands must attempt to build in multilevel metrics to ensure that they retrieve the best data possible so that they can make informed decisions.

Why Measure Return on Investment?

Creating a consistent measurement practice for social media programs is important because most companies primarily view communications as an outbound model for customer relations.[15] It's easy for people who are not used to its communications function to forget that social media tactics can be used for inbound purposes, too. Using social media content of any kind is not a one-way street from company to consumers. It's a two-way street. Not unlike other forms of communication, it deploys a feedback loop a la Shannon and Weaver[16] (see Chapter 3) and extended by Berlo.[17] Feedback from various publics is solicited to measure the effectiveness of the messaging, analyze that information to make macro- or micro-changes in strategy, and then course-correct as needed.

Return on investment (ROI), a performance measure used to evaluate the efficiency of an investment or compare the efficiency of a number of different investments, has become a catch-all metric for those in marketing.[18] Practitioners are quick to pass the baton of judgment to social media to "prove its worth"; the irony is that those very same people are not asking to prove the worth of the billboard on the highway, which has no means of measurement. The truth is, no magic metric illustrates the success of social media. However, hundreds of metrics can be combined and analyzed to create actionable outputs. Your role as a communicator is to craft outcomes from those outputs that take your social strategy and make it better, time after time. Not every organization will be able to directly link social media and revenue, nor should they. However, that doesn't mean that they should not attempt to offer value or arbitrarily spend budget dollars without goals in mind. Adhering to a rigid definition of ROI prevents people and organizations from showing other ways in which their activities are a legitimate investment that is likely paying off. Attributing value is where metrics and analytics come into play. Sometimes organizations will be able to put a pin in cause-effect–related direct line returns, such as a social media post leading to a sale; however, social media is also effective in other, more subtle ways that can be shown through correlative data (summer vacation is around the corner and your seasonal shop picks up foot traffic) or logical relationship-based occurrences. Say a consumer video goes viral and brand followers increase; your brand didn't do this, but it happened, and you can make some assumptions based on the environment that it impacted your brand. You will not always be direct-selling widgets online, so preparing yourself with different forms of analytical prowess is most likely to result in a well-rounded and expertly crafted social media strategy.[19]

KPIs Matter

Implications for avoiding marketing disasters were recommended as a result of an advertising study by Charles R. Taylor of Villanova University. His study proposed that all of the noise and changes of medium along the way can increase communicators' need for e-word-of-mouth research—think of traditional word-of-mouth impacts, but now move it online.[20] One way that organizations can avoid noise as a distraction in measurement is the creation of and adherence to **key performance indicators (KPIs)**,[21] roadmaps for metrics and evaluation (see Figure 11.1). KPIs should align with business goals to create a positive relationship, with attainment of those goals using social media as a tool in the toolbox.[22,23]

TRACKING METRICS, REPORTING ANALYTICS

For all of you who went into communications to avoid math, we have some bad news. You cannot escape metrics and be successful at social media, and metrics involve math. At some point your efforts will need to be reported as a *benchmark* or *metric* (measurement) of the success of your efforts on

FIGURE 11.1

Use of a KPI template like this one can help you track month-to-month and annual goals and objectives from benchmark to success.

SOCIAL MEDIA STRATEGY SCORECARD

BUSINESS GOAL FOR CAMPAIGN:

OBJECTIVE 1

Programs, Initiatives & Actions	Key Performance Indicators & Metrics	Timeframe to Achieve Goals

OBJECTIVE 2

Programs, Initiatives & Actions	Key Performance Indicators & Metrics	Timeframe to Achieve Goals

OBJECTIVE 3

Programs, Initiatives & Actions	Key Performance Indicators & Metrics	Timeframe to Achieve Goals

the platform or platforms that you are using. Metrics are the "what" behind social media: The number of people engaged with a post is just one example. If metrics are the "what," then analytics are the "so what?" or the context of the number of engagements.[24] Understanding and application of metrics yield analytics. Knowing if the number is high, whether it deviated from the same time last month, or if it yielded any conversions (discussed shortly) tells you the "so what?" regarding social media metrics. The real skill lies in your ability to determine why something performed the way it did, either to reproduce the outcome or avoid it by adjusting the input to the social media platform. You can make sense of the analytics through converting analysis of the collected metrics into sound decisions or strategies for success.

Every social media platform carries its own built-in, or native, analytics tool. The lexicon used and the numbers provided differ from platform to platform, but most fall into the following categories:

- Reach and Exposure (impressions; number of people who saw your post; number of times your brand was mentioned; number of followers)
- Engagement (number of likes, shares/retweets, comments/replies, clicks, or video plays)
- Influence (tell a friend; purchase intent; awareness)
- Conversions (number of downloads, sign-ups, sales, new followers)[25]

The following sections identify most of the major players in the digital space along with the top metrics that they track for analytical purposes.

Google Analytics

Google Analytics, a free Web analytics service offered by Internet giant Google, tracks data and reports out website traffic, lets you measure your ROI, creates conversion data when partnered with Google Ads, and helps you optimize any campaign that needs increased metrics to develop a full understanding of a customer journey. All of this makes Google Analytics the "gold standard" in website metrics. Google Analytics allows you to learn more about how consumers are engaging with a brand across multiple platforms and across multiple devices. When people move from tablet to desktop or laptop to mobile device, you can link their behavior and better understand how the data convert across Web pages.[26] Specific actions taken by customers are based on targeted messaging in the online environment. Using the data that Google Analytics collects about your active audience, you can observe how new and returning visitors find and engage with your site, and when they leave it. The top ten data points Google Analytics measures include the following:[27]

1. Real-Time Activity on Site:[28] This data point watches which people are on your site and monitors what they are doing in real time.

2. New versus Returning Visitors:[29] This one shows how often your content brings visitors back to the site.

3. Frequency and Recency:[30] These identify how many times users visit your site (frequency) and the amount of time between visits (recency).

4. Demographics:[31] Data such as age, gender, interest categories, and online purchasing activity provide a reminder that you are engaging with actual people on your site.

5. Benchmarking:[32] Benchmarking compares the performance of your site content to other online companies that share their data with Google.

6. Attribution:[33] If you set up goals in Google Analytics for converting site visitors, based on the visitor's last click you can attribute how the conversion occurred. This gives you the ability to credit a source, allowing you to improve the customer journey with respect to a desired goal or action.

7. Search Console:[34] This feature provides information about what is viewed by a single user in Google search results before they click to visit your site, reporting on the performance of organic-search traffic.

8. Conversions:[35] Like attribution, the setting of conversion goals in Google Analytics is about as close as you can get to drawing a straight line from the consumer to your online goals. Conversions can be used for both paid and unpaid campaigns for which you need to track a result.

9. Site Speed:[36] Speed and ranking have become partners in the online world. The amount of time that your site takes to load impacts the user experience, which impacts your site visibility in search results. You want to be fast *and* relevant.

10. Mobile Traffic:[37] Google's "mobile first" index, introduced in July 2019[38] but officially penalized for lack of submission in January 2020, was intended to ensure that an identical consumer experience could be had on mobile devices and desktops/laptops, proving once again that the consumer experience is top of search results, meaning the first page of Google, for example.

Google Analytics integrates easily with many content management systems and other analytics platforms for seamless integration with e-commerce sites and social media platforms, making it the top tool for analytics. It's simple to set up, highly customizable to your line of business or type of organization, and provides an entire suite of options to create better informed decisions based on data regardless of industry. In addition, training is easy and free; Google Analytics Academy[39] certification training can be performed entirely online through video. It is considered the "gold standard" of metrics software.

YouTube Analytics

With YouTube Analytics, brands can monitor their channels and video performances with metrics and reports in the native YouTube Analytics platform. Much like Google Analytics (they are both owned by Google), information comes by way of different reports that can be examined for watch time, traffic sources, demographic reports (which, like content, can be filtered by a multitude of options), device type, geography/location, date, timeframe, playlist, subscriber status, playback availability, and more. The types of charts in the reports include line charts, multiline charts (of up to twenty-five items), stacked charts (of up to twenty-five items) to identify trends, pie charts to visualize size or impact relative to other variables, bar charts, and bubble charts. In addition, interactive mapping can show where in the world a video is being watched.[40]

Facebook Analytics

Like Google Analytics, entire books and blogs have been dedicated to Facebook Analytics, so a full examination here would be absurd.

Think of our coverage more like Facebook Analytics 101; if you want to immerse yourself in its potential, use the tools included in the Media Sources at the end of this chapter to examine the Facebook Blueprint training guides.

What makes Facebook Analytics different is that it is "the only analytics tool built on insights from Facebook's 2-billion-person community."[41] It's hard to argue with that. For more than a decade, Facebook has been the go-to social network. Even people who do not use it every day have an account. It's almost impossible to be on social media without having some kind of Facebook-related account, especially considering the rate at which the company acquires other cult-follower applications, such as Instagram and WhatsApp. Facebook Analytics, like those in the Google family, uses omni-channel tracking and reporting to gain a more holistic view of the people who come to a channel via multiple devices. Facebook has always used aggregated data from multiple sources to gain a complete picture of the people interested in what your organization does. Those who might be interested in starting a relationship with your organization are captured via targeted advertising tactics such as Facebook Pixel, which integrates with your website to report on actions people take; these results can then piggyback on websites to combine data sources and measure across channels and across devices. From a business perspective, Facebook Analytics is easy to use and has a robust platform manager (called business manager) from which you can manage multiple pages for content purposes, an ads manager that keeps all of your advertising account data in one place and can support multiple payment areas for privacy, and something called creative hub, where you can, quickly and conveniently, edit and make integrated advertising campaigns through the Facebook family of products. Facebook also has its own decision-making smartphone app that can be downloaded with real-time tracking and change capacity.

According to Christina Newberry of social media management platform Hootsuite, Facebook Page Insights helps businesses answer questions related to the following:[42]

- **Reach and engagement**: How many people saw your posts? Who interacted with them? Which posts did people hide? Did people report any posts as spam?
- **Actions**: What actions do people take on your page? How many people click your call-to-action button? How many people click through to your website?
- **People**: What are the demographics of the people who visit your page? (You can dive deeper into this topic with Audience Insights.) When do people visit your page? How do people find your page?
- **Views**: How many people are viewing your page? Which sections are they looking at?
- **Posts**: How are your posts performing over time?

In a nutshell, this data can help you rethink your target audience, adjust your Facebook strategy to better align with your audience, look for trends so you can create better content, and schedule posts at the best times for your audience. It can also create an optimized, data-driven Facebook ads strategy and benchmark and keep data up to date for other business lines in your organization, among other things.

As the advertising side of Facebook evolves, adding even more options for targeting your audience or discovering new ones, it's easy to get lost in all of this. Website Social Media Today, a leader in all things social media related, published a blog that highlighted the top five tricks to running better campaigns on Facebook:[43]

- **Choose an objective that drives business value**: Sound familiar? Aligning your social goals with business goals is critical to helping your organization fulfill its mission and drive value to its audience. An integrated campaign performs best, as it steers various budgets, numbers, and successes toward common goals. On the Facebook ad platform, that translates to advertising objectives such as awareness, consideration, and conversions.[44]
- **Utilize placement optimization**: Facebook ads can be placed anywhere on Facebook but can also trickle over into Instagram feeds and stories, the Messenger app, and to the greater Audience Network, which plays across pages on the greater Internet on other websites that align with the audience interest. Facebook claims that activating all placements optimizes viewing based on audience data. Because Facebook ads "learn" as they go based on a complex algorithm, the more it learns the better it can optimize. However, remember that, as an advertiser, you should be the one driving the bus. Consider each option carefully and pay special attention to where those Audience Network ads are placed. You may wish to make special considerations with regard to placement or privacy, depending on the brand you represent.
- **Learn to love campaign budget optimization**: Take a deep breath, and trust Facebook. We know, we know—but with regard to budgets on Facebook you should throw caution to the wind and leave the efficient and effective use of your money in Facebook's hands. This doesn't mean "set it and forget it," though. You shouldn't micromanage the process, but you should still pay attention to the campaign in case manual adjustments are needed.
- **Embrace mobile-first creative standards and practices**: Focusing on mobile-first will allow you to activate more users into your page experience. We all walk around with that smartphone glued to our hands anyway, right? Making sure that ads look great on mobile and creating short, concise videos will assist your campaigns and bring value to your audience. Don't make stuff just to make stuff. Consider its purpose and value.
- **Understand the difference between broad and specific targeting**: This one may appear to contradict common sense, but bear with us. Here's what Social Media Today's Nathan Mendenhall has to say:

In the past, the goal of Facebook ad targeting was to be as specific as possible. However, due to increased competition and the evolution of the Facebook Ad platform, being super specific in targeting can sometimes lead to more costly results. When you go with super-specific targeting, you're telling the system that you want to serve ads to a certain amount of people no matter what. The Facebook ad system then goes after those people, and you, as the advertiser, are battling budgets for a presumably small amount of people who are also being targeted by other advertisers. This can drive costs up, and Facebook doesn't have much to learn from. When you go a little broader with your targeting, however, Facebook has more touchpoints to learn from, and will automatically optimize to serve your ad to the people in your target audience who are most likely to take your desired objective action. While doing this, the system also looks for the best use of budget in an attempt to drive more results for lower cost. We recommend testing this for yourself—specific targeting always seems great but consider going a little broader when trying to stretch your budget.[45]

The sheer volume of options available to users of Facebook Analytics can leave your head spinning and make you ask yourself, "Where do I start?" Here's where we recommend you begin: The tutorials included in the Facebook BluePrint (see the end-of-chapter Media Sources listing) can help you transition all the way from beginner to expert.

LinkedIn Analytics

LinkedIn has come a long way in just a few years in the sharing of analytics for pages. LinkedIn Page admins have the following information available:[46]

- **Update analytics**: Based on the information posted into a feed/status (which LinkedIn calls an "update"), update analytics evaluate the effectiveness of an update, including the effectiveness of videos.
- **Followers and visitor analytics**: These reveal demographics and sources of a page's followers and visitors.
- **Talent brand analytics**: If you have a career page connected to your brand page, you can access Pipeline Builder metrics, which assist in building a talent pipeline for current or future jobs that your brand may need.

Like other analytics, these can be exported and observed over time. Although this platform's analytical offerings for pages are not as robust, its paid advertisements through the native campaign manager are like those of other social media platforms (see Figure 11.2). In this space you can build brand awareness, drive consideration and engagement, and generate leads and conversions using analytics based on measured conversions, lead generation, performance (clicks, impressions, social actions), and demographics. LinkedIn analytics does this through contact targeting, website retargeting, lead generation forms, and the online audience network.[47]

Finally, through LinkedIn's native publishing platform, basic metrics can show article views, audience, and location-based information. In addition, you can learn whether an article was discovered through LinkedIn search or another method. As shown in Figure 11.3, two of the 238 article views were discovered through a Google search for terms that appeared in the self-published piece.

FIGURE 11.2

Facebook business and/or ad manager shows all campaigns active and not active as well as allows for the user to toggle on or off various reporting metrics in order to isolate variables and determine outcomes. Reports can also be exported.

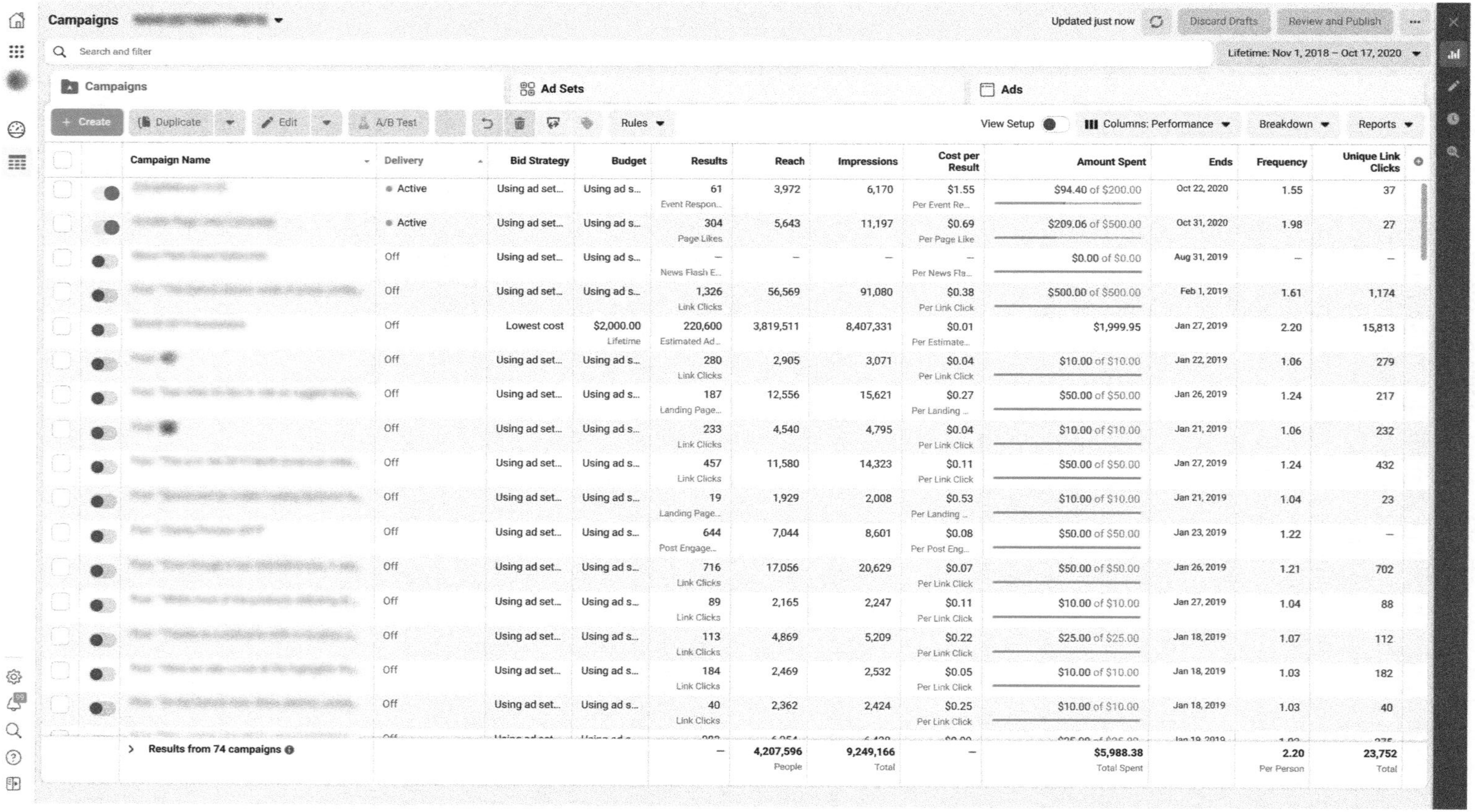

FIGURE 11.3

The LinkedIn paid advertising campaign manager platform organizes data in much the same way as Facebook's business manager. You can toggle to areas to change data filtering options, and it has the ability to export to a supported file type to manipulate data in other ways.

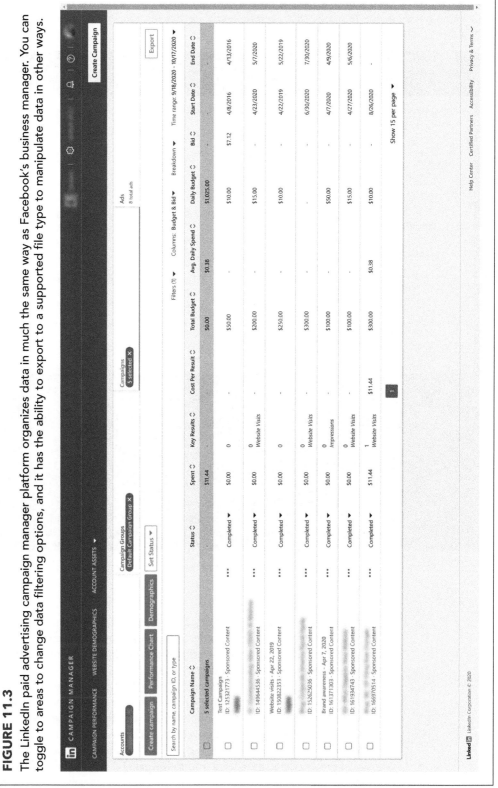

FIGURE 11.4

LinkedIn personal profile pages show engagement metrics for your personal posts, including how the article was discovered.

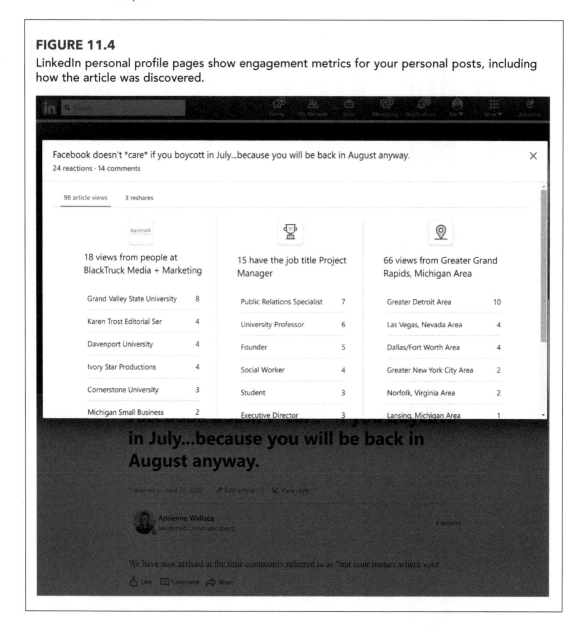

Twitter Analytics

Twitter offers personal analytics and—of course—an arsenal of paid advertising analytics to account holders. As a registered user, everyone has access to personal analytics; these demonstrate month-over-month summaries that change from period to period (see Figure 11.4).

The analysis usually consists of a 28- to 31-day summary of your tweeting activity and has a customizable timeline to examine larger periods of time.[48] Figure 11.5 shows an author-contributed screenshot of her personal Twitter analytics tweets page. Customized to a date range from January 1, 2020, through March (the first-quarter metrics), it includes tweets, tweet impressions, profile visits, mentions, and followers. Twitter will also show you information about your tweets, including the tweets themselves, replies, promoted tweets impressions, engagement metrics, link clicks, retweets, likes, and reply

FIGURE 11.5

Company / business Twitter account analytics page with 28-day summary available to accounts that opt-in.

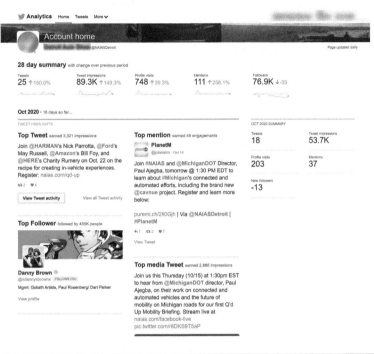

FIGURE 11.6

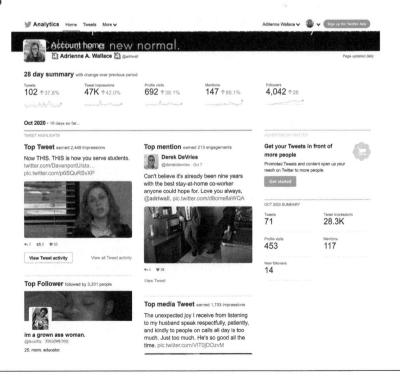

averages for the month. Let's look at this through a personal example (see the Relational/Societal/Self feature).

To use Twitter analytics for business, organizations can use the native Twitter Campaign Dashboard[49] to track the performance of Twitter ads. Twitter offers data on the following: (1) impressions, (2) results (tied to objectives set in the Campaign Dashboard), (3) engagement rate, and (4) cost per result segmented by objective, campaign, individual tweets, and other targeting criteria (see Figure 11.6).

Like most online advertising platforms, Twitter also offers conversion tracking, which continues to track Twitter activity once the user has left Twitter. A click on a campaign tweet may redirect a user to a website or e-commerce platform for sales conversions or lead generation; Twitter analytics can track this activity.

Twitter relies on two common categories of conversion tag options: a Universal Website Tag is a code that tracks across an entire website, and a Single Event Website Tag tracks a single page.[50] Twitter also supports third-party tagging like the popular Google Tag Manager in order to better integrate tools into its advertising toolbox.[51]

Snapchat Analytics

Snapchat keeps it simple. That's most likely why users spend time on the platform. The Snapchat advertising platform includes three objectives from which businesses can choose: drive website traffic to a website for online lead generation, get people to visit your store from a geographic area, and/or drive app installation for, say, a video game. Snapchat's claim to advertising fame is its appeal to those advertisers for which "more than a third of our audience can't be found on Facebook or Instagram."[52] These advertisers can "reach 218 million people on average who use Snapchat everyday."[53] Their audience focus is on Millennials and Gen Z, making Snapchat seem like the perfect place to target new or younger customers.[54] Snapchat native data includes aggregate data from the last 28 days to those with audiences

Relational/Societal/Self: Personal Branding

Your personal social media play a big part in your overall reputation and your personal brand in our digital world. As a result, platforms are moving toward displaying metrics for analytics purposes for both personal and business accounts. This trend can tell you a lot about your own life. You cannot go into a career in communications without thinking about your personal social media habits. Why? In today's world, human resources gives as much weight to your Twitter handle as your references in determining your fit for a job.

Think about It: From a strategic perspective, conduct a personal analytical assessment of one of your own social media channels, such as Twitter or Instagram. What does this analysis reveal about what others might assume about you? Should you make changes to better position yourself personally? Professionally? Share your findings with a friend and ask them how they think your online self compares to the real you.

of greater than 1,000 users. It includes demographics and regions or **designated market areas (DMAs)**, which allow a peek at the population of an area using more traditionally targeted television and radio data.[55] Third-party data, including household income and purchase behavior, are also available through partners.[56]

LATHER, RINSE, REPEAT: BUILDING YOUR OWN FRAMEWORK

A review of best practices for social media reporting could fill hundreds or even thousands of books, so there's no way that it could be covered in a single chapter without leaving the reader wanting more. With the number and speed of changes that occur within social media, a best practices list would need to be rewritten about four times a year in an inevitably vain attempt to keep up. With this in mind, it's best for you to remain flexible when it comes to identifying key areas for measurement. Building a unique framework for measurement that fits your needs includes custom dashboards built on the following broad foundations:

- Social Media Environment Analysis: Conduct a scan of your social media environment to identify where your target audience is, what they share, key conversations they have, and any emerging themes. This analysis should give you a better idea of exactly how your target audience is interacting with your content.
- Social Media Channels: Maintain a list of your social media channels and what you can measure from the brand assets.
- Social Media Tools: Using your goals, identify what you must measure or track over time. Use or advocate for the best, most current tools that are within your budget. Ensure understanding of the measurement of your social media through training. Loop everything back into your objectives and adapt as they grow or change over time. Monitor. Measure. Analyze. Test. Learn. Adapt. Fail. Achieve. Repeat.

By understanding what is happening on their social platforms, individuals and organizations can adopt sound principles and build frameworks that support their objectives.

CHAPTER WRAP-UP

Social media doesn't happen in a vacuum. Most professionals consider it just one of many components of a solid, coherent communications strategy. Firms can use social media in tandem with public relations, marketing, and advertising to integrate their messages. With a methodical, convergent approach that takes advantage of all available metrics and analytics, the possibilities are endless.

CRITICAL-THINKING QUESTIONS

1. Why is there a need for the measurement of social media campaigns?

2. The chapter outlined many of the challenges to measurement. Based on what you have read, how would you describe the best practices for conducting an effective measurement strategy?

3. Is return on investment (ROI) a valid way to measure success with social media? Why or why not? What other ways might be more effective?

4. How do measurement and analytics differ from platform to platform? What consistencies do you see?

5. What variables would you include in your own framework or dashboard for social media reporting?

ACTIVITIES

1. Google Analytics[57] maintains a live feed or demo account for practice use: https://support.google.com/analytics/answer/6367342?hl=en. Using this account, explore the e-commerce website for insightful metrics with the following exercises[58] (you will need to sign up for a Google account via the link prior to accessing the data):

- View all standard reports populated with real data from the Google Merchandise Store.
- View data from Google Ads and Search Console integrations.
- Alter reports by adding filters and secondary dimensions, and by changing the report view.
- Compare date ranges for acquisition, behavior, and conversion data.
- Segment the data using your own custom segments.
- Create your own dashboards, custom reports, and attribution models.
- View predefined dashboards and segments imported from the Solutions Gallery.

2. Using the Google store link in question 1, what are trends in the overall Web traffic for the last three months? Produce a general report of user activity to the website. Include for the given timeframe (the past three months) a few aggregate audience metrics:

- Total number of users/new users
- Page views/pages per session (pages/session)
- Average session duration/bounce rate
- The percent of users that are new visitors versus returning visitors
- The number of users and their percentages for the top three languages
- Analytics reports should contain more than just the data present. You should be able to articulate what the data mean in order to apply it to your client strategy for actionable insights. Anyone can produce a report, but it takes someone skilled to create meaningful interpretation to create actionable intent for a brand.

- What does this data mean?
- How should this brand use this to craft improved social media strategy?
- Are you able to apply aggregate audience metrics to solutions for this brand?

3. Using the KPI template in Figure 11.1, examine a social media brand with your professor. Considering any business statements or mission statements you can find, write KPIs for the selected brand based on written or observed business/mission goals.

KEY CONCEPTS

Designated market area (DMA)
Geolocation
Key performance indicator (KPI)
Metadata
Organic media
Paid media
Return on investment (ROI)
Vanity metrics

MEDIA SOURCES

Google Analytics Academy: https://analytics.google.com/analytics/academy.

Google Analytics Playbook: https://marketingplatform.google.com/about/resources/linking-analytics-and-ads-solution-to-todays-marketing-challenges/?utm_source=google-growth&utm_medium=referral-internal&utm_campaign=2019-q2-gbl-all-gafree-analytics&utm_content=ga-helpcenter-mainguidearticle.

Google Analytics Ecommerce Live Feed: https://support.google.com/analytics/answer/6367342?hl=en.

PESO Certification: https://spinsucks.com/communication/peso-model-certification.

Facebook BluePrint—Free training videos: https://www.facebook.com/business/learn.

Twitter Flight School: https://www.twitterflightschool.com/student/catalog.

Snapchat Ads: https://forbusiness.snapchat.com.

HubSpot Academy: https://academy.hubspot.com.

Amazon Advertising Leaning Console: https://advertising.amazon.com/learn/learning-console.

Pinterest Academy: https://business.pinterest.com/en/pinterest-academy.

Hootsuite Social ROI Calculator: https://hootsuite.com/tools/social-roi-calculator.

Keeping Up with Social Media

SO, YOU WANT TO BE A SOCIAL MEDIA MANAGER?

LEARNING OBJECTIVES

12.1 Describe the skill set that social media strategists must possess.

12.2 Differentiate among career options within social media and identify the tools that help practitioners fulfill their job responsibilities.

12.3 Outline the areas that will play a key role in the future practice of social media.

Positions related to social media are one of the fastest-growing opportunities in the communications field. And that's because social media is a rapidly growing profession. Over the next few years, it is projected that the number of global social media users will top 3.5 billion.[1] This means increased demand for people who understand the various nuances of social media. A quick search for "social media manager" yields well over 36,000 jobs on Indeed, an online job board that aggregates employment postings from a variety of sources, allowing users to search for specific positions.[2] What does it really take to be a social media manager? Is it as simple as posting to Instagram and Snapchat all day? Do you have what it takes to be a good writer? What role do the analytics and data you learned about in Chapter 11 play? These are some of the many topics we'll explore in this chapter.

Keeping current is among the biggest challenges of digital media. You can be a skilled social media marketer or an enthusiastic newbie with digital curiosity surging through your veins, but either way you will have to keep up with trends in this rapidly changing field. This chapter highlights the skills necessary to be a social media manger and offers ideas for strategically managing today's fast-paced, digitally driven environment with grace, speed, and excellence.

WORKING IN SOCIAL MEDIA

In a nutshell, social media managers are responsible for overseeing an organization's activities on social media platforms. Tasks can include everything from social media planning to content creation and publishing to overseeing metrics and analytics (see Figure 12.1). Working in social media can be complex. It's not as easy as posting a pic of your morning coffee or latest food obsession on Instagram or the latest trending dance on TikTok. Careful thought and strategic planning must go into the creation of each and every brand post. Madhura Gaikwad is a contributor for MarTech Advisor, a website dedicated to delivering industry insights. Gaikwad highlighted five areas of importance for today's practitioners,[3] which we've boiled down to three: writing; data, analytics, and trend spotting; and creativity, strategy, and planning.

Writing

Writing is one of the most sought-after skills that employers look for when hiring a new employee. Whether you are applying for a role in public relations, advertising, or marketing, today's practitioners must know how to write—and write well. Because communicating with a target audience is an integral component of any social media strategy, copywriting takes the number one spot in the ranking of skills needed for working in social media. Social media text needs to be not only creative and witty but also grammatically immaculate. Tools such as Hemingway Editor and Grammarly can help practitioners make their writing clear and effective. Watson Tone Analyzer evaluates text messages for tone and sentiment, and Quetext is a plagiarism checker. These are resources that many practitioners use when creating copy.

Resources

- Hemmingway Editor: http://www.hemingwayapp.com.
- Grammarly: https://app.grammarly.com.
- Watson Tone Analyzer: https://www.ibm.com/watson/services/tone-analyzer.
- Quetext (plagiarism checker): https://www.quetext.com.

Data, Analytics, and Trend Spotting

Today, data drives every decision a company makes. From when to launch a product to how best to handle a crisis, analytics plays an integral role. The ability to understand what the data and analytics reveal is critical. As you learned in Chapter 11, social media analytics enable practitioners to spot trends and plan based on current performance. Changes happen almost daily in the social sphere. New platforms are introduced. Viral videos pop up at a moment's notice. Influencers are unpredictable. What does this mean for you

FIGURE 12.1

Is That All? A Day in the Life of a Social Media Manager. Social media managers carry out a brand's integrated strategy on the company's social media channels. They respond to comments, oversee the brand's voice and persona, develop campaigns, and create content while also providing guidance to management surrounding maintaining an online presence.

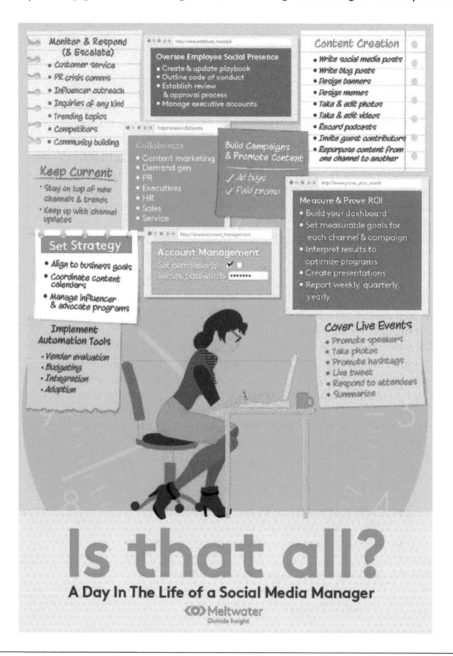

as a social media strategist? You need to understand the numbers and keep current with trends based on your target audience(s).

Aligning content strategy with what is happening in real time takes skill. Data and analytics are a key component. According to Brandwatch, "being the first to know and predicting emerging trends in your industry can give your brand a huge competitive advantage."[4] Data eliminates guessing. Spotting trends is easy when you follow the data. You first learned about *social media dashboards* in the discussion of analytics in Chapter 11. Dashboards such Hootsuite and Cyfe help social media professionals manage social media, analytics, marketing, sales, support, and overall social media infrastructure. Others include Social Mention, Social Studio from Salesforce, Google Trends, Google Analytics, NodeXL, Tableau, and HARO. These online tools organize and streamline a brand's online activity so that you can publish content, respond, monitor, update, and listen from one central log-in.

Resources

- Hootsuite: https://hootsuite.com.
- Cyfe: https://www.cyfe.com.
- Social Mention: https://www.social-searcher.com/social-mention.
- Social Studio from Salesforce: https://www.salesforce.com/products/marketing-cloud/social-media-marketing.
- Google Trends: https://trends.google.com/trends/?geo=US.
- Google Analytics: https://analytics.google.com/analytics/web.
- NodeXL: https://nodexl.com.
- Tableau: https://www.tableau.com.
- HARO (Help a Reporter Out—trend spotting): https://www.helpareporter.com.

Creativity, Strategy, and Planning

The billions of people connected on the social sphere rely heavily on social media channels to obtain news, connect with friends, and be entertained.[5] Breaking through the noise and clutter on social media can be difficult, because competition for a user's time and attention is fierce. That's why being creative is an important quality for a social media strategist to possess. If you're among the many who do not feel creative, there are some tried and true principles that you can count on. The Circular Model of SoMe for Social Communication (Share, Optimize, Manage, Engage) is a great place to start (see Figure 12.2). This model, meant to be the first step in planning a full social media campaign, can help enhance creativity by answering a number of questions:[6,7]

- *Share*: Ask yourself three questions: Where is my audience? On what types of networks are they engaging? Where should our company be sharing content? It is vital for social media strategists to understand how and where their consumers interact. This is a company's opportunity to connect, build trust, and identify channels that allow for true interactions.
- *Optimize*: Ask yourself four questions: Are there issues that need to be addressed? What type of content should be shared? Are there brand influencers and advocates who can spread our message? Where are we being mentioned and how? To optimize any conversation, listening is paramount. A strong communication plan that optimizes strategic content maximizes the impact of messaging, brand, and value for your audience.
- *Manage*: Ask yourself this question: What relevant messaging should we manage, monitor, and measure? By setting up media management

FIGURE 12.2

The Circular Model of SoMe for Social Communication helps social media strategists think about how to share, optimize, manage, and engage when developing a campaign strategy.

systems like Hootsuite, you can keep abreast of conversations happening in real time, respond to consumers instantly, send private messages, share links, monitor conversations, and measure successes/failures. Metrics are integral to managing a social strategy, especially in a corporate setting, where practitioners must illustrate the value of their efforts by reporting the ROI of campaigns to C-level executives.

- *Engage*: Ask yourself two questions: Who should we engage with and how? If we want consumers to take action on what we've shared, what do we want them to do? Cultivating an engagement strategy can be difficult, but once a company realizes the benefits of authentic engagement, true relationships can form.

SoMe-related resources include PESO certification, social media templates, and Trailhead.

Resources

- PESO Certification: http://bit.ly/PESOCertification.
- Social Media Templates: https://www.smartsheet.com/social-media-templates.
- Trailhead (free professional development courses): https://trailhead.salesforce.com.

Successful, long-term social media strategies have clear goals that are aligned with overall organizational goals. Being flexible and agile when developing and executing a sound social media strategy will help practitioners make swift decisions and create real-time solutions should anything unexpected arise.

There are many areas within the communications industry in addition to social media. Many students graduating today will have degrees in public relations, integrated communications, marketing, or advertising, with skills that are transferable across industries. However, social media is changing at a particularly rapid rate. Let's turn our attention now to what the future of social media may hold.

FUTURE OF SOCIAL MEDIA

Judging by recent history, the future of social media is undoubtedly vast. Over the past ten years, social media has changed the landscape of not just public relations, advertising, and marketing, but the world in general. Think about it—social media platforms are used by one in three people in the world. One in three! Just a few short years ago, approximately 2.65 billion people were using social media worldwide; that number is projected to increase to almost 3.5 billion soon[8] (see Figure 12.3).

It's difficult to remember a time before computer-mediated communication (CMC), which as you learned in Chapter 1 is human communication via computers.[9] Computer technology helps achieve communications functions. Special attention now focuses on how computer-mediated communication manages

FIGURE 12.3

This graph depicts the number of monthly active users on every major social media platform between 2004 and 2019.

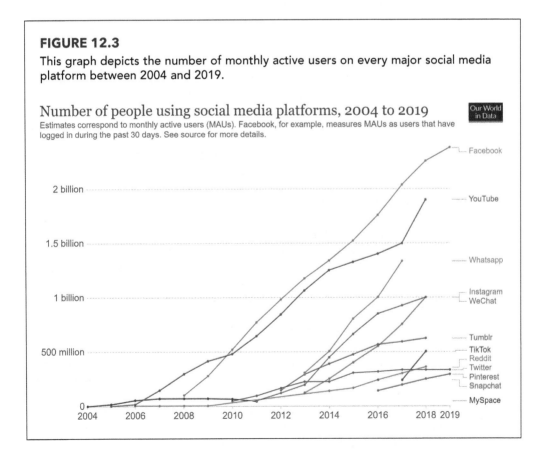

Number of people using social media platforms, 2004 to 2019

Estimates correspond to monthly active users (MAUs). Facebook, for example, measures MAUs as users that have logged in during the past 30 days. See source for more details.

interpersonal interaction, forms impressions, and maintains and sustains relationships through the social networking supported by social media platforms. The social effects of different computer-supported communication technologies impact our daily lives. With the pervasive use of social media, practitioners should take notice of some important areas, including ethics, privacy, the Internet of things, and multimedia. These sections present themes that all practitioners should keep on their radar rather than day-to-day tactical on the job skills.

Ethics of AI

Ethics has always played an important role in a communicator's work. The Public Relations Society of America (PRSA) Code of Ethics, the backbone of the public relations industry, helps practitioners carry out ethical practices for their organizations and their clients.[10] The marketing code of ethics ensures that businesses conduct their affairs with integrity and keep the customer's well-being in mind.[11] The rapid adoption of **Artificial intelligence (AI)** has created a new concern that impacts the data and privacy of users of social media. It was just six or seven years ago that brands began to develop social media guidelines. Over the next few years, development of ethical AI guidelines will become standard practice in the field. Resources related to AI include the Department of Defense Ethical Principles for Artificial Intelligence, the European Commission AI Ethical Guidelines, and Building Ethics into Privacy Frameworks for Big Data and AI.

Resources

- Department of Defense Ethical Principles for Artificial Intelligence: http://bit.ly/DODEthicsAI.
- European Commission AI Ethical Guidelines: http://bit.ly/EUAIEthics.
- Building Ethics into Privacy Frameworks for Big Data and AI: http://bit.ly/DataPrivacyAI.

Privacy and Data

Every time we visit a website, we leave a trail of our digital footsteps, and personal data is collected. When signing up to be on a social platform, we allow collection of data—even something as simple as our email and name—that's important to organizations. Data is also collected whenever we ask Alexa what the weather is like. Essentially everything we share online is collected and stored. That data is worth trillions of dollars to organizations.[12] Over the past few years, there has been an uptick in attempts by consumers to protect their data and their privacy. This effort is likely to amplify in coming years as users gain greater awareness of how their information is used. The first step in this direction was the introduction of the **General Data Protection Regulation (GDPR)**, a law that was created on May 25, 2018, and implemented in 2019 in the European Union (EU) to protect citizens' personal data. GDPR instructs companies of all sizes what they can and cannot do with personal information.[13]

Throughout this book we have discussed the importance of data driving decisions, and it does. However, privacy concerns related to social media and the Internet have always been present and are likely to continue. The future of social media practices means having clear policies in place. It also means taking care of user data, providing user consent outlets, and providing clear outlines of how data is collected, used, and stored.

Resources

- GDPR: https://gdpr-info.eu.
- GDPR for PR and Corporate Communication: http://bit.ly/GDPRComms.
- Privacy Policy Templates: http://bit.ly/PrivacyPolicyTemplates.

Internet of Things (IoT)

We first introduced this concept in Chapter 9. In its simplest form, the Internet of Things (IoT) is everything connected to the Internet, but the term is used increasingly to classify objects that "talk" to each other, including TVs, smart speakers, toys, wearables, and smart appliances.[14] According to WIRED's Matt Burgess, "connected machines and objects in factories offer the potential for a 'fourth industrial revolution,' and experts predict more than half of new businesses will run on the IoT."[15] It is projected that more and more such technologies will continue to come to market. In the next couple of years, one source estimates that there will be 4 billion IoT devices worldwide, bringing with them an economic value of $11 trillion.[16] These devices collect data. As already discussed, ethics, data, and privacy are top priorities for users and lawmakers. Because these areas connect and overlap on the IoT, the future of social media will need to include even more deliberate thought about the importance and concerns of individual users.

Resources

- IoT Case Studies: http://bit.ly/IoTCaseStudies.
- The WIRED Guide to the Internet of Things: http://bit.ly/WiredIoT.
- The Future of IoT (video): http://bit.ly/TedXFutureIoT.

Multimedia Components

Like the IoT, converged media will continue to grow. **Multimedia** is the combination of two or more of five elements of media:[17] text, image, audio, video, and animation.[18] The ability to create meaningful campaigns grounded in the use of multimedia elements is key to success in a social media career. Grouping text with images or video captures and holds the attention of a consumer for a longer period of time and often makes content more shareable. On the social sphere we want our content to be sharable and reach as many users as possible. For example, using a clever **GIF (graphic image file)** with a Tweet is an effortless way to combine two media elements. Multimedia elements can help tell a better story, grab the attention of consumers, assist brands with expressing emotion, and build credibility with consumers. Examples of multimedia include Piktochart, Adobe Spark, Giphy, Canva, and Word Art. For more on how digitally driven our society is, see the Relational/Societal/Self feature.

Resources

- Piktochart: https://piktochart.com.
- Adobe Spark (pages, posts, and videos): https://spark.adobe.com/features.
- Giphy: https://giphy.com/create/gifmaker.
- Canva: https://www.canva.com.
- Word Art: https://wordart.com.

Relational/Societal/Self: Digitally Driven Society

According to the website Our World in Data, US adults "spend more than six hours per day on digital media which consists of apps and websites accessed through mobile phones, tablets, computers and other connected devices such as game consoles."[19] As you have learned throughout this text, social media have a tremendous impact on our personal relationships, on the larger society, and on our sense of self. This is not just a result of the time spent, but of how firmly entrenched social media has become in society today.

Think about It: With this in mind, describe your interactions on social media through the relational, societal, and self lenses. After you review what you've written, answer the following question: Is there such a thing as too much social media? Explain your answer.

CHAPTER WRAP-UP

Social media is the embodiment of two-way communication, which as you learned in Chapter 1 is open access between a brand and its consumers. As a social media manager, it is your responsibility to develop a skill set that best aligns with the goal of reaching your followers, fans, and subscribers. As you can see, the future is both vast and complicated. We hope that this text has provided you with a greater understanding of how to navigate what some consider difficult terrain.

CRITICAL-THINKING QUESTIONS

1. Explain what a social media manager does and the skills necessary to become one.

2. Describe how the Circular Model of SoMe for Social Communication works within the profession and can help practitioners plan campaigns.

3. Unpack this statement: "More valuable than oil, data reigns in today's data economy."[20] What does this mean to you? How does it impact you personally and professionally?

4. What is uses and gratifications theory, and how does it impact the role of social media managers?

5. Matt Burgess from WIRED described the IoT as a "fourth industrial revolution." What does the IoT mean to you, and what does it mean for the future of social media?

ACTIVITIES

1. Safeguarding confidences is a core tenet of the PRSA Code of Ethics. Find the Code on the Internet and relate it to the discussions of privacy and ethics.

2. Find the app Disconnect from the Chrome Web store (http://bit.ly/ ChromeDisconnectApp). Download the app to see a visualization of the websites that track your data and report the results. Were you surprised by what you found?

3. Examine the job descriptions provided in this chapter. Based on the descriptions and skill sets listed, do you feel you are ready to enter the field? Which skills do you already possess? Which do you need to work on?

KEY CONCEPTS

Artificial intelligence (AI)
General Data Protection Regulation (GDPR)
GIF (graphic image file)
Multimedia

MEDIA SOURCES

Sneak Peek—A Day in the Life of a Social Media Manager: https://www .prnewsonline.com/day-in-the-life-social-media-manager.

5 Business Branding Trends to Keep in Mind in 2020: https:// thestoryexchange.org/business-branding-trends-2020/?gclid= Cj0KCQjwx7zzBRCcARIsABPRscM59q_Ayl9gFMKpjHATKrIE_ AZ7pmNk_cW9c3ZL7qEo-igTanTS2qIaApKNEALw_wcB.

What Does GDPR Mean for Social Media Strategies? https:// digitalmarketinginstitute.com/en-us/blog/what-does-gdpr-mean-for-social-media-strategies.

Agenda Setting: The ability to influence the importance placed on the topics of the public agenda.

Amplification: The process of content being shared, either through organic or paid engagement, within social media channels.

Application (or App): A Web-based application that supports information publishing and sharing including text, video, audio, and photo.

Artificial Intelligence (AI): Use of machine learning to mine, collect, and analyze increasing volumes of information to classify and cluster in order to detect patterns for use both commercially and personally.

Big Data: Enormous, almost inconceivable, amounts of information created as a result of online activities.

Boost: A paid tactic that can increase the number of people who see your content on a social media channel.

Bots: An automated program on a network that can interact with users designed to respond or behave like humans.

Brand Identity: How the organization intends for the brand to be perceived.

Brand Image: The way an audience perceives a brand.

Brand Management: A brand is a name, term, design, symbol, or any other feature that identifies one seller's good or service as distinct from those of other sellers.

Browser: A program used to navigate the Internet.

Cambridge Analytica: A British political consulting firm that combined misappropriation of digital assets, data mining, data brokerage, and data analysis with strategic communication during the electoral processes.

Citizen Journalist: Member of the general public (rather than the mainstream media) who provides any type of news gathering and reporting (including writing and publishing articles, posting photographs, and creating videos about newsworthy topics).

Cognitive Mapping Model: A type of mental representation that helps to acquire, code, store, recall, and decode information.

Conflict Perspective: Approaching the study of mass media through the lens of those in control.

Content Aggregator: A Web crawler that gathers information from different online sources powered by individuals or organizations.

Content Analysis: The process of analyzing data including articles, social media posts, or website content.

Content Creation: The generation of a variety of different written and visual communication on behalf of an organization.

Content Curation: Searching for and filtering through content across the social sphere and sharing that information on your social channels.

Content Management System (CMS): A software application that can be used to manage the creation and modification of digital content. An example of this is WordPress.

Converged Media: Within the PESO model, media that overlaps several categories, such as boosted through social media that maintain qualities of both paid and shared content.

Corporate Social Activism: When companies choose to take a public stance on a social or political issue.

Corporate Social Advocacy: A part of CSR, corporate social advocacy is practiced by companies to advance social agendas.

Corporate Social Responsibility (CSR): An organization's commitment to doing business in a socially responsible way through initiatives that support positive resolution of social and environmental issues.

Creative Commons: Licenses that help creators retain copyright while allowing others to copy, distribute, and make some uses of their work, at least noncommercially.

Creativity: The process of attempting to discover new ideas.

Crisis Communication Strategies (CCS): Aids in the use of both traditional and social media in crisis management, response, and recovery of reputation post crisis. The model proposes that social media be used during crises for three purposes: issue relevance, information seeking/sharing, and emotional venting/support.

Crowdfunding: The practice of funding a project or venture by raising many small amounts of money from a large number of people, typically via the Internet.

Crowdsourcing: The practice of obtaining needed services, ideas, or content by soliciting contributions from a large group of people, especially from an online community, rather than from traditional avenues. Wikipedia is the most prominent example of crowdsourcing.

Cyber Activism: The use of electronic communication technologies such as social media, email, videos, blogs, and podcasts for various forms of activism to enable faster and more effective communication by citizen movements, the delivery of particular information to large and specific audiences, as well as coordination.

Cyberbullying: The use of electronic communication to bully a person, typically by sending messages of an intimidating or threatening nature.

Cyfe: A platform to manage social media, analytics, marketing, sales, support, and overall social media infrastructure.

Data: The content analyzed through research.

Deepfakes: Synthetic media in which a person in an existing image or video is replaced with someone else's likeness.

Demographic: A particular sector of a population.

Descriptive Analytics: Gathering and describing social media data in the form of reports and visualizations. Likes, views, and tweets are examples of this type of analytics.

Designated Market Areas (DMA): Allows practitioners to see a population of an area using more traditionally targeted television and radio data.

Diagnosis: Part of the initial stage of campaign planning whereby the organization identifies the problem or opportunity.

Diffusion: Speed of information dissemination over social media networks.

Disinformation: False information that is intended to mislead the public.

Diversity: Differences among people within a group, stemming from variations in factors such as age, gender, ethnicity, religion, sexual preference, and education.

Earned Media: The published coverage of an enterprise, cause, or person's message by a credible third party, such as a journalist, blogger, trade analyst, or industry influencer.

Echo Chamber: Situation in which your own opinions are reinforced by others without introducing new or conflicting content into the mix; limits public discourse and can lead to extremes.

Elites: A small group of people who control a disproportionate amount of wealth or political power.

Email Marketing: The act of sending a commercial message, typically to a group of people, using email. Popular examples of platforms used include MyEmma, MailChimp, and Constant Contact.

Employee Advocacy: Employee-generated exposure that helps increase awareness and reputation for an organization.

Employee Engagement: The feeling of connectedness between employees, and between employees and the employer.

Engagement: Participation in the online community via direct conversations.

Enterprise Social Networks (ESNs): Social networks implemented by organizations to connect and collaborate with internal audiences.

E-sports: Also known as electronic sports; the industry of competitive video gaming.

Ethical Codes: Formalized, written standards of behavior used as procedures for decision making.

Ethics: A set of moral principles that govern a person's behavior or the conducting of an activity.

Exabyte (EB): A multiple of the unit byte for digital information. In the International System of Units, the prefix "exa" indicates multiplication by the sixth power of 1,000. Therefore, one exabyte is one quintillion bytes.

Fake News: Articles that are written and published usually with the intent to mislead in order to damage an agency, entity, or person, and/or gain financially or politically, often using sensationalist, dishonest, or outright fabricated headlines to increase readership.

Fear Of Living Offline (FOLO): Fear of living offline.

Fear Of Missing Out (FOMO): Fear of missing out.

Feed: Frequently updated content published by a website. Feeds are usually used for news and blog websites, as well as for distributing a variety of digital content, including pictures, audio, and video. Feeds can additionally be used to deliver audio content. They are commonly referred to as RSS feeds, XML feeds, syndicated content, Twitter feeds, or Web feeds.

Feminist Perspective: A perspective that calls out the prevalence of the idealization of females in the media as young and svelte, and light-skinned if not white. This represents the culture's accepted standards for female beauty, which reinforces stereotypes and misrepresents actuality in favor of dominant ideologies.

Filter Bubble: A state of intellectual isolation that occurs as a result of algorithms "choosing" what you see and what you will not see. This creates lack of variety of viewpoint and self-isolation as you don't gain viewpoints of opposition ideals.

Formal Research: A systematic collection of information that can be replicated and subject to an analysis of its reliability and validity.

Gatekeeper: The person who make the choices as to what information becomes available for consumption by the public.

General Data Protection Regulation (GDPR): A law that was created in the European Union (EU) to protect the personal data of citizens that went into effect on May 25, 2018.

Generation Z (GenZ): People born between 1997 and 2012; the generation perceived as being familiar with the Internet from a very young age.

Geolocation: The process of detecting geographical locations of a person or device by means of digital information through the Internet.

GIF (Graphic Image File): A computer file format for the compression and storage of visual digital information.

Goodwill: Intangible asset of the organization that adds positive value.

Hacktivism: The use of computer-based techniques such as hacking as a form of civil disobedience to promote a political agenda or social change.

Hashtag Activism: See "slacktivism" and "cyber activism." Use of hashtags to aid online activism.

Hate Speech: Abusive or threatening speech or writing that expresses prejudice against a particular group, especially on the basis of race, religion, or sexual orientation.

Health Communication: Study and practice of communicating promotional health information, such as in public health campaigns, health education, and between doctor and patient. The purpose of disseminating health information is to influence personal health choices by improving health literacy.

Hootsuite: A social media management system that allows brands to streamline social media efforts and campaigns across social networks that include Twitter, Facebook, LinkedIn, WordPress, and Google+ pages. Social strategists collaboratively monitor, engage with, and measure the results of social campaigns from one secure, Web-based dashboard.

Implementation: The point in the campaign process where the campaign plan is put into operation.

Indeed: An online job board that aggregates employment postings from a variety sources, allowing users to search for specific positions.

Influencer: An expert in a specific category that has the most loyal and engaged following.

Influencer Marketing: Use of an expert in a specific category that has a loyal and engaged following that connects with companies regarding a very specific target audience for which to gain influence for a specific purpose, usually sales or other conversion.

Infographic: Also known as an information graphic; a graphically represented image with information in a format designed to make data easily understandable at a glance.

Informal Research: The ability to gather information through conversations and a general assessment of important issues and trends. Informal research does not enjoy a high degree of reliability and validity, often because of its use of nonprobability sampling.

Information Communication Technologies (ICT): Used to refer to the convergence of audiovisual and telephone networks with computer networks through a single cabling or link system. The idea of integration among these technologies is at the forefront of this idea.

Instagram: A photo-sharing application that lets users take photos, apply filters to their images, and share the photos instantly on the Instagram network and other social networks, including Facebook, Flickr, Twitter, Pinterest, and Foursquare.

Integrated Crisis Communication (ICC) Model: Model of crisis management that takes into account integrated organizations, social media, and stakeholders as three main players.

Integrated Marketing Communications: A combination of activities including public relations, communications, advertising, marketing, and social media designed to sell a product, service, or idea. Activities are designed to maintain consistent brand messaging across all communication channels.

Internet of Things (IoT): The interconnection via the Internet of computing devices embedded in everyday objects, enabling them to send and receive data.

Interpersonal-Connection-Behaviors Framework: A structure that examines the relationships based on social network sites that benefit end users when they are used to make connections but harm them when things like isolation and direct social comparison are experienced.

Intranet: Websites created through secured local channels that companies use to organize information for their employees.

Issues Management: Watching for emerging problems in the environment that may affect the organization.

JOMO: The joy of missing out; opposite of FOMO (fear of missing out).

Key Performance Indicator (KPI): A form of measurement connected to a campaign or social media objective to quantify success.

Keywords: Specific words used to describe content that ultimately boosts visibility and rankings on the Web.

Like: An action that can be taken by users on various social media platforms to illustrate appreciation of content shared by others.

Linear Feedback: Direct communication from one entity to another by way of social media (i.e., comments); a direct response.

Listening: Monitoring conversations and activity occurring on the Web.

Livestream: Multimedia that is constantly received by and presented to an end user while being delivered by a provider; also referred to as streaming media.

Machine Learning: The scientific study of algorithms and statistical models that computer systems use to perform specific tasks.

Marketing: The activity, set of institutions, and processes for creating, communicating, delivering, and exchanging offerings that have value for customers, clients, partners, and society at large.

Mass Media: Channels through which communications is intended to reach large groups of people.

Media Relations: Mutually beneficial associations between publicists or public relations professionals and journalists as a condition for reaching audiences with messages of news or features of interest (publicity). The function includes both seeking publicity for an organization and responding to queries from journalists about the organization. Requires maintenance of up-to-date lists of media contacts and a knowledge of media audience interests.

Metadata: A set of data that describes and gives information about other data.

Microblog(ing): The short posts, often including links, images, and video, that characterize social media content on platforms such as Facebook, LinkedIn, and Twitter.

Multimedia: The combination of two or more of the five elements of media: text, image, audio, video, and animation.

News Aggregators: Web applications that pull news stories from different Internet sites into a single location that users can view at their leisure.

Newsgathering: The process of researching news items, especially those for broadcast or publication.

Niche Media: Media channels that are hyper-focused on consumers' viewing, listening, reading, and social interests; a distinct subset of a larger group of media.

Objective: Specific, measurable statement of what needs to be achieved as part of reaching a goal.

Organic Media: Refers to the free, unsponsored content (posts, photos, video, memes, stories, etc.) that all users, including businesses and brands, share with each other on their feeds. Organic content is often partnered with paid content to boost reach.

Owned Media: Content that is produced by and for the organization to share on its "owned" channels, including websites and corporate blog content.

Paid Media: Channels in which money is paid to place messages and control their distribution.

Passion Connection Sites: Sites centered on specific personal interests. Examples include Houzz, Listy, and Foodbuzz.

Pay-to-play: Advertising on social media channels.

PESO: An acronym for paid, earned, shared, and owned. In the PESO model, each channel delivers unique importance.

PESO Model: A public relations planning model based on PESO.

Podcast: An audio file found on the Internet that users can download and listen to.

Predictive Analytics: Analysis of large amounts of data to predict a future event.

Prescriptive Analytics: Application of mathematical and computational sciences to suggest decision options to take advantage of the results of descriptive and predictive analytics. Anticipates what will happen, when it will happen, and why.

Propaganda: Intentional manipulation of public opinion.

Public Relations: A strategic communication process that builds mutually beneficial relationships between organizations and their publics.

Publicity: In media relations, the process of sharing information with journalists with the aim of publishing it for a wider audience.

Qualitative Research: A research method that uses flexible and open-ended questioning, often with a small number of participants/respondents, that cannot be extrapolated to large populations. Examples include in-depth interviews, case studies, and focus groups.

Quantitative Research: A research method that uses standardized and closed-ended questions, often with many participants/respondents, that generally can be extrapolated to large populations. Examples include surveys, content analysis, or experiments.

RACE: A type of four-step communication planning model. RACE: research and planning, action, communication, evaluation.

Real-time Search: The method of indexing content being published online into search engine results with virtually no delay.

Reporting: The analysis of completed or ongoing activities that determine or support a public relations campaign; also known as evaluation.

Research: The methodical collection and explanation of information used to increase understanding of needs.

Return onn Ad Spend (ROAS): A metric that measures the amount of revenue your business earns for each dollar it spends on advertising/paid media.

Return onn Investment (ROI): A performance measure used to evaluate the efficiency of an investment or compare the efficiency of a number of different investments.

Retweet (RT): To share another person's tweet; a great way to spread links exponentially.

ROPE: A type of four-step communication planning model. ROPE: research, objectives, programming, evaluation.

ROSTIR: A public relations planning model that uses research/diagnosis, objectives, strategies, tactics, implementation, and reporting. Tactics utilize paid, earned, shared, and owned media.

RSS Feed: RSS (really simple syndication) is a group of Web-feed formats used to publish frequently updated content such as blogs and videos in a standardized format; allows users to subscribe to the content and read it when they have time, from a location other than the original website or blog, such as a reader or mobile device.

Search Engine Optimization (SEO): The process of improving the volume or quality of traffic to a website from search engines via unpaid or organic search traffic such as Google.

Sentiment: The attitude of user comments related to a brand online.

Shared Media: The pass-along sharing and commenting upon your message by the community through social channels.

Shareholder Activism: A shareholder that uses an equity stake in a corporation to put pressure on its management. A fairly small stake may be enough to launch a successful campaign. In comparison, a full takeover bid is a much more costly and difficult undertaking.

Shortened Message Service (SMS): A text-messaging service component of most telephone, Internet, and mobile device systems. It uses standardized communication protocols to enable mobile devices to exchange short text messages. An intermediary service can facilitate a text-to-voice conversion to be sent to landlines.

Silo Effect: A phrase that is popular in the business and organizational communities to describe a lack of communication and common goals among departments in an organization. Silo maybe defined as groups of employees that tend to work as autonomous units within an organization.

Situational Crisis Communication Theory (SCCT): Methodology for matching strategic crisis responses to the level of crisis responsibility and reputational threat posed by a crisis.

Slactivism: The practice of supporting a political or social cause by means such as social media or online petitions, characterized as involving very little effort or commitment. See also "hacktivism" and "hashtag activism."

SlideShare: An online social network for sharing presentations and documents.

SMART Objectives: Objectives that are written as follows: strategic, measurable, attainable, realistic, and timebound.

Snapchat: A mobile messaging application used to share photos, videos, text, and drawings.

Social Capital: Networking (both online and offline) that provides the social connections and social support to amass status online.

Social Connection: The experience of feeling close and connected to others. It involves feeling loved, cared for, and valued, and forms the basis of interpersonal relationships.

Social Listening: The process of monitoring digital conversations to understand what customers are saying about a brand and industry online.

Social Media: Forms of electronic communication through which users create online communities to share information, ideas, personal messages, and other content.

Social Media Analytics (SMA): The collection and evaluation of data from social media sites and blogs to make business decisions.

Social Media Competitive Analysis: Helps brands identify who their competitors are, which platforms they are using, and how they are using those platforms.

Social Media Crisis Communication (SMCC) model: A model proposing that social media be used during crises for three purposes: issue relevance, information seeking/sharing, and emotional venting/support.

Social Media Dashboard: A user interface that organizes and streamlines online activity so that a person can publish content, respond, monitor, update, and listen from one central place; examples include Hootsuite, Cyfe, Meltwater, and Social Studio.

Social Media Fatigue: User tendency to remove themselves from social when they are feeling overwhelmed or unsafe, or experiencing high anxiety.

Social Media Monitoring: Active monitoring of social media channels for information about a company or organization.

Social Networking Site (SNS): An online platform allowing people to build social networks or social relationships with other people who share similar interests.

Social Sphere: The intertwining of online social spheres constituted by the online social networking ecosystem.

Social Support: A resource that results from development of a network.

Social TV: The simultaneous use of social media while watching television.

Sponsored Content: Online content that is paid for by a company.

Sports Communication: Communication within sport situations; also refers to the study of communications within sport situations.

Sports Marketing: A niche within the marketing industry specializing in the promotion of sport- and nonsport-related events, goods, and services in conjunction with sport-focused individuals and organizations.

Stakeholders: Those persons who are integral to the existence of the organization including employees, customers, and shareholders.

Stakeholder Theory: A theory of organizational management and business ethics that accounts for multiple constituencies impacted by business entities like employees, suppliers, local communities, creditors, and others.

Strategic Sports Communication Model (SSCM): A model created by Pedersen that illustrates the components of sports communications and the process of sports communications.

Strategies: Public specific approaches specifying the channel to send the message to achieve objectives.

Streaming Media: On-demand online entertainment sources for TV shows, movies, and other media.

SWOT Analysis: A process to help organizations define their strengths, weaknesses, opportunities, and threats.

Tactics: Strategy-specific communication products that carry the message to the key publics. Tactics are tangible items such as a press release, social media post, or a website.

Tag: A keyword used to describe content on a blog or in social networks.

Tag Cloud: A visual collection of the most frequent tags produced by a user, blog, profile, page, or descriptions on Web pages.

Terms of Use: The legal agreements between a service provider and a person who wants to use that service.

Thought Leader: Person or organization that is viewed as an expert on a topic and whose opinions and beliefs may influence others.

TL; DR: An acronym that means "too long; didn't read."

Traditional Media: Broadcast and print media channels such as television, radio, and print media.

Traffic: The number of people interacting on a platform.

Troll: A person who provokes or instigates others with negative and sometimes harmful dialogues.

Trolling: The act of being a troll.

Twitter Storm: A period characterized by a sudden increase in the number of posts made on the social media application Twitter about a particular issue, event, etc., especially one that is controversial in nature.

Two-Way Communication: Use of communication to confer with publics, resolve conflict, and promote mutual understanding and respect between the organization and its public(s).

Two-Way Symmetrical Communication: Communication in which a public relations practitioner serves as a liaison between the organization and key publics. The term "symmetrical" is used because the model attempts to create a mutually beneficial situation.

Unified Modeling Language (UML): Approach used in software engineering intended to provide standard visualization of system designs.

User-Generated Content (UGC): Materials publicly gained through promotional efforts other than paid media advertising (publicity gained through advertising), or owned media (branding).

Uses and Gratifications Theory (UGT): Approach to studying communication that focuses on the relationship between an audience and its use of media.

Vanity Metrics: Metrics that do not help brands understand their performance or do not inform future strategies.

Video Connection Sites: Branded video content on platforms such as YouTube.

Views: Number of times that content (including text, photos, and videos) is viewed by people.

Virtual Community (VC): A community of people sharing common interests, ideas, and feelings over the Internet.

Vlogs: Video blogs that are largely YouTube based.

Watchdog: An entity or force intended to prevent others from overstepping a hypothetical boundary.

Website: A location connected to the Internet that maintains one or more pages on the World Wide Web.

Websleuthing: Use of social media networks to aid or avoid disasters.

WeChat: A Chinese multipurpose messaging, social media, and mobile payment app.

Wiki: Web app that allows users to add, modify, or delete content in collaboration with others. Wikipedia is the most well-known Web app.

CHAPTER 1

1. Pathack, Shareen. "How Southwest Airlines turned social media into social business." *Digiday*, December 17, 2015. digiday.com/marketing/southwest-airlines-turned-social-media-social-business.

2. Libby, Christina. "For Southwest Airlines, Culture Determines Who Owns Social Media." *PR News*, August 7, 2017. www.prnewsonline.com/for-southwest-airlines-culture-determines-who-owns-social-media.

3. Fottrell, Quentin. "People spend most of their waking hours staring at screens." *Market Watch*, August 4, 2018. www.marketwatch.com/story/people-are-spending-most-of-their-waking-hours-staring-at-screens-2018-08-01.

4. Smith, Aaron, and Monica Anderson. *Social Media Use in 2018*. The Pew Research Center, March 1, 2018. The Pew Research Center. www.pewinternet.org/2018/03/01/social-media-use-in-2018 (accessed March 12, 2019).

5. Kleinschmit, Matt. Weblog post. Generation Z characteristics: Five infographics on the Gen Z lifestyle. *Vision Critical*, February 10, 2019. Marketing Trends. "Marketing to Generation Z infographic." *Agency Sparks*, 2019. www.agencysparks.com/infographics2/marketing-to-generation-z.

6. Marketing Trends. "Marketing to Generation Z infographic." *Agency Sparks*, 2019. www.agencysparks.com/infographics2/marketing-to-generation-z.

7. *Social Media Fact Sheet*. Pew Research Center Internet and Technology, February 5, 2018. *The Pew Research Center*. www.pewinternet.org/fact-sheet/social-media (accessed March 12, 2019).

8. Merriam-Webster, define social media: https://www.merriam-webster.com/dictionary/social%20media.

9. Cambridge Dictionary, define social media: https://dictionary.cambridge.org/us/dictionary/english/social-media.

10. Dictionary.com, define social media: https://www.dictionary.com/browse/social-media.

11. Safko, L. *The Social Media Bible: Tactics, Tools, and Strategies for Business Success*. Hoboken: John Wiley & Sons, 2012.

12. Luttrell, Regina, and Luke Capizzo. *Public Relations Campaigns: An Integrated Approach*. Thousand Oaks, CA: SAGE Publications, 2018.

13. Jenkins, Henry. *Fans, Bloggers, and Gamers: Exploring Participatory Culture*. NYU Press, 2006.

14. Hlavac, Randy. *Social IMC Social Strategies with Bottom-Line ROI*. Marketing Synergy, Inc., 2014.

15. "News Aggregator." *Wikipedia*, June 2017. en.wikipedia.org/wiki/News_aggregator.

16. Houzz. https://www.houzz.com.

17. "Why Video Is Exploding on Social Media in 2019." *Wyzowl*. www.wyzowl.com/video-social-media-2019 (accessed March 13, 2019).

18. Ibid.

19. Galov, Nick. "How Many Blogs Are There?" *Hosting Tribunal*, February 14, 2019. hostingtribunal.com/blog/how-many-blogs.

20. Luttrell, Regina. *Social Media: How to Engage, Share, and Connect*. 3rd ed., Lanham, MD: Roman & Littlefield Publishers, 2016.

21. McMillin, Paul. "What's the difference between social media and social

networking?" *TechTarget*, Search Unified Communications, 2011. searchunified communications.techtarget.com/ answer/Whats-the-difference-between-social-media-and-social-networking.

22. Merriam-Webster, define website: https:// www.merriam-webster.com/dictionary/ website.

23. Summerfield, Jason. "Mobile website vs. mobile app: Which is best for your organization?" *Human Service Solutions*. www.hswsolutions.com/services/mobile-web-development/mobile-website-vs-apps (accessed March 15, 2019).

24. Kiru. "31 Best News Aggregator Websites of 2019—Top List." *Double Hike Blog*. www.doublehike.com/best-news-aggregator-websites.

25. Howell, Tom. "What Is a Social Media Bot?" *Zignal Blog*, Zignal Labs, August 9, 2018. zignallabs.com/what-is-a-social-media-bot.

26. Varone, Marco. "What Is Machine Learning? A Definition." *Expert System*, 2018. www .expertsystem.com/machine-learning-definition.

CHAPTER 2

1. Wilson, Mark. "The War on What's Real." *Fast Company*, 2018. https://www .fastcompany.com/90162494/the-war-on-whats-real (accessed June 5, 2019).

2. FaceApp. Roose, Kevin. "Here Come the Fake Videos, Too." *New York Times*, March 4, 2018. https://www.nytimes .com/2018/03/04/technology/fake-videos-deepfakes.html (accessed June 5, 2019).

3. Harris, Douglas. "False pornography is here and the law cannot protect you." *Duke L. & Tech. Rev.* 17 (2019): 100.

4. Robitzski, Dan. "DARPA Spent $68 Million on Technology to Spot Deepfakes." *Futurism* (2018). https://futurism.com/ darpa-68-million-technology-deepfakes (accessed June 5, 2019).

5. Brown, Nina I., and Jonathan Peters. "Say this, not that: Government regulation and control of social media." *Syracuse Law Review* 68 (2018): 522 (laws that mandate detection and removal of false content on the basis of its falsity are unconstitutional).

6. 47 U.S.C. § 230.

7. Tomberry. "Slender Man." Know Your Meme [wiki]. Last modified January 3, 2010. https://knowyourmeme.com/memes/ slender-man.

8. Don. "Momo Challenge." Know Your Meme [wiki]. Last modified July 12, 2018. https://knowyourmeme.com/memes/ momo-challenge.

9. Sav. "Cinnamon Challenge." Know Your Meme [wiki]. Last modified January 10, 2010. https://knowyourmeme.com/memes/ cinnamon-challenge.

10. Peacock, Roy. "Tide POD Challenge." Know Your Meme [wiki]. Last modified December 27, 2017. https://knowyourmeme.com/ memes/tide-pod-challenge.

11. Downer, Adam. "Wakanda Forever." Know Your Meme [wiki]. Last modified May 15, 2018. https://knowyourmeme .com/memes/wakanda-forever.

12. Matt. "#WhatTheFluffChallenge." Know Your Meme [wiki]. Last modified June 22, 2018. https://knowyourmeme.com/ memes/whatthefluffchallenge.

13. Rodriguez, Salvador. "Inside Facebook's 'cult-like' workplace, where dissent is discouraged and employees pretend to be happy all the time." CNBC. Last modified January 8, 2019. https:// www.cnbc.com/2019/01/08/ facebook-culture-cult-performance-review-process-blamed.html.

14. Wong, J. C. "Former Facebook executive: Social media is ripping society apart." *The Guardian* (2017). https://www.theguardian .com/technology/2017/dec/11/facebook-former-executive-ripping-society-apart (accessed March 2, 2019).

15. Vincent, James. "Former Facebook exec says social media is ripping apart society." *The Verge*. Last modified December 11, 2017. https://www.theverge.com/2017/12/

11/16761016/former-facebook-exec-ripping-apart-society.

16. Vincent, James. "Former Facebook exec says social media is ripping apart society." *The Verge*. Last modified December 11, 2017. https://www.theverge.com/2017/12/11/16761016/former-facebook-exec-ripping-apart-society.

17. Palihapitiya, Chamath. "Chamath Palihapitiya, Founder and CEO Social Capital, on Money as an Instrument of Change." Interview. Audio file. YouTube. November 13, 2017. https://youtu.be/PMotykw0Slk.

18. Newton, Casey. "Russia's election posts reached 126 million people, Facebook will tell Congress." *The Verge*. Last modified October 30, 2017. https://www.theverge.com/2017/10/30/16578022facebook-senate-testimony-russia-126-million-people.

19. Specia, Megan, and Paul Mozur. "A War of Words Puts Facebook at the Center of Myanmar's Rohingya Crisis." *The New York Times*. Last modified October 27, 2017. https://www.nytimes.com/2017/10/27/world/asia/myanmar-government-facebook-rohingya.html.

20. Levin, Sam. "Facebook promised to tackle fake news. But the evidence shows it's not working." *The Guardian*. Last modified May 16, 2017. https://www.theguardian.com/technology/2017/may/16/facebook-fake-news-tools-not-working.

21. Kietzmann, Jan H., Kristopher Hermkens, Ian P. McCarthy, and Bruno S. Silvestre. "Social media? Get serious! Understanding the functional building blocks of social media." *Business Horizons* 54, no. 3 (2011): 241–251. https://doi.org/10.1016/j.bushor.2011.01.005.

22. Baccarella, Christian V., Timm F. Wagner, Jan H. Kietzmann, and Ian P. McCarthy. "Social media? It's serious! Understanding the dark side of social media." *European Management Journal* 36, no. 4 (2018): 431–438.

23. Kietzmann, Jan H., Kristopher Hermkens, Ian P. McCarthy, and Bruno S. Silvestre. "Social media? Get serious! Understanding the functional building blocks of social media." *Business Horizons* 54, no. 3 (2011): 241–251. https://doi.org/10.1016/j.bushor.2011.01.005.

24. Baccarella, Christian V., Timm F. Wagner, Jan H. Kietzmann, and Ian P. McCarthy. "Social media? It's serious! Understanding the dark side of social media." *European Management Journal* 36, no. 4 (2018): 431–438.

25. Matsa, Katerina, and Elisa Shearer. "News Use Across Social Media Platforms 2018." Pew Internet Research. Last modified September 10, 2018. https://www.journalism.org/2018/09/10/news-use-across-social-media-platforms-2018.

26. Bloomberg Government. "Transcript of Mark Zuckerberg's Senate Hearing." *Washington Post*. Last modified April 10, 2018. https://www.washingtonpost.com/news/the-switch/wp/2018/04/10/transcript-of-mark-zuckerbergs-senate-hearing/?utm_term=.bbcc9965be71.

27. Facebook. "Ad preferences." Facebook. https://www.facebook.com/ads/preferences/?entry_product=ad_settings_screen%20-%20_%3D_#_=_.

28. Hitlin, Paul, and Lee Rainey. "Facebook Algorithms and Personal Data." Pew Research Group. Last modified January 16, 2019. https://www.pewinternet.org/2019/01/16/facebook-algorithms-and-personal-data.

29. Hitlin, Paul, and Lee Rainey. "Facebook Algorithms and Personal Data." Pew Research Group. Last modified January 16, 2019. https://www.pewinternet.org/2019/01/16/facebook-algorithms-and-personal-data.

30. Palos-Sanchez, Pedro, Jose Ramon Saura, and Felix Martin-Velicia. "A study of the effects of programmatic advertising on users' concerns about privacy overtime." *Journal of Business Research* 96 (2019): 61–72.

31. Hitlin, Paul, and Lee Rainey. "Facebook Algorithms and Personal Data." Pew Research Group. Last modified January 16, 2019. https://www.pewinternet.org/2019/01/16/facebook-algorithms-and-personal-data.

32. Smith, Aaron. "Public Attitudes Toward Computer Algorithms." Pew Research Group. Last modified November 16, 2018. https://www.pewinternet.org/2018/11/16/public-attitudes-toward-computer-algorithms.

33. Phan, Anton, and Sinem Yedic. "'This post is a paid sponsorship' Do we care? How consumers perceive brands when social media influencers disclose paid partnerships." (2018).

34. Lou, Chen, and Shupei Yuan. "Influencer marketing: How message value and credibility affect consumer trust of branded content on social media," *Journal of Interactive Advertising* (2018): 1–45.

35. Scott, Megan. "An analysis of how social media influencers utilise trust-building strategies to create advocates." *Journal of Promotional Communications* 6, no. 2 (2018).

36. Atkins, Kasahra, Sophia de Zeeuw, and Samantha Baker. "Examining Social Media Panel: The Role of Influencers in the Digital Era." (2018).

37. Sanchez-Cartas, Juan Manuel, and Gonzalo Leon. "On 'Influencers' and Their Impact on the Diffusion of Digital Platforms." In *International Conference on Practical Applications of Agents and Multi-Agent Systems*, pp. 210–222. Springer, Cham, 2018.

38. Ramirez, Elizabeth. "Social media influencer as a career and how they are reshaping the way we market to Millennials/Generation Z." (2018).

39. Cheng, Xusen, Shixuan Fu, and Gert-Jan DeVreede. "Understanding trust influencing factors in social media communication: A qualitative study." *International Journal of Information Management* 37, no. 2 (April 2017): 25–35. https://doi.org/10.1016/j.ijinfomgt.2016.11.009.

40. Chien, Shu-Hua, Yin-Hueih Chen, and Jyh-Jeng Wu. "Building online transaction trust through a two-step flow of information communication." *Journal of Global Information Technology Management* 16, no. 4 (2013): 6–20. https://search-proquest-com.ezproxy.gvsu.edu/docview/1461726501?pq-origsite=summon.

41. Dewan, Sanjeev, and Jui Ramaprasad. "Social media, traditional media, and music sales." *MIS Quarterly* 38, no. 1 (March 2014): 101–121. http://ezproxy.gvsu.edu/login?url=http://search.ebscohost.com/login.aspx?direct=true&db=bsu&AN=94003208&site=ehost-live&scope=site.

42. Daniel Hunt, David Atkin, and Archana Krishnan. "The influence of computer-mediated communication apprehension on motives for facebook use." *Journal of Broadcasting & Electronic Media* 56 (2012): 2, 187–202. https://doi.org/10.1080/08838151.2012.678717.

43. Wang, Xia, Chunling Yu, and Yujie Wei. "Social media peer communication and impacts on purchase intentions: A consumer socialization framework." *Journal of Interactive Marketing* 26, no. 4 (November 2012): 198–208. https://doi.org/10.1016/j.intmar.2011.11.004.

44. Kim, Young Ae, and Muhammad A. Ahmad. "Trust, distrust and lack of confidence of users in online social media-sharing communities." *Knowledge-Based Systems* 37 (January 2013): 438–450. https://doi.org/10.1016/j.knosys.2012.09.002.

45. Eden, Colin. "Cognitive mapping and problem structuring for system dynamics model building." *System Dynamics Review* 10, nos. 2–3 (Fall 1994): 257–76. https://doi.org/10.1002/sdr.4260100212.

46. Larsen, Tor J., Fred Niederman, Moez Limayem, and Joyce Chan. "The role of modelling in achieving information systems success: UML to the rescue?" *Information Systems Journal* 19, no. 1 (January 2009): 83–117. https://doi.org.ezproxy.gvsu.edu/10.1111/j.1365-2575.2007.00272.x.

47. Cheng, Xusen, Shixuan Fu, and Gert-Jan DeVreede. "Understanding trust influencing factors in social media communication: A qualitative study." *International Journal of Information Management* 37, no. 2 (April 2017): 25–35. https://doi.org/10.1016/j.ijinfomgt.2016.11.009.

48. Cheng, Xusen, Shixuan Fu, and Gert-Jan DeVreede. "Understanding trust influencing factors in social media communication: A qualitative study." *International Journal of Information Management* 37, no. 2 (April 2017): 25–35. https://doi.org/10.1016/j.ijinfomgt.2016.11.009.

49. Cheng, Xusen, Shixuan Fu, and Gert-Jan DeVreede. "Understanding trust influencing factors in social media communication: A qualitative study." *International Journal of Information Management* 37, no. 2 (April 2017): 25–35. https://doi.org/10.1016/j.ijinfomgt.2016.11.009.

50. Warner-Sonderholm, Gillian, Andy Bertsch, Everlyn Sawe, Dwight Lee, Trina Wolfe, Josh Meyer, Josh Engle, and Uepati Normann Fatilua. "Who trusts social media?" *Computers in Human Behavior* 81 (April 2018): 303–315. https://doi.org/10.1016/j.chb.2017.12.026.

51. Phan, Anton, and Sinem Yedic. "'This post is a paid sponsorship' Do we care? How consumers perceive brands when social media influencers disclose paid partnerships." (2018). https://www.diva-portal.org/smash/record.jsf?pid=diva2%3A1221954&dswid=-5119.

52. Leslie, Fair. "Three FTC actions of interest to influencers." Federal Trade Commission. Last modified September 2017. https://www.ftc.gov/news-events/blogs/business-blog/2017/09/three-ftc-actions-interest-influencers.

53. "Federal Trade Commission 16 CFR Part 255." Federal Trade Commission. Last modified 2017. https://www.ftc.gov/sites/default/files/attachments/press-releases/ftc-publishes-final-guides-governing-endorsements-testimonials/091005revisedendorsementguides.pdf.

54. Ingram, David, and Diane Bartz. "FTC demands endorsement info from Instagram 'influencers.'" Reuters. Last modified September 13, 2017. https://www.reuters.com/article/us-usa-ftc-celebrities/ftc-demands-endorsement-info-from-instagram-influencers-idUSKCN1BO2TE.

55. "Federal Trade Commission 16 CFR Part 255." Federal Trade Commission. Last modified 2017. https://www.ftc.gov/sites/default/files/attachments/press-releases/ftc-publishes-final-guides-governing-endorsements-testimonials/091005revisedendorsementguides.pdf.

56. Sabin, Sam. "A Year after Major Actions, FTC's Influencer Marketing Guidelines Still Overlooked." Morning Consult. Last modified October 4, 2018. https://morningconsult.com/2018/10/04/a-year-later-ftcs-influencer-marketing-guidelines-still-largely-ignored.

57. Scott, Megan. "An analysis of how social media influencers utilise trust-building strategies to create advocates." *Journal of Promotional Communications* 6, no. 2 (2018).

58. Lou, Chen, and Shupei Yuan. "Influencer marketing: How message value and credibility affect consumer trust of branded content on social media." *Journal of Interactive Advertising* (2018): 1–45.

59. Bradshaw, Samantha, and Philip N. Howard. "Challenging truth and trust: A global inventory of organized social media manipulation." *The Computational Propaganda Project* (2018).

60. Siegel, Rachel. "Unilever's plan to combat the 'dark side' of social media advertising." *Washington Post.* Last modified June 19, 2018. https://www.chicagotribune.com/business/ct-biz-unilever-social-media-advertising-20180619-story.html.

61. Siegel, Rachel. "Unilever's plan to combat the 'dark side' of social media advertising." *Washington Post.* Last modified June 19, 2018. https://www

.chicagotribune.com/business/ct-biz-unilever-social-media-advertising-20180619-story.html.

62. Mitchell, Amy, Michael Barthel, and Jesse Holcomb. "Many Americans Believe Fake News Is Sowing Confusion." Pew Research Center. Last modified December 15, 2016. https://www.journalism.org/2016/12/15/many-americans-believe-fake-news-is-sowing-confusion.

63. Bradshaw, Samantha, and Philip N. Howard. "Challenging truth and trust: A global inventory of organized social media manipulation." *The Computational Propaganda Project* (2018).

64. Bradshaw, Samantha, and Philip Howard. "Troops, trolls and troublemakers: A global inventory of organized social media manipulation." (2017). https://ora.ox.ac.uk/objects/uuid:cef7e8d9-27bf-4ea5-9fd6-855209b3e1f6.

65. de Cock Buning, Madeleine. *A multidimensional approach to disinformation: Report of the independent High Level Group on fake news and online disinformation.* Publications Office of the European Union, 2018.

66. Bradshaw, Samantha, and Philip N. Howard. "Challenging truth and trust: A global inventory of organized social media manipulation." *The Computational Propaganda Project* (2018).

67. Anderson, Monica. "A Majority of Teens Have Experienced Some Form of Cyberbullying." Pew Research Group. Last modified September 27, 2018. https://www.pewinternet.org/2018/09/27/a-majority-of-teens-have-experienced-some-form-of-cyberbullying.

68. Smith, Peter K., Jess Mahdavi, Manuel Carvalho, Sonja Fisher, Shanette Russell, and Neil Tippett. "Cyberbullying: Its nature and impact in secondary school pupils." *Journal of Child Psychology and Psychiatry* 49, no. 4 (2008): 376–385.

69. Kowalski, Robin M., S. P. Limber, and P. W. Agatston. *Cyber Bullying: Bullying in the Digital Age.* Malden, MA: Blackwell Publishing, 2008.

70. Olweus, Dan. "Bullying or peer abuse at school: Facts and intervention." *Current Directions in Psychological Science* 4, no. 6 (1995): 196–200.

71. Slonje, Robert, and Peter K. Smith. "Cyberbullying: Another main type of bullying?" *Scandinavian Journal of Psychology* 49, no. 2 (2008): 147–154.

72. Bauman, Sheri. "Cyberbullying in a rural intermediate school: An exploratory study." *The Journal of Early Adolescence* 30, no. 6 (2010): 803–833.

73. Payne, Allison Ann, and Kirsten L. Hutzell. "Old wine, new bottle? Comparing interpersonal bullying and cyberbullying victimization." *Youth & Society* 49, no. 8 (2017): 1149–1178.

74. Duggan, Maeve. "Online Harassment 2017." Pew Research Center. Last modified July 11, 2017. https://www.pewinternet.org/2017/07/11/other-types-of-negative-experiences-online.

75. Dictionary.com. "Hate Speech." https://www.dictionary.com/browse/hate-speech?s=t (accessed February 17, 2020).

76. Hoffman, Beth L., Elizabeth M. Felter, Kar-Hai Chu, Ariel Shensa, Chad Hermann, Todd Wolynn, Daria Williams, and Brian A. Primack. "It's not all about autism: The emerging landscape of anti-vaccination sentiment on Facebook." *Vaccine.* https://doi.org/10.1016/j.vaccine.2019.03.003 (accessed March 27, 2019).

77. PBS News Hour. "How social media platforms reacted to viral video of New Zealand shootings." Online video. March 18, 2019. https://www.pbs.org/newshour/show/how-social-media-platforms-reacted-to-viral-video-of-new-zealand-shootings.

78. Boot, Max. "Why social media and terrorism make a perfect fit." *Washington Post.* Last modified March 16, 2019. https://www.washingtonpost.com/opinions/2019/03/16/why-social-media-terrorism-make-perfect-fit/?utm_term=.f3bc5a7b3187.

79. Lumb, David. "YouTube bans Neo-Nazi group following backlash over hate

speech." *Engadget.* Last modified February 28, 2018. https://www.engadget.com/2018/02/28/youtube-bans-neo0-nazi-group-following-backlash-over-hate-speech.

80. Hosseini, Hossein, Sreeram Kannan, Baosen Zhang, and Radha Poovendran. "Deceiving Google's perspective API built for detecting toxic comments." *arXiv preprint arXiv:1702.08138* (2017).

81. Dellinger, A. J. "Facebook will cooperate with French hate speech investigation." *Engadget.* Last modified November 12, 2018. https://www.engadget.com/2018/11/12/facebook-france-investigation-moderation-hate-speech.

82. Tarantola, Andrew. "Facebook bans 22 more pages linked to Alex Jones." *Engadget.* Last modified February 5, 2019. https://www.engadget.com/2019/02/05/facebook-bans-22-more-pages-linked-to-alex-jones.

83. Mosendz, Polly, and Gerrit DeVynck. "Facebook and Google are guilty of a failure to take ownership." *Bloomberg.* Last modified March 21, 2019. https://www.bloomberg.com/news/articles/2019-03-21/facebook-and-google-are-guilty-of-a-failure-to-take-ownership.

84. Mosendz, Polly, and Gerrit DeVynck. "Facebook and Google are guilty of a failure to take ownership." *Bloomberg.* Last modified March 21, 2019. https://www.bloomberg.com/news/articles/2019-03-21/facebook-and-google-are-guilty-of-a-failure-to-take-ownership.

85. Allcott, Hunt, Luca Braghieri, Sarah Eichmeyer, and Matthew Gentzkow. *The Welfare Effects of Social Media.* No. w25514. National Bureau of Economic Research, 2019.

86. Blackwell, David, Carrie Leaman, Rose Tramposch, Ciera Osborne, and Miriam Liss. "Extraversion, neuroticism, attachment style and fear of missing out as predictors of social media use and addiction." *Personality and Individual Differences* 116 (2017): 69–72.

87. Fromm, Jeff, and Angie Reid. *Marketing to Gen Z: The Rules for Reaching This Vast—and Very Different—Generation of Influencers.* New York: AMACOM, 2018.

88. Dhir, Amandeep, Yossiri Yossatorn, Puneet Kaur, and Sufen Chen. "Online social media fatigue and psychological wellbeing—A study of compulsive use, fear of missing out, fatigue, anxiety and depression." *International Journal of Information Management* 40 (2018): 141–152.

89. Dhir, Amandeep, Yossiri Yossatorn, Puneet Kaur, and Sufen Chen. "Online social media fatigue and psychological wellbeing—A study of compulsive use, fear of missing out, fatigue, anxiety and depression." *International Journal of Information Management* 40 (2018): 141–152.

90. "Brian Solis—Why You're Addicted to Social Media—SXSW 2018." Video file, 41:32. YouTube. Posted by SXSW, June 20, 2018. https://www.youtube.com/watch?v=aB2WUYNqFHQ&feature=youtu.be.

91. Osatuyi, Babajide, and Ofir Turel. "Tug of war between social self-regulation and habit: Explaining the experience of momentary social media addiction symptoms." *Computers in Human Behavior* 85 (2018): 95–105.

92. Lin, Liu Yi, Jaime E. Sidani, Ariel Shensa, Ana Radovic, Elizabeth Miller, Jason B. Colditz, Beth L. Hoffman, Leila M. Giles, and Brian A. Primack. "Association between social media use and depression among US young adults." *Depression and Anxiety* 33, no. 4 (2016): 323–331.

93. Kross, E., P. Verduyn, E. Demiralp, J. Park, D. S. Lee, and N. Lin. "Facebook use predicts declines in subjective well-being in young adults." *PloS One* 8 (8), e69841 (2013).

94. Robinson, Anthony, Aaron Bonnette, Krista Howard, Natalie Ceballos, Stephanie Dailey, Yongmei Lu, and Tom Grimes. "Social comparisons, social media addiction, and social interaction: An examination of specific social media behaviors related to major depressive

disorder in a millennial population." *Journal of Applied Biobehavioral Research* (2019): e12158.

95. Hawi, Nazir, and Maya Samaha. "Identifying commonalities and differences in personality characteristics of Internet and social media addiction profiles: Traits, self-esteem, and self-construal." *Behaviour & Information Technology* 38, no. 2 (2019): 110–119.

96. Kuss, Daria, and Mark Griffiths. "Social networking sites and addiction: Ten lessons learned." *International Journal of Environmental Research and Public Health* 14, no. 3 (2017): 311.

97. Salim, Saima. "How much time do you spend on social media?" Digital Information World. Last modified January 4, 2019. https://www.digitalinformation world.com/2019/01/how-much-time-do-people-spend-social-media-infographic.html#.

98. National Sleep Foundation. "How Much Sleep Do You Need." https://www.sleepfoundation.org/excessive-sleepiness/support/how-much-sleep-do-we-really-need.

99. Salim, Saima. "How much time do you spend on social media?" Digital Information World. Last modified January 4, 2019. https://www.digitalinformationworld.com/2019/01/how-much-time-do-people-spend-social-media-infographic.html#.

100. Ahmad, Irfan. "The most popular social media platforms of 2019." Digital Information World. Last modified January 1, 2019. https://www.digital informationworld.com/2019/01/most-popular-global-social-networks-apps-infographic.html.

101. Anderson, Monica, and Jingjing Jiang. "Teens, social media & technology 2018." Washington, DC: Pew Internet & American Life Project.

102. Brooks, Stoney. "Does personal social media usage affect efficiency and well-being?" *Computers in Human Behavior* 46 (2015): 26–37.

103. Page, X., P. Wisniewski, B. P. Knijnenburg, and M. Namara. "Social media's have-nots: An era of social disenfranchisement." *Internet Research* 28, no. 5 (2018): 1253–1274.

104. Page, X., P. Wisniewski, B. P. Knijnenburg, and M. Namara. "Social media's have-nots: An era of social disenfranchisement." *Internet Research* 28, no. 5 (2018): 1253–1274.

105. Fotrell, Quenten. "People spend most of their waking hours staring at screens." *Market Watch* (blog). Entry posted August 4, 2018. https://www.market watch.com/story/people-are-spending-most-of-their-waking-hours-staring-at-screens-2018-08-01.

CHAPTER 3

1. Pacauskas, Darius, Risto Rajala, Mika Westerlund, and Matti Mäntymäki. "Harnessing user innovation for social media marketing: Case study of a crowdsourced hamburger." *International Journal of Information Management* 43 (2018): 319–327.

2. Chozick, Amy. "Keeping up with the Kardashian cash flow." *The New York Times.* Last modified March 30, 2019. https://www.nytimes.com/2019/03/30/style/kardashians-interview.html.

3. Lopez, Kathryn Jean. "Adopting social media miracles." *National Review.* Last modified March 26, 2018. https://www.nationalreview.com/2018/03/facebook-social-media-can-help-families-in-crisis.

4. Laxen, Jacob. "How one Fort Collins girl gave hope to 86,000 people with blood cancers." *USA Today/Coloradoan.* Last modified September 27, 2018. https://www.coloradoan.com/story/news/2018/09/27/fort-collins-blood-cancer-leukemia-bone-marrow-transplant/1379659002.

5. Hudson, Alexander. "When does public participation make a difference? Evidence from Iceland's crowdsourced constitution." *Policy & Internet* 10, no. 2 (2018): 185–217.

6. Mezzofiore, Gianluca. "A 95-year-old World War II veteran took 4 buses to attend a march after the New Zealand mosque attacks." CNN. Last modified March 27, 2019. https://www.cnn.com/2019/03/27/asia/world-war-ii-veteran-racism-march-new-zealand-trnd/index.html.

7. Walker-Ford, Mark. "This is what happens in an Internet minute in 2019 [Infographic]." *Social Media Today.* Last modified March 29, 2019. https://www.socialmediatoday.com/news/this-is-what-happens-in-an-internet-minute-in-2019-infographic/551391.

8. Kawachi, Ichiro, and Lisa F. Berkman. "Social ties and mental health." *Journal of Urban Health* 78, no. 3 (2001): 458–467.

9. Cohen, Sheldon. "Social relationships and health." *American Psychologist* 59, no. 8 (2004): 676.

10. House, James S., Karl R. Landis, and Debra Umberson. "Social relationships and health." *Science* 241, no. 4865 (1988): 540–545.

11. Cacioppo, John T., and Stephanie Cacioppo. "Social relationships and health: The toxic effects of perceived social isolation." *Social and Personality Psychology Compass* 8, no. 2 (2014): 58–72.

12. Porter, Constance Elise, and Naveen Donthu. "Cultivating trust and harvesting value in virtual communities." *Management Science* 54, no. 1 (2008): 113–128.

13. Shen, Yung-Cheng, Chun-Yao Huang, Chia-Hsien Chu, and Hui-Chun Liao. "Virtual community loyalty: An interpersonal-interaction perspective." *International Journal of Electronic Commerce* 15, no. 1 (2010): 49–73.

14. de Valck, Kristine, Gerrit H. van Bruggen, and Berend Wierenga. "Virtual communities: A marketing perspective." *Decision Support Systems* 47, no. 3 (2009): 185–203.

15. Lu, Yaobin, Ling Zhao, and Bin Wang. "From virtual community members to C2C e-commerce buyers: Trust in virtual communities and its effect on consumers' purchase intention." *Electronic Commerce Research and Applications* 9, no. 4 (2010): 346–360.

16. Triandis, H. C. "Nebraska symposium on motivation, 1979: Beliefs, attitudes and values." (1980).

17. Douglas, Jack D. *FIRO: A Three-Dimensional Theory of Interpersonal Behavior.* Vol. 66, University of Chicago Press, 1961.

18. Lerner, Arthur. "Firo: A three-dimensional theory of interpersonal behavior." *Personnel Journal (Pre-1986)* 37, no. 10 (1959): 388.

19. Li, Honglei, and Kun Chang Lee. "An interpersonal relationship framework for virtual community participation psychology: From covert to overt process." *Social Science Computer Review* 31, no. 6 (2013): 703–724.

20. Rheingold, Howard Lee. "Virtual community." *Encyclopædia Britannica.* Encyclopædia Britannica, Inc., April 13, 2018. https://www.britannica.com/topic/virtual-community.

21. Li, Honglei, and Kun Chang Lee. "An interpersonal relationship framework for virtual community participation psychology: From covert to overt process." *Social Science Computer Review* 31, no. 6 (2013): 703–724.

22. Li, Honglei, and Kun Chang Lee. "An interpersonal relationship framework for virtual community participation psychology: From covert to overt process." *Social Science Computer Review* 31, no. 6 (2013): 703–724.

23. Clark, Jenna L., Sara B. Algoe, and Melanie C. Green. "Social network sites and well-being: The role of social connection." *Current Directions in Psychological Science* 27, no. 1 (February 2018): 32–37. https://doi.org/10.1177/0963721417730833.

24. Wellman, Barry. "Computer networks as social networks." *Science* 293, no. 5537 (2001): 2031–2034.

25. Bourdieu, Pierre, and Richard Nice. *Outline of a Theory of Practice.* Vol. 16. Cambridge: Cambridge University Press, 1977.

26. Poteyeva, Margarita. "Social capital." *Encyclopædia Britannica.* Encyclopædia Britannica, Inc., December 17, 2018. https://www.britannica.com/topic/social-capital.

27. Qi, Jiayin, Emmanuel Monod, Binxing Fang, and Shichang Deng. "Theories of social media: Philosophical foundations." *Engineering* 4, no. 1 (2018): 94–102.

28. Lin, Nan. "Building a network theory of social capital." In *Social Capital*, pp. 3–28. Routledge, 2017. https://www.taylorfrancis.com/books/e/9781315129457/chapters/10.4324/9781315129457-1.

29. "Social Connection." Wikipedia. Wikimedia Foundation, February 14, 2020. https://en.wikipedia.org/wiki/Social_connection.

30. Ellison, N. B., C. Steinfield, and C. Lampe. (2007). "The benefits of Facebook "friends": Social capital and college students' use of online social network sites." *Journal of Computer-Mediated Communication,* 12: 1143–1168. https://doi.org/10.1111/j.1083–6101.2007.00367.x.

31. Clark, Jenna L., Sara B. Algoe, and Melanie C. Green. "Social network sites and well-being: The role of social connection." *Current Directions in Psychological Science* 27, no. 1 (February 2018): 32–37. https://doi.org/10.1177/0963721417730833.

32. Liu, C.-Y., and C.-P. Yu. (2013). "Can Facebook use induce well-being?" *Cyberpsychology, Behavior, and Social Networking* 16: 674–678. https://doi.org/10.1089/cyber.2012.0301.

33. Ahn, D., and D.-H. Shin. (2013). "Is the social use of media for seeking connectedness or for avoiding social isolation? Mechanisms underlying media use and subjective well-being." *Computers in Human Behavior* 29: 2453–2462. https://doi.org/10.1016/j.chb.2012.12.022.

34. Deters, F. G., and M. R. Mehl. (2013). Does posting Facebook status updates increase or decrease loneliness? An online social networking experiment. *Social Psychological & Personality Science* 4: 579–586. https://doi.org/10.1177/1948550612469233.

35. Burke, Moira, and Robert E. Kraut. "The relationship between Facebook use and well-being depends on communication type and tie strength." *Journal of Computer-Mediated Communication* 21, no. 4 (2016): 265–281.

36. Clark, Jenna L., Sara B. Algoe, and Melanie C. Green. "Social network sites and well-being: The role of social connection." *Current Directions in Psychological Science* 27, no. 1 (February 2018): 32–37. https://doi.org/10.1177/0963721417730833.

37. Procidano, M., and K. Heller. (1983) Measures of perceived social support from friends and from family: Three validation studies. *American Journal of Community Psychology* 11: 1–24.

38. Appel, L., P. Dadlani, and M. Dwyer (2014) Testing the validity of social capital measures in the study of information and communication technologies. *Information, Communication & Society* 17: 398–416.

39. Goulet LS. *Friends in All the Right Places: Social Resources and Geography in the Age of Social Network Sites.* Philadelphia, PA: Annenberg School for Communication, University of Pennsylvania, 2012.

40. Hampton, K. N., L. S. Goulet, and L. Rainie. *Social Networking Sites and Our Lives: How People's Trust, Personal Relationships, and Civic and Political Involvement Are Connected to Their Use of Social Networking Sites and Other Technologies.* Washington, DC: Pew Research Center, 2011.

41. Oh, Sanghee, and Sue Yeon Syn. "Motivations for sharing information and social support in social media: A comparative analysis of Facebook, Twitter, Delicious, YouTube, and Flickr." *Journal of the Association for Information Science and Technology* 66, no. 10 (2015): 2045–2060.

42. Lin, Nan, Karen S. Cook, and Ronald S. Burt (eds.). *Social Capital: Theory and Research.* Transaction Publishers, 2001.

43. Lin, Nan. "Building a network theory of social capital." In *Social Capital*, pp. 3–28.

Routledge, 2017. https://www.taylorfrancis
.com/books/e/9781315129457/
chapters/10.4324/9781315129457-1.

44. Hampton, K. N., C. J. Lee, and E. J. Her.
How new media afford network diversity:
Direct and mediated access to social
capital through participation in local
social settings. *New Media & Society* 13
(2011): 1031–1049.

45. Hampton, K. N., L. Sessions, and E. Ja
Her. Core networks, social isolation,
and new media: Internet and mobile
phone use, network size, and diversity.
Information, Communication & Society
14 (2011): 130–155.

46. Lu, Weixu, and Keith N. Hampton. "Beyond
the power of networks: Differentiating network structure from social media affordances for perceived social support."
New Media & Society 19, no. 6 (June
2017): 861–879. https://doi.org/10.1177/
1461444815621514.

47. Olapic. "How user-generated content drives
engagement & purchase decisions."
Last modified 2017. www.olapic.com/
resources/user-generated-content-drives-
engagement-purchase-decisions.

48. "Earned Media." Wikipedia. Wikimedia
Foundation, October 20, 2019. https://en
.wikipedia.org/wiki/Earned_media.

49. Olapic. "How user-generated content
drives engagement & purchase decisions."
Last modified 2017. www.olapic.com/
resources/user-generated-content-drives-
engagement-purchase-decisions.

50. Halliday, Sue Vaux. "User-generated content
about brands: Understanding its creators
and consumers." *Journal of Business
Research* 69, no. 1 (2016): 137–144.

51. Chari, Simos, George Christodoulides,
Caterina Presi, Jil Wenhold, and John
P. Casaletto. "Consumer trust in user⊠
generated brand recommendations on
Facebook." *Psychology & Marketing* 33,
no. 12 (2016): 1071–1081.

52. Ryan, Damian. *Understanding Digital
Marketing: Marketing Strategies for
Engaging the Digital Generation.* Kogan
Page Publishers, 2016.

53. Hackley, Chris, and Rungpaka Amy
Hackley. *Advertising and Promotion.*
Sage, 2017.

54. Olapic. "How user-generated content
drives engagement & purchase decisions"
Last modified 2017. www.olapic.com/
resources/user-generated-content-drives-
engagement-purchase-decisions.

55. Olapic. "How user-generated content
drives engagement & purchase decisions."
Last modified 2017. www.olapic.com/
resources/user-generated-content-drives-
engagement-purchase-decisions.

56. Knoll, Johannes. "Advertising in social
media: A review of empirical evidence."
International Journal of Advertising 35,
no. 2 (March 2016): 266–300. https://doi
.org/10.1080/02650487.2015.1021898.

57. Stieglitz, Stefan, and Linh Dang-Xuan.
"Emotions and information diffusion in
social media—sentiment of microblogs
and sharing behavior." *Journal of
Management Information Systems* 29,
no. 4 (2013): 217–248.

58. Yagan, Osman, Dajun Qian, Junshan Zhang,
and Douglas Cochran. "Conjoining speeds
up information diffusion in overlaying
social-physical networks." *IEEE Journal on
Selected Areas in Communications* 31, no.
6 (2013): 1038–1048.

59. Iyengar, Raghuram, Christophe Van den
Bulte, and Thomas W. Valente. "Opinion
leadership and social contagion in new
product diffusion." *Marketing Science*
30, no. 2 (2011): 195–212.

60. Stewart, Margaret C., and Cory Young.
"Revisiting STREMII: Social media
crisis communication during Hurricane
Matthew." *Journal of International Crisis
and Risk Communication Research* 1, no.
2 (2018): 5.

61. Alexander, David E. "Social media
in disaster risk reduction and crisis
management." *Science and Engineering
Ethics* 20, no. 3 (2014): 717–733.

62. Stieglitz, Stefan, and Linh Dang-Xuan.
"Emotions and information diffusion in
social media—sentiment of microblogs
and sharing behavior." *Journal of*

Management Information Systems 29, no. 4 (2013): 217–248.

63. Dong, Rongsheng, Libing Li, Qingpeng Zhang, and Guoyong Cai. "Information diffusion on social media during natural disasters." *IEEE Transactions on Computational Social Systems* 5, no. 1 (2018): 265–276.

64. Kim, Jooho, Juhee Bae, and Makarand Hastak. "Emergency information diffusion on online social media during storm Cindy in US." *International Journal of Information Management* 40 (2018): 153–165.

65. Imran, Muhammad, Carlos Castillo, Fernando Diaz, and Sarah Vieweg. "Processing social media messages in mass emergency: Survey summary." In *Companion of the The Web Conference 2018 on The Web Conference 2018*, pp. 507–511. International World Wide Web Conferences Steering Committee, 2018.

66. Jurgens, Manon, and Ira Helsloot. "The effect of social media on the dynamics of (self) resilience during disasters: A literature review." *Journal of Contingencies and Crisis Management* 26, no. 1 (2018): 79–88.

67. Yardley, Elizabeth, Adam George, Thomas Lynes, David Wilson, and Emma Kelly. "What's the deal with 'websleuthing'? News media representations of amateur detectives in networked spaces." *Crime, Media, Culture* 14, no. 1 (2018): 81–109.

68. Zimmer, Franziska, Katrin Scheibe, and Wolfgang G. Stock. "A model for information behavior research on social live streaming services (SLSSs)." In *International Conference on Social Computing and Social Media*, pp. 429–448. Springer, Cham, 2018.

69. Artwick, Claudette G. *Social Media Livestreaming: Design for Disruption?* Routledge, 2018.

70. Chung, Deborah S., Seungahn Nah, and Masahiro Yamamoto. "Conceptualizing citizen journalism: US news editors' views." *Journalism* 19, no. 12 (2018): 1694–1712.

71. Bruns, Axel. *Gatewatching and News Curation: Journalism, Social Media, and the Public Sphere*. Peter Lang, 2018.

72. Hermida, Alfred. "The existential predicament when journalism moves beyond journalism." *Journalism* 20, no. 1 (2019): 177–180.

73. Hirst, Martin. *Navigating Social Journalism: A Handbook for Media Literacy and Citizen Journalism*. Routledge, 2018.

74. Zubiaga, Arkaitz. "Mining social media for newsgathering." *arXiv preprint arXiv:1804.03540* (2018).

75. "Newsgathering." Dictionary.com. https://www.dictionary.com/browse/newsgathering?s=t (accessed February 17, 2020).

76. Bergström, Annika, and Maria Jervelycke Belfrage. "News in social media: Incidental consumption and the role of opinion leaders." *Digital Journalism* 6, no. 5 (2018): 583–598.

77. Zhou, Xinyi, Reza Zafarani, Kai Shu, and Huan Liu. "Fake news: Fundamental theories, detection strategies and challenges." In *Proceedings of the Twelfth ACM International Conference on Web Search and Data Mining*, pp. 836–837. ACM, 2019.

78. Hornmoen, Harald, Klas Backholm, Anna Grøndahl Larsen, Joachim Högväg, Julian Ausserhofer, Elsebeth Frey, and Gudrun Reimerth. "Crises, rumours and reposts: Journalists' social media content gathering and verification practices in breaking news situations." *Media and Communication* 5, no. 2 (2017): 67–76.

79. Shannon, C. E. "A mathematical theory of communication." *The Bell System Technical Journal* 27, no. 4 (1948): 623–656.

80. "Shannon and Weaver's Model." Oxford Reference, November 3, 2019. https://www.oxfordreference.com/view/10.1093/oi/authority.20110803100459436.

81. Westley, Bruce H., and Malcolm S. MacLean. "A conceptual model for

communications research." *Educational Technology Research and Development* 3, no. 1 (1955): 3–12.

82. DeFleur, Melvin Lawrence, Patricia Kearney, and Timothy G. Plax. *Mastering Communication in Contemporary America: Theory, Research, and Practice.* Mayfield Publishing Company, 1993.

83. Bever, Lindsey. "H&M apologizes for showing Black child wearing a 'monkey in the jungle' sweatshirt." *Washington Post.* Last modified January 18, 2018. https://www.washingtonpost.com/news/business/wp/2018/01/08/hm-apologizes-for-showing-black-child-wearing-a-monkey-in-the-jungle-sweatshirt/?noredirect=on&utm_term=.e293fe6039f1.

84. Holecombe, Madeline. "Gucci apologizes after social media users say sweater resembles blackface." *CNN* (blog). Entry posted February 8, 2018. https://www.cnn.com/2019/02/07/us/gucci-blackface-sweater/index.html.

85. Datafloq. "A Short History of Big Data." Last modified January 6, 2019. https://datafloq.com/read/big-data-history/239.

86. Ghani, Norjihan Abdul, Suraya Hamid, Ibrahim Abaker, Targio Hashem, and Ejaz Ahmed. "Social media big data analytics: A survey." *Computers in Human Behavior* (2018).

87. Liu, Bing. *Sentiment Analysis: Mining Opinions, Sentiments, and Emotions.* Cambridge University Press, 2015.

88. Ghani, Norjihan Abdul, Suraya Hamid, Ibrahim Abaker, Targio Hashem, and Ejaz Ahmed. "Social media big data analytics: A survey." *Computers in Human Behavior* (2018).

89. Gama, João, Indrė Žliobaitė, Albert Bifet, Mykola Pechenizkiy, and Abdelhamid Bouchachia. "A survey on concept drift adaptation." *ACM Computing Surveys (CSUR)* 46, no. 4 (2014): 44.

90. Lim, Sunghoon, Conrad S. Tucker, and Soundar Kumara. "An unsupervised machine learning model for discovering latent infectious diseases using social media data." *Journal of Biomedical Informatics* 66 (2017): 82–94.

91. Jansson, Patrick, and Shuhua Liu. "Distributed representation, LDA topic modeling and deep learning for emerging named entity recognition from social media." In *Proceedings of the 3rd Workshop on Noisy User-Generated Text*, pp. 154–159. 2017. https://www.aclweb.org/anthology/W17-4420.pdf.

92. Nguyen, Dat Tien, Shafiq Joty, Muhammad Imran, Hassan Sajjad, and Prasenjit Mitra. "Applications of online deep learning for crisis response using social media information." *arXiv preprint arXiv:1610.01030* (2016).

93. Cambria, Erik, Dheeraj Rajagopal, Daniel Olsher, and Dipankar Das. "Big social data analysis." *Big Data Computing* 13 (2013): 401–414.

94. Cohen, Sheldon, and S. Leonard Syme. "Issues in the study and application of social support." *Social Support and Health* 3 (1985): 3–22.

95. Cohen, Sheldon, Benjamin H. Gottlieb, and Lynn G. Underwood. "Social relationships and health: Challenges for measurement and intervention." *Advances in Mind-Body Medicine* (2001).

96. Buechel, Eva C., and Jonah Berger. "Microblogging and the value of undirected communication." *Journal of Consumer Psychology* 28, no. 1 (2018): 40–55.

97. Buechel, Eva C., and Jonah Berger. "Microblogging and the value of undirected communication." *Journal of Consumer Psychology* 28, no. 1 (2018): 40–55.

98. Buechel, Eva C., and Jonah Berger. "Microblogging and the value of undirected communication." *Journal of Consumer Psychology* 28, no. 1 (2018): 40–55.

99. Grieve, Rachel, Michaelle Indian, Kate Witteveen, G. Anne Tolan, and Jessica Marrington. "Face-to-face or Facebook: Can social connectedness be derived online?" *Computers in Human Behavior* 29, no. 3 (2013): 604–609.

100. Weinstein, Emily. "The social media see-saw: Positive and negative influences on adolescents' affective well-being." *New Media & Society* 20, no. 10 (2018): 3597–3623.

101. Krishen, Anjala S., Orie Berezan, Shaurya Agarwal, and Pushkin Kachroo. "The generation of virtual needs: Recipes for satisfaction in social media networking." *Journal of Business Research* 69, no. 11 (2016): 5248–5254.

102. Wenninger, Helena, Hanna Krasnova, and Peter Buxmann. "Activity matters: Investigating the influence of Facebook on life satisfaction of teenage users." (2014). https://aisel.aisnet.org/ecis2014/proceedings/track01/13.

103. Ong, Chorng-Shyong, Shu-Chen Chang, and Shwn-Meei Lee. "Development of WebHapp: Factors in predicting user perceptions of website-related happiness." *Journal of Business Research* 68, no. 3 (2015): 591–598.

104. Ong, Chorng-Shyong, Shu-Chen Chang, and Shwn-Meei Lee. "Development of WebHapp: Factors in predicting user perceptions of website-related happiness." *Journal of Business Research* 68, no. 3 (2015): 591–598.

105. Wu, Jiao, and Mark Srite. "Benign Envy, Social Media, and Culture" (2015). DIGIT 2015 Proceedings. 1. http://aisel.aisnet.org/digit2015/1

106. Fuller, Kristen, MD. "JOMO: The joy of missing out." *Psychology Today.* Last modified July 26, 2018. https://www.psychologytoday.com/us/blog/happiness-is-state-mind/201807/jomo-the-joy-missing-out.

CHAPTER 4

1. Potter, W. James. "Synthesizing a working definition of 'mass' media." *Review of Communication Research* 1, no. 1 (2013): 1–30. https://doi.org/10.12840/issn.2255-4165_2013_01.01_001 (accessed August 19, 2019).

2. Wright, C. R. *Mass Communication: A Sociological Perspective,* 3rd ed. New York: Random House, 1986.

3. Glynn, Carroll J., Susan Herbst, Mark Lindeman, Garrett J. O'Keefe, and Robert Y. Shapiro. *Public Opinion,* 3rd ed. Boulder, CO: Westview Press, 2016.

4. Kerbel, Matthew Robert. *Remote and Controlled: Media Politics in a Cynical Age.* Routledge, 2018.

5. Reporters without Borders. "Our values." Last modified 2019. https://rsf.org/en/our-values.

6. Ryerson, William. "The effectiveness of entertainment mass media in changing behavior." Unpublished manuscript. Population Media Center, 2008. http://www.populationmedia.org/wp-content/uploads/2008/02/effectiveness-of-entertainment-education-112706.pdf (accessed April 30, 2020).

7. Shoemaker, Pamela J., and Tim P. Vos. *Gatekeeping Theory.* London, United Kingdom: Routledge, 2009.

8. McCombs, Maxwell. *Setting the Agenda: Mass Media and Public Opinion,* 2nd ed. Cambridge, United Kingdom: Polity Press, 2014.

9. McCombs, Maxwell E., and Donald L. Shaw. "The agenda-setting function of mass media." *Public Opinion Quarterly* 36, no. 2 (Summer 1972): 176–187. https://doi.org/10.1086/267990.

10. Ibid., 3.

11. Byerly, Carolyn M., and Karen Ross. *Women and Media: A Critical Introduction.* Hoboken, NJ: Wiley-Blackwell, 2006.

12. Ravelry. "About." https://www.ravelry.com/about (accessed September 30, 2020).

13. McCracken, Grant. "Who is the celebrity endorser? Cultural foundations of the endorsement process." *Journal of Consumer Research* 16, no. 3 (December 1989): 310–321.

14. Deloitte, Comp. *The Deloitte Global Millennial Survey 2019.* San Francisco, CA: Deloitte, 2019. https://www2

.deloitte.com/us/en/insights/topics/talent/deloitte-millennial-survey.html.

15. Bor, Kristen. *Bearfoot Theory Media Kit.* Salt Lake City, UT: Bearfoot Theory, 2018.

16. Ibid., 2.

17. Ibid., 3.

18. Rothfeld, Lindsay. "18 Quirky, Niche Businesses." *Mashable* (blog). Entry posted June 6, 2014. https://mashable.com/2014/06/06/niche-businesses/.

CHAPTER 5

1. Miller, Grace. "Positively Good Marketing: Warby Parker." Campaign Monitor. Last modified December 12, 2018. https://www.campaignmonitor.com/blog/email-marketing/2018/12positively-good-marketing-warby-parker (accessed September 9, 2019).

2. Kerpen, Dave. "How Strategic Communications Puts Your Company Ahead of the Pack." Inc. (blog). https://www.inc.com/dave-kerpen/how-strategic-communications-puts-your-company-ahead-of-the-pack.html (accessed September 9, 2019).

3. Ibid.

4. Hootsuite. Global Digital Report, 2019. https://p.widencdn.net/kqy7ii/Digital2019-Report-en.

5. Ibid.

6. Ibid., 19.

7. Grunig, L., J. Grunig, and D. Dozier. *Excellent Organizations and Effective Organizations: A Study of Communication Management in Three Countries.* Mahwah, NJ: Lawrence Erlbaum, 2002.

8. Amatulli, Jenna. "Gucci Apologizes for Black Balaclava Sweater That Resembles Blackface Caricatures." HuffPost, February 7, 2019. https://www.huffpost.com/entry/gucci-apologizes-for-black-balaclava-top-that-resembled-blackface-caricatures_n_5c5bb5cbe4b09293b20b6a0b (accessed September 9, 2019).

9. Interbrand. "Q&A with Marco Bizzarri, President and CEO, Gucci." https://www.interbrand.com/best-brands/best-global-brands/2017/ranking/gucci/qa-with-marco-bizzarri-president-and-ceo-gucci (accessed 2016).

10. Twaronite, Karen. "The surprising power of simply asking coworkers how they're doing." *Harvard Business Review.* Last modified February 28, 2019. https://hbr.org/2019/02/the-surprising-power-of-simply-asking-coworkers-how-theyre-doing.

11. The Radiacati Group, Inc. Email Statistics Report, 2015–2019. https://www.radicati.com/wp/wp-content/uploads/2015/02/Email-Statistics-Report-2015-2019-Executive-Summary.pdf.

12. International Association of Business Communicators. "Are Email Open Rates Misleading Your Internal Communications Team?" IABC World Conference. https://wc.iabc.com/are-email-open-rates-misleading-your-internal-communications-team.

13. Twaronite, Karen. "The surprising power of simply asking coworkers how they're doing." *Harvard Business Review.* Last modified February 28, 2019. https://hbr.org/2019/02/the-surprising-power-of-simply-asking-coworkers-how-theyre-doing.

14. Ewing, Michelle, Linjuan Rita Men, and Julie O'Neill. "Using social media to engage employees: Insights from internal communication managers." *International Journal of Strategic Communication* 13, no. 2 (2019): 110–132. https://doi.org/libezproxy2.syr.edu/10.1080/553118X.2019.1575830.

15. Hutchinson, Andrew. "The Power of the Employee Influencer [Infographic]." Social Media Today. Last modified July 9, 2019. https://www.socialmediatoday.com/news/the-power-of-the-employee-influencer-infographic/558304.

16. Edelman. *Edelman Trust Barometer Global Report.* Research Report No. 19. New York: Edelman, 2019.

17. The L'Oréal Group. "Key Figures." https://www.loreal.com/group/our-activities/key-figures.

18. Simpson, Jack. "How L'Oréal Uses Social Media to Increase Employee Engagement." Econsultancy (blog). Entry posted October 22, 2015. https://econsultancy.com/how-l-oreal-uses-social-media-to-increase-employee-engagement.

19. Fournier, Susan, and Jill Avery. "The uninvited brand." *Business Horizons* 54, no. 3 (2011): 193–207. https://doi.org/10.1016/j.bushor.2011.01.001.

20. Freaker. "Story Time." FreakerUSA.com. https://www.freakerusa.com/pages/story.

21. Cone Communications. 2017 Cone Communications CSR Study. Boston, MA: Cone Communications, 2017.

22. Ibid.

23. Sen, Sankar, C. B. Bhattacharya, and Daniel Korschun. "The role of corporate social responsibility in strengthening multiple stakeholder relationships: A field experiment." *Journal of the Academy of Marketing Science* 34, no. 2 (Spring 2006): 158–166.

24. Chernev, Alexander, and Sean Blair. "Doing well by doing good: The benevolent halo of corporate social responsibility." *Journal of Consumer Research* 41, no. 6 (2015): 1412–1425.

25. Eichholtz, P., N. Kok, and J. M. Quigley. "Doing well by doing good? Green office buildings." *The American Economic Review* 100, no. 5 (2010):2492–2509.

26. The LEGO® Group. "Policies and Reporting." https://www.lego.com/en-us/aboutus/responsibility/our-policies-and-reporting.

27. Pride in London. "Pride in London Announces Family Area as Space for LGBT+ Youth and Families." Last modified June 25, 2019. https://prideinlondon.org/news-and-views/pride-in-london-announces-family-area-as-space-for-lgbt-youth-and-families.

28. Ben & Jerry's. "A New Flavor "For The People"—Literally! Join Us for the Big Reveal." Last modified May 9, 2016. https://www.benjerry.com/whats-new/2016/democracy-flavor-launch-event.

29. B the Change. "Activism as Brand Identity: Part of Ben & Jerry's Flavor and a Lesson for Other Mission-Driven Companies." Last modified December 13, 2016. https://bthechange.com/activism-as-brand-identity-part-of-ben-jerrys-flavor-and-a-lesson-for-other-mission-driven-companies-cf7d61d0860e.

30. Admati, Anat R., Paul Pfleiderer, and Josef Zechner. "Large shareholder activism, risk sharing, and financial market equilibrium." *Journal of Political Economy* 102, no. 6 (1994): 1097–1130.

31. Ibid.

32. Thompson, Gareth. "Social gains from the public relations voice of activist investors: The case of Herbalife and Pershing Square Capital Management." *Public Relations Review* 44, no. 4 (2018): 481–489.

33. The Digital Hyve. "About." Last modified July 10, 2019. https://www.digitalhyve.com.

34. Dietrich, G. *Communication and Reputation Management in the Digital Age*. Que Publishing: Pearson Education, 2014.

35. Casper. "About." Last modified 2019. https://casper.com/about.

36. Red Antler. "Casper Case Study." https://redantler.com/work/casper.

CHAPTER 6

1. Carroll, Dave. YouTube. https://www.youtube.com/watch?time_continue=1&v=5YGc4zOqozo. Last modified 2009. https://www.youtube.com/watch?time_continue=1&v=5YGc4zOqozo (accessed May 12, 2019).

2. Ayres, Chris. "Revenge is best served cold—On YouTube: How a broken guitar became a smash hit." *The Times Online*

UK (UK), July 22, 2009. https://www
.thetimes.co.uk/article/revenge-is-best-
served-cold-on-youtube-2dhbsh6jtp5
(accessed August 10, 2019).

3. Stoll, John. "Did Twitter help ground the
Boeing 737 MAX? Corporate executives
must respond in real time or risk being
overrun by criticism." *The Wall Street
Journal*. Last modified March 15, 2019.
https://www.wsj.com/articles/ill-tweet-
to-that-social-media-gives-consumers-
newfound-reach-11552667731
(accessed June 13, 2019).

4. Root, Al. "What Boeing stock shows
about managing risk in a social media
world." *Barron's*. Last modified March 28,
2019. https://www.barrons.com/articles/
what-boeing-stock-shows-about-
managing-risk-in-a-social-media-world-
51553767200 (accessed July 12, 2019).

5. "Twitter storm | Definition of Twitter
storm in English by Oxford Dictionaries."
Oxford Dictionaries | English. https://
en.oxforddictionaries.com/definition/
twitter_storm.

6. Bedrock. "We screwed up …" Facebook.
Last modified July 23, 2017. https://
www.facebook.com/BedrockDetroit/
posts (accessed October 1, 2019).

7. Coombs, W. Timothy. "Choosing the right
words: The development of guidelines
for the selection of the 'appropriate'
crisis-response strategies." *Management
Communication Quarterly* 8, no. 4 (1995):
447–476.

8. Coombs, W. Timothy. "Crisis communi-
cation and social media." Essential
Knowledge Project, Institute for Public
Relations (2008).

9. Fearn-Banks, Kathleen. *Crisis Communi-
cations: A Casebook Approach*, 3rd ed.
Taylor & Francis Group, 2014. ProQuest
Ebook.

10. Fearn-Banks, Kathleen. *Crisis Communi-
cations: A Casebook Approach*, 3rd ed.
Taylor & Francis Group, 2014. ProQuest
Ebook.

11. Edelman Intelligence. "Edelman trust
barometer global report." *Edelman*. Last
modified January 20, 2019. https://www

.edelman.com/sites/g/files/aatuss191/
files/2019-02_2019_Edelman_Trust_
Barometer_Global_Report.pdf (accessed
August 1, 2019).

12. Edelman Intelligence. "2016 Edelman
trust barometer." *Edelman*. Last modified
January 16, 2016. https://www.edelman
.com/research/2016-edelman-trust-
barometer (accessed August 1, 2019).

13. Edelman Intelligence. "2017 Edelman
trust barometer." *Edelman*. Last modified
January 20, 2017. https://www.edelman
.com/research/2017-edelman-trust-
barometer (accessed August 1, 2019).

14. Edelman Intelligence. "2018 Edelman
trust barometer." *Edelman*. Last modified
January 21, 2018. https://www.edelman
.com/research/2018-edelman-trust-
barometer (accessed August 1, 2019).

15. Edelman Intelligence. "2019 Edelman
trust barometer." *Edelman*. Last modified
January 20, 2019. https://www.edelman
.com/trust-barometer (accessed August
1, 2019).

16. Institute for Public Relations. "Crisis
management and communications."
Institute for Public Relations. Last
modified October 30, 2007. https://
instituteforpr.org/crisis-management-and-
communications (accessed May 1, 2019).

17. Frandsen, Finn, and Winni Johansen.
*Organizational Crisis Communication: A
Multivocal Approach*. Sage, 2016.

18. Fearn-Banks, Kathleen. *Crisis Communi-
cations: A Casebook Approach*, 3rd ed.
Taylor & Francis Group, 2014. ProQuest
Ebook.

19. Institute for Public Relations. "Crisis
management and communications."
Institute for Public Relations. Last
modified October 30, 2007. https://
instituteforpr.org/crisis-management-
and-communications (accessed May 1,
2019).

20. Frandsen, Finn, and Winni Johansen.
*Organizational Crisis Communication: A
Multivocal Approach*. Sage, 2016.

21. Fearn-Banks, Kathleen. *Crisis Communications: A Casebook Approach*, 3rd ed.

Taylor & Francis Group, 2014. ProQuest Ebook.

22. Barton, Laurence. *Crisis in Organizations,* 2nd ed. Cincinnati, Ohio: South-Western College Publishing, 2001.

23. Barton, Laurence. *Crisis in Organizations.* Cincinnati, OH: South-Western, 1993.

24. Barnhart, Brent. "Benefits of Social Media." *Sprout Social* (blog). Entry posted July 15, 2019. https://sprout-social.com/insights/benefits-of-social-media (accessed October 2, 2019).

25. Newberry, Christina, and Sarah Dawley. "How to manage a social media crisis: A practical guide for brands." *Hootsuite.* Last modified February 6, 2019. https://blog.hootsuite.com/social-media-crisis-management (accessed September 27, 2019).

26. Culp, Ron (ed.). *The New Rules of Crisis Management,* 2nd ed. Vol. 2. In Case of Crisis. RockDove Solutions, 2018. PDF.

27. Culp, Ron (ed.). *The New Rules of Crisis Management,* 2nd ed. Vol. 2. In Case of Crisis. RockDove Solutions, 2018. PDF.

28. Newberry, Christina, and Sarah Dawley. "How to manage a social media crisis: A practical guide for brands." *Hootsuite.* Last modified February 6, 2019. https://blog.hootsuite.com/social-media-crisis-management (accessed September 27, 2019).

29. Coombs, W. Timothy. "Choosing the right words: The development of guidelines for the selection of the 'appropriate' crisis-response strategies." *Management Communication Quarterly* 8, no. 4 (1995): 447–476.

30. Page, Tyler G. "Beyond attribution: Building new measures to explain the reputation threat posed by crisis." *Public Relations Review* 45, no. 1 (2019): 138–152.

31. Mason, Alicia. "Media frames and crisis events: Understanding the impact on corporate reputations, responsibility attributions, and negative affect." *International Journal of Business Communication* 56, no. 3 (2019): 414–431.

32. Zamani, Efpraxia D., George M. Giaglis, and Anna E. Kasimati. "Public relations crisis and social media: An investigation into extant and prospective consumers' perceptions through the lens of attribution theory." *Journal of Theoretical and Applied Electronic Commerce Research* 10, no. 2 (2015): 32–52.

33. Wei, Jiuchang, Zhe Ouyang, and Haipeng (Allan) Chen. "Well known or well liked? The effects of corporate reputation on firm value at the onset of a corporate crisis." *Strategic Management Journal* 38, no. 10 (2017): 2103–2120.

34. Jin, Yan, and Brooke Fisher Liu. "The blog-mediated crisis communication model: Recommendations for responding to influential external blogs." *Journal of Public Relations Research* 22, no. 4 (2010): 429–455.

35. Austin, Lucinda, Brooke Fisher Liu, and Yan Jin. "How audiences seek out crisis information: Exploring the social-mediated crisis communication model." *Journal of Applied Communication Research* 40, no. 2 (2012): 188–207.

36. Bates, L., and C. Callison. (2008, August). "Effect of Company Affiliation on Credibility in the Blogosphere." Paper presented at the Association for Education in Journalism and Mass Communication Conference, Chicago.

37. Cheng, Yang. "How social media is changing crisis communication strategies: Evidence from the updated literature." *Journal of Contingencies and Crisis Management* 26, no. 1 (2018): 58–68.

38. Timothy Coombs, W., and Sherry Jean Holladay. "How publics react to crisis communication efforts: Comparing crisis response reactions across sub-arenas." *Journal of Communication Management* 18, no. 1 (2014): 40–57.

39. Baer, Jay, and Lauren Teague. "Don't be scared, be prepared: How to manage a social media crisis." *Convince & Convert* (blog). Entry posted 2018. https://www.convinceandconvert.com/social-media-strategy/dont-be-scared-

be-prepared-how-to-manage-a-social-media-crisis (accessed October 3, 2019).

40. Frandsen, Finn, and Winni Johansen. *Organizational Crisis Communication: A Multivocal Approach*. Sage, 2016.

CHAPTER 7

1. Mike Tirico, email message to author, February 2020.

2. Allen, M. (ed.). *The SAGE Encyclopedia of Communication Research Methods*. SAGE Publications, 2017.

3. Pedersen, Paul M., Pamela C. Laucella, Edward Kian, and Andrea Nicole Geurin. *Strategic Sport Communication*, 2nd ed. Champaign, IL: Human Kinetics, Inc., 2016.

4. Paulsen. "Ratings: Spelling Bee, PGA Tour, Senior PGA, WNBA." Sports Media Watch. Last modified May 31, 2019. https://www.sportsmediawatch.com/2019/05/spelling-bee-viewership-pga-tour-wnba.

5. Knauss, Jeff. "Millennials: Changing the Landscape of Public Relations." Lecture, S.I. Newhouse of Public Communications at Syracuse University, Syracuse, NY, March 19, 2019.

6. LaLiga. "LaLiga Community." La Liga Facebook profile. https://www.facebook.com/LaLiga (accessed February 10, 2020).

7. Real Madrid. "Community." Real Madrid Facebook profile. https://www.facebook.com/RealMadrid (accessed February 10, 2020).

8. Real Madrid. "Twitter Profile." Real Madrid Twitter profile. https://twitter.com/realmadrid (accessed February 10, 2020).

9. Kleinschmidt, Jessica. "Thanks to Orbit, We Found Out Ronald Guzman has Some Pretty Solid Dance Moves." Cut4. Last modified July 28, 2018. https://www.mlb.com/cut4/ronald-guzman-danced-with-orbit-c287804074.

10. ChurchPOP Editor. "ESPN Nominates Dominican Sister Who Threw Curveball at WhiteSox Game for ESPY Award: "It's Kind of Surreal." ChurchPOP. Last modified June 26, 2019. https://churchpop.com/2019/06/26/espy-awards-nominates-dominican-sister-who-threw-curveball-at-white-sox-game-its-kind-of-surreal.

11. Boren, Cindy. "Superfan Laila Anderson was the best part of the Blues' Stanley Cup celebration." *The Washington Post* (Washington, DC), June 13, 2019. https://www.washingtonpost.com/sports/2019/06/13/superfan-laila-anderson-was-best-part-blues-stanley-cup-celebration.

12. Butler, Elise. "Blues Search for Bone Marrow Match for Young Fan." St. Louis Blues. Last modified November 13, 2018. https://www.nhl.com/blues/news/blues-search-for-bone-marrow-donor-match-for-young-fan-laila-anderson/c-301889204.

13. Twiford, Kristin. "7 College Sports Teams Share Their Social Media Secrets." Libris. Last modified 2017. https://librisblog.photoshelter.com/college-football-playoff-national-championship-2017-on-social-media/?utm_source=blog&utm_medium=content&utm_campaign=college-sports-qa.

14. Thamel, Pete. "Ohio State, Clemson competing in Fiesta Bowl … and on social media." *Sports Illustrated*. Last modified December 28, 2016. https://www.si.com/college/2016/12/29/ohio-state-clemson-social-media-fiesta-bowl-playoff-semifinal.

15. Ehalt, Matt. "Inside the MLB Social Program that Pete Alonso and Others Are Embracing." Yahoo! Sports. Last modified August 23, 2019. https://sports.yahoo.com/inside-the-mlb-social-program-that-pete-alonso-and-others-are-embracing-234633181.html.

16. Greenfly. "MLB Uses Greenfly to Drive Deeper Fan Connections on Social." Greenfly. https://www.greenfly.com.

17. Greenfly. "Greenfly for Sports." Last modified 2020. https://www.greenfly.com/solutions/sports.

18. Ibid., 16.

19. Barrabi, Thomas. "Colin Kaepernick and Nike: A timeline of ex-NFL QB's relationship with brand." Fox Business. Last modified July 3, 2019. https://www.foxbusiness.com/retail/colin-kaepernick-nike-timeline.

20. Wang, Amy B., and Rachel Siegel. "Trump: Nike 'getting absolutely killed' with boycotts over Colin Kaepernick's 'Just Do It' campaign." *The Washington Post* (Washington, DC), September 5, 2018, Business. https://www.washingtonpost.com/business/2018/09/04/people-are-destroying-their-nike-gear-protest-colin-kaepernicks-just-do-it-campaign.

21. Ibid., 19.

22. Ibid., 19.

23. Setty, Ganesh. "Colin Kaepernick's New Nike Shoe Sells Out on the First Day." CNBC. Last modified December 23, 2019. https://www.cnbc.com/2019/12/23/colin-kaepernicks-new-nike-shoe-sells-out-on-the-first-day.html.

24. Baxter, Kevin. "Column: Megan Rapinoe making good use of her platform as US soccer star." *LA Times*. Last modified September 1, 2018. https://www.latimes.com/sports/soccer/la-sp-soccer-baxter-20180901-story.html.

25. Mc Near, Clare. "Enes Kanter and the NBA Model of Activism." The Ringer. Last modified May 22, 2017. https://www.theringer.com/2017/5/22/16036916/enes-kanter-oklahoma-city-thunder-nba-political-activism-368e1a6b3bf0.

26. Shank, Matthew D., and Mark R. Lyberger. *Sports Marketing: A Strategic Perspective*, 5th ed. New York: Routledge, 2015.

27. Olivia Stomski, email message to author, January 12, 2020.

28. Ibid., 26.

29. Ibid., 26.

30. FIFA. "Russia 2018 Most Engaging FIFA World Cup Ever." FIFA.com. Last modified July 20, 2018. https://www.fifa.com/worldcup/news/russia-2018-most-engaging-fifa-world-cup-ever.

31. Ibid., 29.

32. Ibid., 29.

33. Ibid., 29.

34. Ibid., 29.

35. Ibid., 29.

36. Newzoo. Global Esports Market Report. 2018. https://resources.newzoo.com/hubfs/Factsheets/Newzoo_Global_Esports_Market_Report_Factsheet.pdf?hsCtaTracking=3a4cc3a4-5b97-46cd-89fb-e25a7f3fea2d|80a504c2-6c7e-4198-acaa-de102e2e48cd.

37. Borowy, Michael, and Dal Yong Jin. "Pioneering e-sport: The experience economy and the marketing of early 1980s arcade gaming contests." *International Journal of Communication* 7 (2013): 2254–2274.

38. AtariWomen. "Rebecca Heineman." http://www.atariwomen.org/stories/rebecca-heineman.

39. LOLEsportsStaff. "2019 World Championship Hits Record Viewership." League of Legends Esports (blog). Entry posted December 23, 2019. https://nexus.leagueoflegends.com/en-us/2019/12/2019-world-championship-hits-record-viewership.

40. Sykes, Tom. "US Government Recognises League of Legends Pros as Professional Athletes." PC Gamer. Last modified July 13, 2013. https://www.pcgamer.com/us-government-recognises-league-of-legends-pros-as-professional-athletes.

41. Justin.tv. "Justin.tv Launches TwitchTV, the World's Largest Competitive Video Gaming Network." BusinessWire. Last modified June 6, 2011. https://www.businesswire.com/news/home/20110606005437/en/Justin.tv-Launches-TwitchTV-World's-Largest-Competitive-Video.

42. Ibid., 40.

43. Iqbal, Mansoor. "Twitch Revenue and Usage Statistics (2019)." Business of Apps. Last modified February 27, 2019. https://www.businessofapps.com/data/twitch-statistics.

44. Newzoo, and Global Esports. "Newzoo Global Esports Market Report 2020: Light Version." Newzoo. https://newzoo .com/insights/trend-reports/newzoo- global-esports-market-report-2020- light-version (accessed April 27, 2020).

45. World Economic Forum. "The Explosive Growth of eSports." World Economic Forum. Last modified July 2018. https:// www.weforum.org/agenda/2018/07/ the-explosive-growth-of-esports.

46. Gillette. "Gillette® and Twitch Announce the Gillette Gaming Alliance." PG. Last modified March 6, 2019. https://news .pg.com/press-release/pg-corporate- announcements/gillette-and-twitch- announce-gillette-gaming-alliance.

47. Sweeney, Erica. "Red Bull Partners with Pro Gamer Ninja on Experiential Contest." Marketing Dive. Last modified March 28, 2019. https://www.marketingdive.com/ news/red-bull-partners-with-pro-gamer- ninja-on-experiential-contest/551486.

CHAPTER 8

1. Stieglitz, Stefan, and Linh Dang-Xuan. "Social media and political communication: A social media analytics framework." *Social Network Analysis and Mining* 3, no. 4 (2013): 1277–1291.

2. Stieglitz, Stefan, and Linh Dang-Xuan. "Women's March on Washington." Facebook. Last modified 2016. https://www .facebook.com/events/2169332969958991 (accessed February 9, 2020).

3. The Women's March. "The Women's March." Last modified n.d.. https:// womensmarch.com (accessed February 9, 2020).

4. Women's March. "Mission and Principles—Women's March 2020." Women's March. https://womensmarch .com/mission-and-principles (accessed February 11, 2020).

5. Luttrell, Regina. *Social Media: How to Engage, Share, and Connect.* Lanham: Rowman & Littlefield, 2019.

6. Campbell, Scott W., and Nojin Kwak. "Mobile communication and civic life: Linking patterns of use to civic and political engagement." *Journal of Communication* 60, no. 3 (2010): 536–555.

7. Weiss, Inbar, Pamela Paxton, Kristopher Velasco, and Robert W. Ressler. "Revisiting declines in social capital: Evidence from a new measure." *Social Indicators Research* 142, no. 3 (2019): 1015–1029.

8. Huang, Chiungjung. "Internet use and psychological well-being: A meta-analysis." *Cyberpsychology, Behavior, and Social Networking* 13, no. 3 (2010): 241–249.

9. Nie, Norman H., and Lutz Erbring. "Internet and society: A preliminary report." *IT & Society* 1, no. 1 (2002): 275–283.

10. Hampton, Keith, and Barry Wellman. "Long distance community in the network society: Contact and support beyond Netville." *American Behavioral Scientist* 45, no. 3 (2001): 476–495.

11. Bail, Christopher A., Lisa P. Argyle, Taylor W. Brown, John P. Bumpus, Haohan Chen, M. B. Fallin Hunzaker, Jaemin Lee, Marcus Mann, Friedolin Merhout, and Alexander Volfovsky. "Exposure to opposing views on social media can increase political polarization." *Proceedings of the National Academy of Sciences* 115, no. 37 (2018): 9216–9221.

12. Lee, Jae Kook, Jihyang Choi, Cheonsoo Kim, and Yonghwan Kim. "Social media, network heterogeneity, and opinion polarization." *Journal of Communication* 64, no. 4 (2014): 702–722.

13. Bail, Christopher A., Lisa P. Argyle, Taylor W. Brown, John P. Bumpus, Haohan Chen, M. B. Fallin Hunzaker, Jaemin Lee, Marcus Mann, Friedolin Merhout, and Alexander Volfovsky. "Exposure to opposing views on social media can increase political polarization." *Proceedings of the National Academy of Sciences* 115, no. 37 (2018): 9216–9221.

14. Barberá, Pablo. "How social media reduces mass political polarization.

Evidence from Germany, Spain, and the US." *Job Market Paper, New York University* 46 (2014).

15. Spohr, Dominic. "Fake news and ideological polarization: Filter bubbles and selective exposure on social media." *Business Information Review* 34, no. 3 (2017): 150–160.

16. Ibid.

17. Spohr, Dominic. "Fake news and ideological polarization: Filter bubbles and selective exposure on social media." *Business Information Review* 34, no. 3 (2017): 150–160.

18. Wong, Julia Carrie. "The Cambridge Analytica scandal changed the world—but it didn't change Facebook." *The Guardian.* Last modified March 18, 2019. https://www.theguardian.com/technology/2019/mar/17/the-cambridge-analytica-scandal-changed-the-world-but-it-didnt-change-facebook (accessed January 9, 2020).

19. Internet Live Stats. "Google Search Statistics." Last modified 2019. https://www.internetlivestats.com/google-search-statistics (accessed February 8, 2020).

20. Oberlo. "Search Engine Market Share in 2019." Last modified 2019. https://www.oberlo.com/statistics/search-engine-market-share (accessed February 8, 2020).

21. Statcounter. "Browser Market Share Worldwide." StatCounter. Last modified 2020. https://gs.statcounter.com (accessed January 8, 2020).

22. Coelho, Patrícia M. F., Pedro Pereira Correia, and Irene Garcia Medina. "Social media: A new way of public and political communication in digital media." *International Journal of Interactive Mobile Technologies (iJIM)* 11, no. 6 (2017): 150–157.

23. Jenkins, Henry. *Fans, Bloggers, and Gamers: Exploring Participatory Culture.* NYU Press, 2006.

24. Rheingold, Howard. *Using Participatory Media and Public Voice to Encourage Civic Engagement.* MacArthur Foundation Digital Media and Learning Initiative, 2008.

25. Sydney Tarrow. *Power in Movement: Social Movements and Contentious Politics,* 2nd ed. New York: Cambridge University Press, 1998, 16.

26. Goffman, Erving. *Frame Analysis: An Essay on the Organization of Experience.* Cambridge, MA: Harvard University Press, 1974.

27. Goffman, Erving. *Frame Analysis: An Essay on the Organization of Experience.* Cambridge, MA: Harvard University Press, 1974.

28. Shaw, Eugene F. "Agenda-setting and mass communication theory." *Gazette* 25, no. 2 (1979): 96–105.

29. McCombs, Maxwell E., Donald L. Shaw, and David H. Weaver. "New directions in agenda-setting theory and research." *Mass Communication and Society* 17, no. 6 (2014): 781–802.

30. Young, Amber, Lisen Selander, and Emmanuelle Vaast. "Digital organizing for social impact: Current insights and future research avenues on collective action, social movements, and digital technologies." *Information and Organization* 29, no. 3 (2019): 100257.

31. Carty, Victoria. "New information communication technologies and grassroots mobilization." *Information, Communication & Society* 13, no. 2 (2010): 155–173.

32. Kevin DeLuca, Sean Lawson, and Le Sun. "OWS on the public screens of social media." *Communication, Culture, & Critique* 5 (2012): 483–509. https://doi.org/10.1111/j.1753–9137.2012.01141.x.483–509.

33. Yochai Benkler. *The Wealth of Networks: How Social Production Transforms Markets and Freedom.* New Haven, CT: Yale University Press, 2006, 151.

34. Carty, Victoria, and Francisco G. Reynoso Barron. "Social movements and new technology: The dynamics of cyber activism in the digital age."

In *The Palgrave Handbook of Social Movements, Revolution, and Social Transformation*, pp. 373–397. Palgrave Macmillan, Cham, 2019.

35. Robert McChesney. *Rich Media, Poor Democracy*. New York: The New Press, 1999, 15–78.

36. Ilten, Carla, and Paul-Brian McInerney. "Social movements and digital technology a research agenda." *digitalSTS: A Field Guide for Science & Technology Studies* (2019): 198.

37. Chung, Deborah S., Seungahn Nah, and Masahiro Yamamoto. "Conceptualizing citizen journalism: US news editors' views." *Journalism* 19, no. 12 (2018): 1694–1712.

38. Rosen, Jay. "Audience Atomization Overcome: Why the Internet Weakens the Authority of the Press." Press Think (blog). January 12, 2009. http://archive.pressthink.org/2009/01/12/atomization.html.

39. Rosen. "Audience Atomization Overcome: Why the Internet Weakens the Authority of the Press."

40. Rosen. "Audience Atomization Overcome: Why the Internet Weakens the Authority of the Press."

41. Plantek, Lea, Kamil Baluk, and Hanna Pincus. "New tools for new movements: Using social media for civil good." *EuroNews*. October 17, 2013. www.euronews.com/2013/10/17/new-tools-for-new-movements-using-social-media-for-civil-good.

42. Tocchi, Claudio. "Journal-activism: A new species or a dangerous hybrid?" *EuroNews*. October 17, 2013. www.euronews.com/2013/10/17/new-tools-for-new-movements-using-social-media-for-civil-good.

43. "CNBC's Rick Santelli's Chicago Tea Party." Video file. YouTube. Posted by The Heritage Foundation, February 19, 2009. https://www.youtube.com/watch?v=zp-Jw-5Kx8k (accessed February 8, 2020).

44. Shirky, Clay. "Political power of social media—technology, the public sphere, and political change." *Foreign Affairs* 28, no. 32 (January/February 2011). www.foreignaffairs.com/articles/67038/clay-shirky/the-political-power-of-social-media.

45. Bennett, W. Lance, Christian Breunig, and Terri Givens. "Communication and political mobilization: Digital media and the organization of the anti-Iraq War demonstrates in the US." *Political Communication* 25 (2008): 269–289. https://doi.org/10.1080/10584600802197434.

46. Vragra, Emily, Leticia Bode, Chris Wells, Devin Driscoll, and Kjerstin Thorson. "The rules of engagement: Comparing two social protest movements on YouTube." *Cyberpsychology, Behavior, and Social Networking* (2013): 133–140. https://doi.org/10.1089/cyber.2013.0117.

47. Earl, Jennifer Earl. "The dynamics of protest-related diffusion on the Web." *Information, Communication, & Society* 13 (2010): 209–225. https://doi.org/10.1080/13691180902934170.

48. Earl, Jennifer, Katrina Kimport, Greg Prieto, Carly Rush, and Kimberly Reynoso. "Changing the world one webpage at a time: Conceptualizing and explaining Internet activism." *Mobilization: An International Journal*, 15 (2010): 425–446.

49. Bennett, Breunig, and Bivens, "Communication and political mobilization: Digital media and the organization of the anti-Iraq War demonstrates in the US." 269–289.

50. Vragra, et al. "The rules of engagement: Comparing two social protest movements on YouTube." 133–140.

51. Olson. *The Logic of Collective Action: Public Goods and the Theory of Groups.* 5–8, 14–16, 123–125, 128–129.

52. Earl. "The dynamics of protest-related diffusion on the Web." 209–225.

53. Benkler. *The Wealth of Networks: How Social Production Transforms Markets and Freedom*, 151.

54. VanLaer, Jeroen, and Peter VanAelst. "Internet and social movement action

repertoires: Opportunities and limitations." *Information, Communication, & Society* 13 (2010):1146–1171.https://doi.org/10.1080/13691181003628307.

55. Sayre, Ben, Leticia Bode, Dave Wilcox, Dhavan Shah, and Chirag Shah. "Agenda setting in a digital age: Tracking attention to California Proposition 8 in social media, online news, and conventional news." *Policy & Internet,* 2 (2010): 7–32. https://doi.org/10.2202/1944-2866.1040.

56. Bimber, Brucer, Andrew Flanagin, and Cynthia Stohl. "Reconceptualizing collective action in the contemporary media environment." *Communication Theory* 15 (2005): 365–388. https://doi .org/10.1093/ct/15.4.365.

57. Bennett, W. Lance. "The uncivic culture: Communication, identity, and the rise of lifestyle politics." *Political Science & Politics* 31 (1998): 741–761. https://doi .org/10.1017/S1049096500053270.

58. Giddens, Anthony. *Modernity and Self-Identity: Self and Society in the Late Modern Age.* Stanford, CA: Stanford University Press, 1991, 187–201.

59. Bennett. "The uncivic culture: Communication, identity, and the rise of lifestyle politics." 741–761.

60. Rainie and Wellman. *Networked: The New Social Operating System.* 3–22.

61. Macafee, Timothy, and J. J. Simone. "Killing the bill online? Pathways to young people's protest engagement via social media."*CyberPsychology, Behavior, & Social Networking* 15 (2012): 579–584. https://doi.org/10.1089/cyber.2012.0153.

62. Rainie, Harrison, and Barry Wellman. *Networked: The New Social Operating System.* Cambridge, MA: MIT Press, 2012, 3–22.

63. Wojcieszak, Magdalena, and Hernando Rojas. "Correlates of party, ideology and issue based extremity in an era of egocentric publics." *International Journal of Press/Politics* 16 (2011): 488–507. https://doi.org/10.1177/1940161211418226.

64. Goldman, Jason. "Meeting People Where They Are." White House Official. Last modified January 10, 2016. https://obamawhitehouse.archives.gov/blog/2016/01/10/meeting-people-where-they-are (accessed February 9, 2020).

65. Goldman, Jason. "Meeting People Where They Are: How the White House Office of Digital Strategy Is Preparing for the 2016 State of the Union Address." Medium (blog). Entry posted January 10, 2016. https://medium.com/@Goldman44/meeting-people-where-they-are-9e396744bc43 (addressed February 9, 2020).

66. Garunay, Melanie. "When Is the 2016 State of the Union?" White House. Last modified November 30, 2015. https://obamawhitehouse.archives.gov/blog/2015/11/30/when-2016-state-union (accessed February 9, 2020).

67. The White House. "President Obama's Final State of the Union." Facebook. Last modified January 12, 2016. https://www .facebook.com/events/470650513119401 (accessed February 9, 2020).

68. The White House. "Meeting People Where They Are: How the White House Office of Digital Strategy Is Preparing for the 2016 State of the Union Address." Medium (blog). Entry posted January 10, 2016. https://medium.com/@Goldman44 (accessed February 9, 2020).

69. Garunay, Melanie. "When Is the 2016 State of the Union?" White House. Last modified November 30, 2015. https://obamawhitehouse.archives.gov/blog/2015/11/30/when-2016-state-union (accessed February 9, 2020).

70. Garunay, Melanie. "Meeting People Where They Are: How the White House Office of Digital Strategy Is Preparing for the 2016 State of the Union Address." Medium (blog). Entry posted January 10, 2016.https://medium.com/@Goldman44 (accessed February 9, 2020).

71. Mills, Chris. "The 2016 State of the Union Will Be Streamed by Amazon." Gizmodo. Last modified January 10, 2016. https://

gizmodo.com/tips-from-entrepreneurs-for-staffing-up-fast-without-s-1840466523 (accessed February 9, 2020).

72. Fingas, John. "Genius for Android Shows Lyrics for Whatever You're Playing." Engadget. Last modified December 22, 2015. https://www.engadget.com/2015/12/22/genius-for-android-lyrics-matching (accessed February 9, 2020).

73. Goldman, Jason. "Meeting People Where They Are." White House Official. Last modified January 10, 2016. https://obamawhitehouse.archives.gov/blog/2016/01/10/meeting-people-where-they-are (accessed February 9, 2020).

74. Ingraham, Nathan. "President Obama Is the White House's First Social Media Ninja." Engadget. Last modified January 12, 2016. https://www.engadget.com/2016/01/12/president-obama-social-networking-the-white-house (accessed February 9, 2020).

75. Ingraham, Nathan. "President Obama Is the White House's First Social Media Ninja." Engadget. Last modified January 12, 2016. https://www.engadget.com/2016/01/12/president-obama-social-networking-the-white-house (accessed February 9, 2020).

76. Kanalley, Craig. "Occupy Wall Street: Social Media's Role in Social Change." Huffington Post. October 6, 2011. http://www.huffingtonpost.com/2011/10/06/occupy-wall-street-social-media_n_999178.html.

77. Kanalley. "Occupy Wall Street: Social Media's Role in Social Change."

78. Shirky. "Political power of social media—technology, the public sphere, and political change."

79. Castells, Manuel. *Networks of Outrage and Hope: Social Movements in The Internet Age.* Malden, MA: Polity Press, 2012, 159–219.

80. Shirky, Clay. *Here Comes Everybody: The Power of Organizing without Organizations.* New York: Penguin Press, 2008, 172.

81. Gladwell, Malcom. "Small Change. Why the Revolution Will Not Be Tweeted."

The New Yorker. October 4, 2010. http://www.newyorker.com/reporting/2010/10/04/101004fa_fact_gladwell.

82. Gladwell. *"Small Change. Why the Revolution Will Not Be Tweeted."*

83. Gladwell, Malcom. *Outliers.* New York: Little, Brown & Company, 2008, 47.

84. Gladwell. *Outliers,* 46.

85. Gladwell. *Outliers,* 49.

86. Gladwell. *Outliers,* 49.

87. Morozov, Evengy. "Iran: Downside to the 'Twitter revolution.'" *Dissent* 56, no. 4 (2009): 10–14.

88. Morozov. "Iran: Downside to the 'Twitter revolution.'" 10–14.

89. Shirky. "Political power of social media—technology, the public sphere, and political change."

90. Shirky. "Political power of social media—technology, the public sphere, and political change."

91. Shirky. "Political power of social media—technology, the public sphere, and political change."

92. Morozov. "Iran: Downside to the 'Twitter Revolution.'" 10–14.

93. Shirky. "Political power of social media—technology, the public sphere, and political change."

94. Shirky. "Political power of social media—technology, the public sphere, and political change."

95. Yang, Guobin. "Narrative agency in hashtag activism: The case of #Black LivesMatter." *Media and Communication* 4, no. 4 (2016): 13.

96. Moscato, Derek. "Media portrayals of hashtag activism: A framing analysis of Canada's #Idlenomore Movement." *Media and Communication* 4, no. 2 (2016): 3.

97. Misra, Sutapa. "New media & social networks: A contemporary public sphere for social change." *International Journal of Research in Social Sciences* 9, no. 6 (2019): 324–334.

CHAPTER 9

1. Pross, Katrina. "Diabetics from Minnesota find insulin at one-tenth the price … In Canada." *Twin Cities Pioneer Press.* Last modified July 7, 2019. https://www .twincities.com/2019/07/07/minnesotans-trek-to-canada-in-search-of-affordable-insulin (accessed February 23, 2020).

2. Ember, Sydney. "Bernie Sanders heads to Canada for affordable insulin." *New York Times.* Last modified July 28, 2019. https://www.nytimes.com/2019/07/28/ us/politics/bernie-sanders-prescription-drug-prices.html (accessed February 23, 2020).

3. National Communication Association. "What Is Communication?" Last modified n.d. https://www.natcom.org/about-nca/ what-communication?id=236&terms= health%20communication (accessed February 10, 2020).

4. National Health Council (United States of America) and Helen Neal. *Better Communications for Health.* Helen Neal (ed.). [Based mainly upon the 1961 National Health Forum Proceedings and the reports of the Pre-Forum Workshops.] Columbia University Press, 1962.

5. International Communication Association. "History." Last modified n.d. https:// www.icahdq.org/page/History (accessed February 10, 2020).

6. Centers for Disease Control and Prevention. "What Is Health Communication?" Last modified 2019. https:// www.cdc.gov/healthcommunication/ healthbasics/whatishc.html#What (accessed February 10, 2020).

7. Centers for Disease Control and Prevention. "Vaccines and Immunizations." Last modified 2020. https://www.cdc.gov/ vaccines/index.html (accessed February 23, 2020).

8. Shots Heard around the World. "When Anti-Vaxxers Attack, We Fight Back. Shots Heard Round the World. Last modified 2017. https://www.shotsheard .com (accessed February 23, 2020).

9. Shots Heard Around the World. "When Anti-Vaxxers Attack, We Fight Back." Shots Heard Round the World. Last modified 2017. https://www.shotsheard .com (accessed February 23, 2020).

10. Haglage, Abby. "Scientists debunk coronavirus conspiracy, say it 'threatens to undermine' global efforts to stop it." *Yahoo News.* Last modified February 21, 2020. https://www.yahoo .com/lifestyle/scientists-debunk-coronavirus-conspiracy-say-it-threatens-to-undermine-global-efforts-to-stop-it-220044983.html (accessed February 23, 2020).

11. Target Network. Exabyte definition: https://searchstorage.techtarget.com/ definition/exabyte.

12. Beall, Anne-Lindsay. "Big data in health care—How three organizations are using big data to improve patient care and more." SAS. Last modified 2019. https:// www.sas.com/en_us/insights/articles/ big-data/big-data-in-healthcare.html (accessed January 2, 2020).

13. SAS. "Emerging topics in health care." Last modified 2019. https://www.sas .com/content/dam/SAS/en_us/doc/ whitepaper1/emerging-topics-health-care-109815.pdf. (accessed December 30, 2019).

14. Walker, Elizabeth. "New Associate Benefits Aim to Simplify Health Care and Focus on Appropriate Care." Walmart. Last modified October 3, 2019. https://corporate .walmart.com/newsroom/2019/10/03/ new-associate-benefits-aim-to-simplify-health-care-and-focus-on-appropriate-carez. (accessed January 5, 2020).

15. Nathan-Kazis, Josh. "Walmart could disrupt health care the same way it did retail, analyst says." *Barron's.* Last modified September 3, 2019. https://www .barrons.com/articles/walmart-stock-health-care-stand-alone-health-clinic-51567522182 (accessed January 5, 2020).

16. Walker, Elizabeth. "New Associate Benefits Aim to Simplify Health Care and Focus on Appropriate Care." Walmart.

Last modified October 3, 2019. https://corporate.walmart.com/newsroom/2019/10/03 (accessed January 5, 2020).

17. Carroll, Christopher L., Kristi Bruno, and Pradeep Ramachandran. "Building community through a #pulmcc Twitter chat to advocate for pulmonary, critical care, and sleep." *Chest* 152, no. 2 (2017): 402–409.

18. Dutta, Mohan J., and Uttaran Dutta. "Voices of the poor from the margins of Bengal: Structural inequities and health." *Qualitative Health Research* 23, no. 1 (2013): 14–25.

19. Strekalova, Yulia A. "Health risk information engagement and amplification on social media: News about an emerging pandemic on Facebook." *Health Education & Behavior* 44, no. 2 (2017): 332–339.

20. Dutta, Mohan Jyoti, Agaptus Anaele, and Christina Jones. "Voices of hunger: Addressing health disparities through the culture⊠centered approach." *Journal of Communication* 63, no. 1 (2013): 159–180.

21. Keller, Michelle Sophie, Sasan Mosadeghi, Erica R. Cohen, James Kwan, and Brennan Mason Ross Spiegel. "Reproductive health and medication concerns for patients with inflammatory bowel disease: Thematic and quantitative analysis using social listening." *Journal of Medical Internet Research* 20, no. 6 (2018): e206.

22. Matthews, Nicole, and Naomi Sunderland. *Digital Storytelling in Health and Social Policy: Listening to Marginalised Voices.* Routledge, 2017.

23. Stough, Laura, Kayla Sweet, Jennifer K. LeBlanc, and Noelle W. Sweany. "Community building and knowledge sharing by individuals with disabilities using social media." (2019).

24. Stough, Laura, Kayla Sweet, Jennifer K. LeBlanc, and Noelle W. Sweany. "Community building and knowledge sharing by individuals with disabilities using social media." (2019).

25. Chen, Jason I., Elizabeth R. Hooker, Meike Niederhausen, Heather E. Marsh, Somnath Saha, Steven K. Dobscha, and Alan R. Teo. "Social connectedness, depression symptoms, and health service utilization: A longitudinal study of Veterans Health Administration patients." *Social Psychiatry and Psychiatric Epidemiology* (2019): 1–9.

26. Huisman, Martijn. "Doctor Google and the shifting dynamics of the older adult patient-physician relationship." In *Etmaal van de Communicatiewetenschap 2019.* 2019. https://biblio.ugent.be/publication/8612514.

27. Seo, Hyunjin, Joseph Erba, Mugur Geana, and Crystal Lumpkins. "Calling doctor Google? Technology adoption and health information seeking among low-income African-American older adults." (2017). https://journals.flvc.org/jpic/article/view/104561.

28. Duquesne School of Nursing. "How Health Communicators Use Social Media in Interactive Marketing." Last modified n.d. https://onlinenursing.duq.edu/blog/health-communicators-use-social-media-interactive-marketing (accessed February 23, 2020).

29. Duquesne School of Nursing. "How Health Communicators Use Social Media in Interactive Marketing." Last modified n.d. https://onlinenursing.duq.edu/blog/health-communicators-use-social-media-interactive-marketing (accessed February 23, 2020).

30. Kind, Terry. "Professional guidelines for social media use: A starting point." *AMA Journal of Ethics* 17, no. 5 (2015): 441–447.

31. Martin, Dan. "HIMSS19: Recap and Insights of Top Trends and Takeaways." Pan Communication. Last modified February 21, 2019. https://www.pancommunications.com/blog/himss19-recap-and-insights-of-top-trends-and-takeaways (accessed February 23, 2020).

32. Martin, Dan. "HIMSS19: Recap and Insights of Top Trends and Takeaways." Pan Communication. Last modified February 21, 2019. https://www.pan

communications.com/blog/himss19-recap-and-insights-of-top-trends-and-takeaways (accessed February 23, 2020).

33. Martin, Dan. "HIMSS19: Recap and Insights of Top Trends and Takeaways." Pan Communication. Last modified February 21, 2019. https://www.pancommunications.com/blog/himss19-recap-and-insights-of-top-trends-and-takeaways (accessed February 23, 2020).

34. Office of the National Coordinator for Health Information Technology (ONC). "Home Page." Last modified 2020; "A Shared Nationwide Interoperability Roadmap Version 1.0." Last modified March 28, 2019. https://www.healthit.gov/sites/default/files/hie-interoperability/nationwide-interoperability-roadmap-final-version-1.0.pdf; https://www.healthit.gov/topic/about-onc (accessed February 23, 2020).

35. Office of the National Coordinator for Health Information Technology (ONC). "Home Page." Last modified 2020. (accessed February 23, 2020).

36. Martin, Dan. "HIMSS19: Recap and Insights of Top Trends and Takeaways." Pan Communication. Last modified February 21, 2019. https://www.pancommunications.com/blog/himss19-recap-and-insights-of-top-trends-and-takeaways (accessed February 23, 2020).

37. Martin, Dan. "HIMSS19: Recap and Insights of Top Trends and Takeaways." Pan Communication. Last modified February 21, 2019. https://www.pancommunications.com/blog/himss19-recap-and-insights-of-top-trends-and-takeaways (accessed February 23, 2020).

38. Albalawi, Yousef, and Jane Sixsmith. "Agenda setting for health promotion: Exploring an adapted model for the social media era." JMIR Public Health and Surveillance 1, no. 2 (2015): e21.

39. Lippmann W. Public Opinion. New York: Macmillan, 1922.

40. Lasswell, Harold, and Lyman Bryson. "The Communication of Ideas: A Series of Addresses." (1948): 37. https://openlibrary.org/books/OL6031494M/The_communication_of_ideas.

41. McCombs, Maxwell E., and Donald L. Shaw. "The agenda-setting function of mass media." The Public Opinion Quarterly 36, no. 2 (1972): 176–187.

42. Rogers, E., and J. Dearing. Agenda-setting research: Where has it been? Where is it going? In J. Anderson (ed.). Communication Yearbook, 11th ed. Newbury Park, CA: Sage; 1988. pp. 555–594.

43. Kozel, Charles T., William M. Kane, Michael T. Hatcher, Anne P. Hubbell, James W. Dearing, Sue Forster-Cox, Sharon Thompson, Frank G. Pérez, and Melanie Goodman. "Introducing health promotion agenda-setting for health education practitioners." Californian Journal of Health Promotion 4, no. 1 (2006): 32–40.

44. Albalawi, Yousef, and Jane Sixsmith. "Agenda setting for health promotion: Exploring an adapted model for the social media era." JMIR Public Health and Surveillance 1, no. 2 (2015): e21.

CHAPTER 10

1. Abidor, Jen. "All of Taylor Swift's Social Media Accounts Are Gone and People Are Freaking Out." BuzzFeed. Last modified August 18, 2017. https://www.buzzfeed.com/jenniferabidor/taylor-swift-just-purged-all-of-her-social-media-accounts.

2. Jordynville. "I Woke Up Literally 7 Minutes Ago: What in the World Is Going On with Taylor Swift." Twitter. August 18, 2017, 11:51 A.M. https://twitter.com/parksandrep/status/898573077109407744.

3. Bruner, Raisa. "Are you ready for Taylor Swift's long-anticipated new music release? Here's everything we know so far." TIME. Last modified August 23, 2017. https://time.com/4911005/taylor-swift-new-music-details.

4. Bruner, Raisa. "Are you ready for Taylor Swift's long-anticipated new music

release? Here's everything we know so far." *TIME*. Last modified August 23, 2017. https://time.com/4911005/taylor-swift-new-music-details.

5. Caulfield, Keith. "Taylor Swift's 'Reputation' debuts at no. 1 on Billboard 200 Albums Chart." Billboard. Last modified November 20, 2017. https://www.billboard.com/articles/columns/chart-beat/8039679/taylor-swift-reputation-debuts-no-1-billboard-200-albums.

6. Boothby, Erica J., Leigh K. Smith, Margaret S. Clark, and John A. Bargh. "Psychological distance moderates the amplification of shared experience." *Personality and Social Psychology Bulletin* 42, no. 10 (2016): 1431–1444.

7. Wakefield, Lane T., and Gregg Bennett. "Sports fan experience: Electronic word-of-mouth in ephemeral social media." *Sport Management Review* 21, no. 2 (2018): 147–159.

8. Wakefield, Lane T., and Gregg Bennett. "Sports fan experience: Electronic word-of-mouth in ephemeral social media." *Sport Management Review* 21, no. 2 (2018): 147–159.

9. Ng, Hou Hong, Haroon Abdullah Saleem, Kim Yew Lim, and Chee Hoo Wong. "The influence of electronic word of mouth in social media on generation Z purchase intentions: A review." *INTI Journal*, no. 4 (2019).

10. Katz, E., and J. G. Blumler. *Utilization of Mass Communications by the Individual.* M. Gurevitch, J. G. Blumler, and E. Katz (eds.). Beverly Hills, CA: Sage, 1974.

11. Turney, Sarah. Sarah Turney. 2016. Uses and Gratifications Theory and Its Connection to Public Relations, 473. https://sites.psu.edu/sarahturney/uses-and-gratifications-theory.

12. Lariscy, Ruthann Weaver, Spencer F. Tinkham, and Kaye D. Sweetser. "Kids these days: Examining differences in political uses and gratifications, Internet political participation, political information efficacy, and cynicism on the basis of age." *American Behavioral Scientist* 55, no. 6 (2011): 749–764. https://doi.org/10.1177/0002764211398091.

13. Palmgreen, Philip, and J.D. Rayburn. "Uses and gratifications and exposure to public television." *Communication Research* 6, no. 2 (1979): 155–179. https://doi.org/10.1177/009365027900600203.

14. Whiting, Anita, and David Williams. "Why people use social media: A uses and gratifications approach." *Qualitative Market Research: An International Journal* (2013).

15. Katz, E., and J. G. Blumler. *Utilization of Mass Communications by the Individual.* M. Gurevitch, J. G. Blumler, and E. Katz (eds.). Beverly Hills, CA: Sage, 1974.

16. Whiting, Anita, and David Williams. "Why people use social media: A uses and gratifications approach." *Qualitative Market Research: An International Journal* (2013).

17. Bartsch, Anne, and Reinhold Viehoff. "The use of media entertainment and emotional gratification." *Procedia Social and Behavioral Sciences* 5 (2010): 2247–2255.

18. Twenge, Jean M., Gabrielle N. Martin, and Brian H. Spitzberg. "Trends in US adolescents' media use, 1976–2016: The rise of digital media, the decline of TV, and the (near) demise of print." *Psychology of Popular Media Culture* 8, no. 4 (2019): 329.

19. García-Avilés, Jose A. "Reinventing television news: Innovative formats in a social media environment." In *Journalistic Metamorphosis*, pp. 143–155. Springer, Cham, 2020.

20. Craig, David, and Stuart Cunningham. "Social media entertainment: The new intersection of Hollywood and Silicon Valley. *NYU Press*, 2019.

21. Habes, Mohammed. "The influence of personal motivation on using social TV: A uses and gratifications approach." *Int. J. Inf. Technol. Lang. Stud* 3, no. 1 (2019): 32–39.

22. Campbell, Colin, and Pamela E. Grimm. "The challenges native advertising

poses: Exploring potential federal trade commission responses and identifying research needs." *Journal of Public Policy & Marketing* 38, no. 1 (2019): 110–123.

23. Fossen, Beth L., and David A. Schweidel. "Social TV, advertising, and sales: Are social shows good for advertisers?" *Marketing Science* 38, no. 2 (2019): 274–295.

24. Hur, Johnson. "History of the Television." From the 1800s to Current Time. December 4, 2018. https://bebusinessed .com/history/history-of-the-television.

25. McDonough School of Business. "The Impact of Social TV on How We Consume Advertisements." Georgetown University. Last modified 2019. https:// msb.georgetown.edu/news-story/ social-tv.

26. Bulkeley, William. "10 Breakthrough Techologies." *MIT Technology Review*. Last modified April 20, 2010. http://www2 .technologyreview.com/news/418541/ tr10-social-tv (accessed March 5, 2020).

27. De Michele, Roberta, Stefano Ferretti, and Marco Furini. "On helping broadcasters to promote TV shows through hashtags." *Multimedia Tools and Applications* 78, no. 3 (2019): 3279–3296.

28. Chen, Gina Masullo. "Tweet this: A uses and gratifications perspective on how active Twitter use gratifies a need to connect with others." *Computers in Human Behavior* 27 (2011): 755–762.

29. Spangler, Todd. "Nielsen now tracks celebs' social-media touts of TV shows." *Variety*. Last modified September 19, 2019. https://variety.com/2019/digital/ news/nielsen-talent-celebrity-social- media-tv-shows-1203341097.

30. Rogers, Everett M. *Diffusion of Innovations*, 5th ed. New York, NY: Simon & Schuster, 2003.

31. Vena, Danny. "Is Coronavirus Boosting Netflix's Subscriber Growth?" Nasdaq, March 8, 2020. https://www.nasdaq .com/articles/is-coronavirus-boosting- netflixs-subscriber-growth-2020-03-08.

32. Clark, Travis. "Netflix is still growing wildly, but its market share has fallen to an estimated 19 percent as new competitors emerge." *Business Insider*. January 24, 2020. https://www.businessinsider.com/ netflix-market-share-of-global-streaming- subscribers-dropping-ampere-2020-1.

33. FIPP. *Global Digital Subscription Snapshot*. London, UK: FIPP, 2019.

34. Sherman, Alex. "NBC's Streaming Service Peacock Will Have Free Version and Two Subscription Tiers Starting at $4.99." CNBC. Last modified January 16, 2020. https://www.cnbc.com/2020/01/16/nbc- peacock-price-launch-date-and-shows .html.

35. Alexander, Julia. "Quibi tries to explain what Quibi is in a new Super Bowl commercial." *The Verge*. Last modified January 31, 2020. https://www .theverge.com/2020/1/31/21116642/ quibi-super-bowl-commercial-jeffrey- katzenberg-meg-whitman-streaming- service-chance-rapper.

36. Pallotta, Frank. "Short clips, big risk: This mysterious startup wants to turn streaming on its head." *CNN Business*. Last modified October 11, 2019. https:// www.cnn.com/2019/10/03/business/ quibi-whitman-katzenberg-risk-takers/ index.html.

37. Alexander, Julia. "Quibi tries to explain what Quibi is in a new Super Bowl commercial." *The Verge*. Last modified January 31, 2020. https://www .theverge.com/2020/1/31/21116642/ quibi-super-bowl-commercial-jeffrey- katzenberg-meg-whitman-streaming- service-chance-rapper.

38. Aquilina, Tyler. "All the projects coming to Quibi, Jeffrey Katzenberg's bite-size streaming service." *Entertainment Weekly*. Last modified March 6, 2020. https://ew.com/tv/2019/06/13/ quibi-projects-jeffrey-katzenberg.

39. Pallotta, Frank. "Short clips, big risk: This mysterious startup wants to turn streaming on its head." *CNN Business*. Last modified October 11, 2019. https://

www.cnn.com/2019/10/03/business/quibi-whitman-katzenberg-risk-takers/index.html.

40. Crupnick, Russ. "Music scores a gold record on the social media charts." *Music Watch*. Last modified August 6, 2018. https://www.musicwatchinc.com/blog/music-scores-a-gold-record-on-the-social-media-charts.

41. Naveed, Kashif, Chihiro Watanabe, and Pekka Neittaanmaki. "Co-evolution between streaming and live music leads a way to the sustainable growth of music industry: E-lessons from the US experiences." *Technology in Society* 50 (2017): 1–19.

42. Richter, Felix. "From Tape Deck to Tidal: 30 Years of US Music Sales." Statista. Last modified February 27, 2020. https://www.statista.com/chart/17244/us-music-revenue-by-format.

43. Crupnick, Russ. "Music scores a gold record on the social media charts." *Music Watch*. Last modified August 6, 2018. https://www.musicwatchinc.com/blog/music-scores-a-gold-record-on-the-social-media-charts.

44. Saboo, Alok R., V. Kumar, and Girish Ramani. "Evaluating the impact of social media activities on human brand sales." *International Journal of Research in Marketing* 33, no. 3 (2016): 524–541.

45. Crupnick, Russ. "Music scores a gold record on the social media charts." *Music Watch*. Last modified August 6, 2018. https://www.musicwatchinc.com/blog/music-scores-a-gold-record-on-the-social-media-charts.

46. Wikipedia. "Lil Xan." Wikimedia Foundation, March 29, 2020. https://en.wikipedia.org/wiki/Lil_Xan.

47. Stechnij, Tanner. "Lil Xan on tour life, sobriety, and his rise to fame." *Phoenix New Times*. February 7, 2018. https://www.phoenixnewtimes.com/music/lil-xan-10111742.

48. Click, Melissa A., Hyunji Lee, and Holly Willson Holladay. "Making monsters:

Lady Gaga, fan identification, and social media." *Popular Music and Society* 36, no. 3 (2013): 360–379.

49. Beaudoin, Kate. "The Story of How Adele Became Famous Will Make You Love Her Even More." Mic. Last modified June 16, 2015. https://www.mic.com/articles/120804/the-story-behind-how-adele-became-the-defining-british-artist-of-the-2010s.

50. "W5: Rare Interview before Justin Bieber Was a Star." Video file, 19:46. YouTube. Posted by CTV W5, April 7, 2017. https://www.youtube.com/watch?v=bvtbstYPdOk.

51. "W5: Rare Interview before Justin Bieber Was a Star." Video file, 19:46. YouTube. Posted by CTV W5, April 7, 2017. https://www.youtube.com/watch?v=bvtbstYPdOk.

52. "How Justin Bieber Was Discovered." Video file, 02:35. YouTube. Posted by CBS News, March 16, 2010. https://www.youtube.com/watch?v=X_XopFLciYQ.

53. Hoffman, Jan. "Justin Bieber is living the dream." *The New York Times*. Last modified December 31, 2009. https://www.nytimes.com/2010/01/03/fashion/03bieber.html.

54. Vena, Jocelyn. "Justin Bieber Hits 6 Million Followers on Twitter." MTV. Last modified November 9, 2010. http://www.mtv.com/news/1651843/justin-bieber-hits-6-million-twitter-followers.

55. Boyd, Joshua. "The Most Followed Accounts on Twitter." Brandwatch. Last modified February 28, 2020. https://www.brandwatch.com/blog/most-twitter-followers.

56. Bieber, Justin. "Justin Bieber Channel." YouTube. https://www.youtube.com/user/kidrauhl.

57. Bieber, Justin. "Justin Bieber Channel." YouTube. https://www.youtube.com/user/kidrauhl.

58. Rosenblatt, Kalhan. "How TikTok Became the Music Discovery Platform for the Smartphone Generation."

NBC News. Last modified July 28, 2019. https://www.nbcnews.com/tech/tech-news/how-tiktok-became-music-discovery-platform-smartphone-generation-n1035246.

59. Rosenblatt, Kalhan. "How TikTok Became the Music Discovery Platform for the Smartphone Generation." NBC News. Last modified July 28, 2019.https://www.nbcnews.com/tech/tech-news/how-tiktok-became-music-discovery-platform-smartphone-generation-n1035246.

60. Rosenblatt, Kalhan. "How TikTok Became the Music Discovery Platform for the Smartphone Generation." NBC News. Last modified July 28, 2019. https://www.nbcnews.com/tech/tech-news/how-tiktok-became-music-discovery-platform-smartphone-generation-n1035246.

61. Oesterle, Ulf. *Interview.* Syracuse University, Syracuse, NY: February 28, 2020.

62. Starling, Lakin. "Lil Nas X talks fame, going viral, and more in his first cover story." *Teen Vogue.* Last modified June 3, 2019. https://www.teenvogue.com/story/lil-nas-x-june-2019-cover.

63. Starling, Lakin. "Lil Nas X talks fame, going viral, and more in his first cover story." *Teen Vogue.* Last modified June 3, 2019. https://www.teenvogue.com/story/lil-nas-x-june-2019-cover.

64. Starling, Lakin. "Lil Nas X talks fame, going viral, and more in his first cover Story." *Teen Vogue.* Last modified June 3, 2019. https://www.teenvogue.com/story/lil-nas-x-june-2019-cover.

65. Strapagiel, Lauren. "How TikTok Made 'Old Town Road' Become Both a Meme and a Banger." BuzzFeed News. Last modified April 9, 2019. https://www.buzzfeednews.com/article/laurenstrapagiel/tiktok-lil-nas-x-old-town-road.

66. Starling, Lakin. "Lil Nas X talks fame, going viral, and more in his first cover story." *Teen Vogue.* Last modified June 3, 2019. https://www.teenvogue.com/story/lil-nas-x-june-2019-cover.

67. Chow, Andrew R. "Lil Nas X talks 'Old Town Road' and the Billboard controversy." *TIME.* https://time.com/5561466/lil-nas-x-old-town-road-billboard.

68. Trust, Gary. "Lil Nas X's 'Old Town Road' Leaps to No. 1 on Billboard Hot 100." Billboard. Last modified April 8, 2019. https://www.billboard.com/articles/columns/chart-beat/8506256/lil-nas-x-old-town-road-number-one-hot-100.

69. Starling, Lakin. "Lil Nas X talks fame, going viral, and more in his first cover story." *Teen Vogue.* Last modified June 3, 2019.https://www.teenvogue.com/story/lil-nas-x-june-2019-cover.

70. Nair, Lekha R., Sujala D. Shetty, and Siddhant Deepak Shetty. "Streaming big data analysis for real-time sentiment based targeted advertising." *International Journal of Electrical and Computer Engineering* 7, no. 1 (2017): 402.

71. Spotify. "Media Kit." Spotify. Last modified 2020. https://downloads.ctfassets.net/ziwa9xqm84y1/4YF1oeZTpNgnd7qpSKEwS0/d7b2791bdad7f1867d70f961bfbf4894/Media_Kit_Q1_2020_-_US.pdf.

72. Spotify for Brands. "AXE Gold Shines with Hilariously Fresh Videos." https://www.spotifyforbrands.com/en-US/ad-experiences/axe-gold-shines-with-hilariously-fresh-videos (accessed April 1, 2020).

73. Spotify for Brands. "AXE Gold Shines with Hilariously Fresh Videos." https://www.spotifyforbrands.com/en-US/ad-experiences/axe-gold-shines-with-hilariously-fresh-videos (accessed April 1, 2020).

74. Neustar. *Do Movie Marketing Budgets Need a Digital Reboot?* Sterling, VA: Neustar, 2018.

75. Neustar. *Do Movie Marketing Budgets Need a Digital Reboot?* Sterling, VA: Neustar, 2018.

76. Neustar. *Do Movie Marketing Budgets Need a Digital Reboot?* Sterling, VA: Neustar, 2018.

77. Big Commerce. "What is ROAS? Calculating return on ad spend." *Big Commerce*. Last modified 2020. https://www.bigcommerce.com/ecommerce-answers/what-is-roas-calculating-return-on-ad-spend (accessed March 5, 2020).

78. Neustar. *Do Movie Marketing Budgets Need a Digital Reboot?* Sterling, VA: Neustar, 2018.

79. Moore, Kaleigh. "Ecommerce 101 + The history of online shopping: What the past says about tomorrow's retail challenges." *Big Commerce*. Last modified n.d. https://www.bigcommerce.com/blog/ecommerce (accessed March 5, 2020).

80. Jarvey, Natalie. "A closer look at 'Star wars: The force awakens' social media chatter." *The Hollywood Reporter*. Last modified December 21, 2015. https://www.hollywoodreporter.com/news/a-closer-look-at-star-850615.

81. Burney, Kara. "The star wars marketing force awakens on social media with 234 million interactions." *TrackMaven*. Last modified 2015. https://trackmaven.com/blog/star-wars-marketing-force-awakens-on-social-media.

82. D'Alessandro, Anthony. "'The Force Awakens' Blasts 667M+ on Social Media before Opening, in Line with 2015's Other Top Franchises." Deadline. Last modified December 16, 2015. https://deadline.com/2015/12/star-wars-the-force-awakens-social-media-box-office-1201668176.

83. Maglio, Tony. "'Star Wars: The Force Awakens' Trailer Anticipation Peaks 'Monday Night Football' Ratings." The Wrap. Last modified October 20, 2015. https://www.thewrap.com/star-wars-the-force-awakens-episode-vii-trailer-monday-night-football-tv-ratings-eagles-giants.

84. Guinness World Records Limited. "Most Viewed Movie Trailer on YouTube in 24 Hours." Last modified April 16, 2015. https://www.guinnessworldrecords.com/world-records/377645-most-viewed-movie-trailer-on-youtube-in-24-hours.

85. Jarvey, Natalie. "A closer look at 'Star Wars: The force awakens' social media chatter." *The Hollywood Reporter*. Last modified December 21, 2015. https://www.hollywoodreporter.com/news/a-closer-look-at-star-850615.

86. Jarvey, Natalie. "A closer look at 'Star Wars: The force awakens' social media chatter." *The Hollywood Reporter*. Last modified December 21, 2015. https://www.hollywoodreporter.com/news/a-closer-look-at-star-850615.

87. Moraski, Lauren. "Star Wars' Fans Crash Websites, Line Up for Tickets for 'The Force Awakens.'" CBS News. Last modified October 20, 2015. https://www.cbsnews.com/news/star-wars-fans-crash-websites-line-up-for-tickets-for-the-force-awakens.

88. McMillan, Graeme. "Lucasfilm reveals brand partnerships for 'Star Wars: The force awakens.'" *The Hollywood Reporter*. Last modified August 13, 2013. https://www.hollywoodreporter.com/heat-vision/lucasfilm-reveals-brand-partnerships-star-815160.

89. Franklin, M. J. "Interview: Chrissy Teigen, on How to Definitively Win the Internet." Mashable. Last modified August 4, 2017. https://mashable.com/2017/08/04/chrissy-teigen-wins-the-Internet.

90. Legault, Amanda. "Chrissy Teigen—The Sarcastic, Social Media Mastermind." Medium. Last modified April 19, 2018. https://medium.com/rta902/chrissy-teigen-the-sarcastic-social-media-mastermind-491596420471.

91. Howe, Rebecca L. "@chrissyteigen but seriously when you're done with that red dress from this week's @SpikeLSB can I have it please ☺."Twitter. December 22, 2016, 9:36 P.M. https://twitter.com/rebeccahowe/status/812124780363214849.

92. Teigen, Christine. "I am done. DM me your address!" Twitter. December 22, 2016, 9:38 P.M. https://twitter.com/chrissyteigen/status/812125125923352577.

93. Manning, Charles. "Chrissy Teigen gave a fan the dress off her back just because

she asked." *Cosmopolitan*. Last modified December 23, 2016. https://www.cosmo politan.com/style-beauty/fashion/a8531721/chrissy-teigen-twitter-dress-gift.

94. TIME Staff. "The 25 Most Influential People on the Internet." Last modified June 26, 2017. https://time.com/4815217/most-influential-people-Internetz.

95. 60 Minutes. "Kim Kardashian Attributes Career to Social Media." CBS News. Last modified October 21, 2016. https://www.cbsnews.com/news/kim-kardashian-social-media-career-60-minutes.

96. Taylor, Kate. "Kim Kardashian revealed in a lawsuit that she demands up to half a million dollars for a single Instagram post and other details about how much she charges for endorsement deals." *Business Insider*. Last modified May 9, 2019. https://www.businessinsider.com/how-much-kim-kardashian-charges-for-instagram-endorsement-deals-2019-5 (accessed March 19, 2020).

97. Harper's Bazaar Arabia. "Here's how much the Kardashians get paid for one Instagram post." *Harper's Bazaar Arabia*. Last modified July 25, 2019. https://www.harpersbazaararabia.com/people/the-a-list/heres-how-much-the-kardashians-get-paid-for-one-instagram-post.

98. Rodriguez, Karla. "The most influential celebrities on social media." *US Weekly*. Last modified February 27, 2020. https://www.usmagazine.com/celebrity-news/pictures/the-most-influential-celebrities-on-social-media/ariana-grande-2-4.

99. Johnson, Dwayne. "Verified: The name Is Official: Ladies and Gents, I Proudly Bring You, TEREMANA TEQUILA." Instagram. October 30, 2019. https://www.instagram.com/p/B4PdNg_Fkts.

CHAPTER 11

1. *The Economist*. "Instagram may offer clues about the spread of the new coronavirus." Last modified March 17, 2020. https://www.economist.com/graphic-detail/2020/03/17/instagram-may-offer-clues-about-the-spread-of-the-new-coronavirus (accessed March 27, 2020).

2. *The Economist*. "Instagram may offer clues about the spread of the new coronavirus." Last modified March 17, 2020. https://www.economist.com/graphic-detail/2020/03/17/instagram-may-offer-clues-about-the-spread-of-the-new-coronavirus (accessed March 27, 2020).

3. *The Economist*. "Instagram may offer clues about the spread of the new coronavirus." Last modified March 17, 2020. https://www.economist.com/graphic-detail/2020/03/17/instagram-may-offer-clues-about-the-spread-of-the-new-coronavirus (accessed March 27, 2020).

4. Marr, Bernard. "Coronavirus fake news: How Facebook, Twitter, and Instagram are tackling the problem." *Forbes*. Last modified March 27, 2020. https://www.forbes.com/sites/everbridge/2020/03/20/four-steps-businesses-can-take-to-reduce-coronavirus-impact/#454115385754 (accessed March 27, 2020).

5. Clegg, Nick. "Combating COVID-19 misinformation across our apps." *Facebook*. Last modified March 25, 2020. https://about.fb.com/news/2020/03/combating-covid-19-misinformation (accessed March 27, 2020).

6. Jensen, Klaus Bruhn, and Rasmus Helles. "Speaking into the system: Social media and many-to-one communication." *European Journal of Communication* 32, no. 1 (2017): 16–25.

7. Khan, Gohar, Manar Mohaisen, and Matthias Trier. "The network ROI." *Internet Research* (2019).

8. Martínez-Rolán, Xabier, and Teresa Piñeiro-Otero. "6 Marketing analytics: Why measuring Web and social media matters." *Business Intelligence and Analytics in Small and Medium Enterprises* (2019): 75–88.

9. Bonner, Mehera. "An influencer with 2 million followers couldn't sell 36 T-shirts

and Twitter is not okay." *Cosmopolitan.* Last modified May 29, 2019. https://www.cosmopolitan.com/entertainment/celebs/a27623334/influencer-arii-36-shirts-2-million-followers (accessed March 22, 2020).

10. Pearl, Diana. "Arii has over 2 million followers. So why did her clothing line fail?" *AdWeek.* Last modified June 5, 2019. https://www.adweek.com/brand-marketing/arii-has-over-2-million-followers-so-why-did-her-clothing-line-fail (accessed March 22, 2020).

11. Kelly, Kevin. "1,000 True Fans." The Technium (blog). Entry posted March 24, 2012. https://kk.org/thetechnium/1000-true-fans (accessed March 22, 2020).

12. Kelly, Kevin. "1,000 True Fans." The Technium (blog). Entry posted March 24, 2012. https://kk.org/thetechnium/1000-true-fans (accessed March 22, 2020).

13. Blanchard, Olivier. *Social Media ROI: Managing and Measuring Social Media Efforts in Your Organization.* Pearson Education, 2011.

14. Marrs, Megan. "How to measure the ROI of social media (No, it's not impossible!)." *WordStream.* Last modified January 18, 2019. https://www.wordstream.com/blog/ws/2013/04/25/social-media-roi (accessed March 22, 2020).

15. Minsky, Laurence, and Keith A. Quesenberry. "How B2B sales can benefit from social selling." *Harvard Business Review* 8 (2016).

16. Shannon, Claude E. "A mathematical theory of communication." *Bell System Technical Journal* 27, no. 3 (1948): 379–423.

17. Berlo, David K. *The Process of Communication.* New York: Holt, Rinehart and Winston (1960): 30.

18. Lal, Banita, Elvira Ismagilova, Yogesh K. Dwivedi, and Shirumisha Kwayu. "Return on investment in social media marketing: Literature review and suggestions for future research." In *Digital and Social Media Marketing*, pp. 3–17. Springer, Cham, 2020.

19. Treem, Jeffrey W., and Paul M. Leonardi. "Social media use in organizations: Exploring the affordances of visibility, editability, persistence, and association." *Annals of the International Communication Association* 36, no. 1 (2013): 143–189.

20. Taylor, Charles R. "How to avoid marketing disasters: Back to the basic communications model, but with some updates illustrating the importance of e-word-of-mouth research." *International Journal of Advertising* 36, no. 4 (2017): 515–519.

21. Gräve, Jan-Frederik. "What KPIs are key? Evaluating performance metrics for social media influencers." *Social Media+ Society* 5, no. 3 (2019). https://journals.sagepub.com/doi/full/10.1177/2056305119865475. https://doi.org/10.1177/2056305119865475.

22. Mukesh, Mudra, and Anand Rao. "Social media measurement and monitoring." In *Contemporary Issues in Social Media Marketing*, pp. 184–205. Routledge, 2017.

23. Chuang, Shu-Hui. "Co-creating social media agility to build strong customer-firm relationships." *Industrial Marketing Management* 84 (2020): 202–211.

24. Chen, Jenn. "The most important social media metrics to track." *Sprout Social.* Last modified January 10, 2020. https://sproutsocial.com/insights/social-media-metrics (accessed March 26, 2020).

25. Chen, Jenn. "The most important social media metrics to track." *Sprout Social.* Last modified January 10, 2020. https://sproutsocial.com/insights/social-media-metrics (accessed March 26, 2020).

26. Google. "Linking Analytics and Ads." Last modified 2019. https://services.google.com/fh/files/misc/analytics_ads_guide.pdf (accessed March 25, 2020).

27. Martin, James. "Top 10 things to measure in Google Analytics in 2018." *CMS Wire.* Last modified March 21, 2019. https://www.cmswire.com/analytics/top-10-things-to-measure-in-google-analytics-in-2018 (accessed March 25, 2020).

28. Google. "About Real-Time." Last modified 2020. https://support.google .com/analytics/answer/1638635?hl=en (accessed March 25, 2020).

29. Analytics Edge. Last modified 2020. https://help.analyticsedge.com/ article/misunderstood-metrics-new-vs-returning-visitors (accessed March 25, 2020).

30. Analytics Edge. "Overview of Audience Reports." Google. Last modified 2020. https://support.google.com/analytics/ answer/1012034?hl=en (accessed March 25, 2020).

31. Google. "About Demographics and Interests." Last modified 2020. https:// support.google.com/analytics/answer/ 2799357?hl=en (accessed March 25, 2020).

32. Google. "About Benchmarking." Last modified 2020. https://support.google .com/analytics/answer/6086666?hl=en (accessed March 25, 2020).

33. Google. "Attribution Model." Last modified 2020. https://support.google .com/analytics/answer/6086214?hl=en (accessed March 25, 2020).

34. Google. "About Search Console." Last modified 2020. https://support.google .com/analytics/answer/1308617?hl=en (accessed March 25, 2020).

35. Google. "Conversions." Last modified 2020. https://support.google.com/analytics/ answer/6317518?hl=en (accessed March 25, 2020).

36. Google. "Site Speed." Last modified 2020. https://support.google.com/analytics/ answer/1205784?hl=en (accessed March 25, 2020).

37. Google. "Mobile Traffic." Last modified 2020. https://support.google.com/ analytics/answer/2587086?hl=en (accessed March 25, 2020).

38. Schwartz, Barry. "Starting July 1, all new sites will be indexed using Google's mobile-first indexing." Search Engine Land. Last modified May 28, 2019. https://searchengineland.com/july-1-new-sites-will-be-indexed-using-googles-mobile-first-indexing-317490 (accessed March 25, 2020).

39. Google. "Google Academy." Last modified 2020. https://analytics.google .com/analytics/academy (accessed March 25, 2020).

40. Google. "YouTube Studio." YouTube. Last modified 2020. https://support.google .com/youtube/answer/1714323?hl=en (accessed March 25, 2020).

41. Facebook. "Facebook Analytics." Last modified 2020. https://analytics .facebook.com (accessed March 27, 2020).

42. Newberry, Christina. "The Beginner's Guide to Facebook Analytics." Hootsuite. Last modified January 20, 2020. https:// blog.hootsuite.com/facebook-analytics-insights-beginners-guide (accessed March 27, 2020).

43. Mendenhall, Nathan. "5 best practices for Facebook ads—From Facebook." *Social Media Today.* Last modified March 19, 2019. https://www.socialmediatoday .com/news/5-best-practices-for-facebook-ads-from-facebook/550680 (accessed March 27, 2020).

44. Facebook. "Fundamentals: A Beginners Guide." Facebook. Last modified 2020. https://www.facebook.com/ business/help/1438417719786914 ?id=802745156580214 (accessed March 27, 2020).

45. Mendenhall, Nathan. "5 best practices for Facebook ads—From Facebook." *Social Media Today.* Last modified March 19, 2019. https://www.socialmediatoday .com/news (accessed March 27, 2020).

46. LinkedIn. "LinkedIn Page Analytics—Overview." Last modified November 2019. https://www.linkedin.com/help/ linkedin/answer/4499/linkedin-page-analytics-overview?lang=en (accessed March 26, 2020).

47. LinkedIn. "Reporting and Analytics Measure the ROI of Your LinkedIn Ads." Last modified November 2019. https:// business.linkedin.com/marketing-solutions/reporting-analytics (accessed March 26, 2020).

48. Twitter. "Analytics Page for User AdriWall." Last modified 2020. https://analytics.twitter.com (accessed March 26, 2020).

49. Twitter. "Campaign Dashboard." Last modified 2020. https://business.twitter.com/en/analytics/campaign-dashboard.html (accessed March 26, 2020).

50. Twitter. "Advanced Conversion Tracking." Last modified 2020. https://business.twitter.com/en/solutions/twitter-ads/website-clicks/advanced-conversion-tracking.html (accessed March 26, 2020).

51. Twitter. "How to Set Up Conversion Tracking." Last modified 2020. https://business.twitter.com/en/solutions/twitter-ads/website-clicks/set-up-conversion-tracking.html (accessed March 26, 2020).

52. Snapchat. "Snapchat Ads." Last modified 2020. https://forbusiness.snapchat.com (accessed March 27, 2020).

53. Snapchat. "Snapchat Ads." Last modified 2020. https://forbusiness.snapchat.com (accessed March 27, 2020).

54. Snapchat. "Snapchat Ads." Last modified 2020. https://forbusiness.snapchat.com (accessed March 27, 2020).

55. Nielsen. "Nielsen DMA." Last modified 2020. https://www.nielsen.com/us/en/intl-campaigns/dma-maps (accessed March 27, 2020).

56. Snapchat. "Audience Insights FAQs." Last modified 2020. https://businesshelp.snapchat.com/en-US/article/audience-insights-faq (accessed March 27, 2020).

57. Google. "Learn by Experimenting with Data from the Google Merchandise Store." Last modified 2020. https://support.google.com/analytics/answer/6367342?hl=en (accessed March 27, 2020).

58. Google. "Learn by Experimenting with Data from the Google Merchandise Store." Last modified 2020. https://support.google.com/analytics/answer/6367342?hl=en (accessed March 27, 2020).

CHAPTER 12

1. Clement, J. "Number of Social Media Users Worldwide 2010–2021." Statista. August 14, 2019. https://www.statista.com/statistics.

2. Hayes, Adam. "Indeed vs. LinkedIn: What's the Difference?" Investopedia. January 29, 2020. https://www.investopedia.com/articles/personal-finance.

3. Gaikwad, Madhura. "10 Key Roles of a Social Media Manager in 2020." MarTech Advisor. January 2, 2020. https://www.martechadvisor.com/articles/social-media-marketing-2.

4. Pougatch, Sam. "Why Your Business Should Use Predictive Trend Spotting." Brandwatch. August 8, 2019. https://www.brandwatch.com/blog/predictive-trend-spotting.

5. Crawford, Charles. "7 Creative Social Media Strategies to Really Get You Noticed." *Social Media Week*. September 3, 2017. https://socialmediaweek.org/blog/2017/09/7.

6. Luttrell, Regina. *Social Media: How to Engage, Share, and Connect.* Lanham: Rowman & Littlefield, 2019.

7. Luttrell, Regina. "The Circular Model of SoMe for Social Communication." January 5, 2015. https://ginaluttrellphd.com/.

8. Ortiz-Ospina, Esteban. "The Rise of Social Media." Our World in Data. September 18, 2019. https://ourworldindata.org/rise-of-social-media.

9. Siegel, Jane, Vitaly Dubrovsky, Sara Kiesler, and Timothy W. McGuire. "Group processes in computer-mediated communication." *Organizational Behavior and Human Decision Processes* 37, no. 2 (1986): 157–187.

10. PRSA. "Ethics." Public Relations Society of America, 2000. https://www.prsa.org/about/ethics.

11. Paige, Alyson. "Marketing Code of Ethics." Small Business—Chron.com. November 21, 2017. https://smallbusiness.chron.com/marketing-code-ethics.

12. Fogg, Simon, K. J. Dearie, Zachary Paruch, Felix Sebastian, and Simon Fogg. "GDPR for Dummies: The Beginner's Guide to GDPR." Termly. February 4, 2020. https://termly.io/resources/articles/gdpr-for-dummies.

13. Ibid.

14. Rouse, Margaret. "What Is IoT Devices (Internet of Things Devices)?—Definition from WhatIs.com." IoT Agenda. TechTarget. March 29, 2018. https://internetofthingsagenda.techtarget.com/definition/IoT-device#.

15. Burgess, Matt. "What Is the Internet of Things? WIRED Explains." Wired. Last modified February 16, 2018. https://www.wired.co.uk/article/internet-of-things-what-is-explained-iot (accessed April 2, 2020).

16. Petrov, Christo. "40 Internet of Things Statistics from 2020 to Justify the Rise of IoT." Tech Jury. February 19, 2020. https://techjury.net/stats-about/internet-of-things-statistics/.

17. Kelleher, Tom. *Public Relations*. New York: Oxford University Press, 2021.

18. Sarokin, David. "5 Components of Multimedia." Small Business—Chron.com. April 9, 2019. https://smallbusiness.chron.com/5-components-multimedia-28279.html.

19. Ortiz-Ospina, Esteban. "The Rise of Social Media." Our World in Data. September 18, 2019. https://ourworldindata.org/rise-of-social-media.

20. Fauerbach, Therese. "Data Reigns in Today's Data Economy." The Northridge Group, November 11, 2019. https://www.northridgegroup.com/blog/more-valuable-than-oil-data-reigns-in-todays-data-economy.

CREDITS

CHAPTER 1

3 iStock: hocus-focus. **5** iStock: Melpomenem.

CHAPTER 2

13 Getty: jozefmicic. **17** *Business Horizons* 54 / Issue 3, Jan H. Keitzmann et al., "Social media? Get serious! Understanding the functional building blocks of social media," 241–51. Copyright 2011, with permission from Elsevier. **18** Elisa Shearer and Katerina Eva Matsa, Pew Research Center: https://www.journalism.org/2018/09/10/news-use-across-social-media-platforms-2018/. **21** Paul Hitlin and Lee Rainie, Pew Research Center: https://www.pewresearch.org/internet/2019/01/16/facebook-algorithms-and-personal-data/. **23** *International Journal of Information Management* 37 / Issue 2, Xusen Cheng et al., "Understanding trust influencing factors in social media communication: A qualitative study," 25–35. Copyright 2017, with permission from Elsevier. **26** Monica Anderson, Pew Research Center: https://www.pewinternet.org/2018/09/27/a-majority-of-teens-have-experienced-some-form-of-cyberbullying. **29** Saima Salim, DigitalInformationWorld.com. Reprinted with permission from https://www.digitalinformationworld.com/2019/01/how-much-time-do-people-spend-social-media-infographic.html. **30** SensorTower.com. February 21, 2020: https://sensortower.com/blog/top-social-media-apps-worldwide-january-2020.

CHAPTER 3

33 Reprinted with permission of 8ThirtyFour Integrated Communications. **35** Red Website Design: @LoriLewis and @Officially Chad: https://blog.red-website-design.co.uk/2019/03/27/internet-minute-2019-infographic/. **39** CommunicationTheory.org: https://www.communicationtheory.org/shannon-and-weaver-model-of-communication/. **40** HelpfulProfessor.com: https://helpful-professor.com/westley-maclean-model. **41** Communication Theory.org https://www.communicationtheory.org/de-fleur-model-of-communication/. **42** https://knowyourmeme.com/photos/1330532-hms-coolest-monkey-in-the-jungle-ad.

CHAPTER 4

51 Getty: 1055437636. **54** iStock: frimufilms. **56** Prem Samy, RSF Press Index. Reprinted with permission from index@rsf.org.

CHAPTER 5

64 iStock: Rawpixel. **67** Modified from J. Grunig and T. Hunt, *Managing Public Relations*, Holt, Rinehart and Winston, 1984, p. 141. **72** Finances Online: Reviews for Business. **74** (top) Freaker USA. Reprinted with permission of Freaker USA; (bottom) Adidas-Group.com: https://www.adidas-group.com/en/sustainability/managing-sustainability/general-approach/. **76** London P. **78** Developed by Gini Dietrich.

CHAPTER 6

82 April 4, 2020. Press briefing with Dr. Anthony Fauci. Getty: Jonathan Newton/*The Washington Post*. **83** United B. **86** 2019 Edelman Trust Barometer: Used with permission of Daniel J. Edelman Holdings, Inc. **87** The Noggin Blog. Used with permission of Noggin: https://www.noggin.io/blog/the-stages-of-crisis-understanding-the-crisis-management-lifecycle. **91** Modified from Jin, Yan, and Brooke Fisher Liu. "The blog-mediated crisis communication model: Recommendations for responding to influential external blogs." *Journal of Public Relations Research* 22, no. 4 2010. 429–455.

CHAPTER 7

95 Getty: graphicnoi. **96** Photo © Mike Tirico. Used with permission. **101** Getty: Icon Sportswire. **104** Getty: Michael Zagaris. **107** Shutterstock: RHONA WISE. **109** Getty: Mirrorpix

CHAPTER 8

115 Getty: Malte Mueller. **120** Pexels: Asad Photo Maldives.

CHAPTER 9

128 Getty: zubada. **129** Twitter, February 22, 2019. https://twitter.com/QuinnNystrom. **130** Twitter, January 11, 2020.https://twitter.com/NicoleB_MD. **131** Twitter, January 11, 2020. https://twitter.com/NicoleB_MD. **132** Facebook, January 17, 2020. https://www.facebook.com/DrNicole-Baldwin. **138** Modified from Albalawi, Yousef and Jane Sixsmith. "Agenda Setting for Health Promotion: Exploring an Adapted Model for the Social Media Era." *JMIR Public Health and Surveillance* 1, no. 2 2015. 39.

CHAPTER 10

141 Getty: yanyong. **146** Russ Crupnick, Music Watch. Reprinted with permission: https://www.musicwatchinc.com/blog/music-scores-a-gold-record-on-the-social-media-charts/. **147** RIAA data visualized by Feliz Richter. **149** Bieber, Justin. "Justin Bieber Channel." YouTube. https://www.youtube.com/user/ Kidrauhl. **151** https://newsroom.tiktok.com/en-us/. **152** Modified from Neustar whitepaper "Do Movie Market Budgets Need a Digital Reboot?" **154** Trackmaven Blog: https://trackmaven.com/blog/star-wars-marketing-force-awakens-on-social-media/.

CHAPTER 12

182 Getty: scyther5. **187** Esteban Ortiz-Ospina "The Rise in Social Media" https://ourworldindata.org/rise-of-social-media.

INDEX